"Laxmi is a woman after my own heart. I felt like I was reading my own mind. Her raw yet light-hearted, hilarious approach to the depth and complexity of spirituality awakened a desire to deepen my relationship with a higher power.

I tore into the pages, devouring each concept like my happiness depended on it. Each engaging lesson creates a roadmap to inner peace. Laxmi and Laurent have expertly woven timeless wisdom into delicious little bites that can be enjoyed the first time and the hundredth time. Their storytelling creates a visceral experience that will evoke every emotion from belly laughs to tears.

21SL21C is everything other spiritual books aren't: relatable, applicable, and truly arresting."

—Olivia, Founder of the Activation Project
  (Austin, TX)

"*21 Spiritual Lessons for the 21st Century* is both grounding and uplifting. In a world where so many self-help books and leaders promise escape, transcendence, or greener grass, these authors provide accessible tools to embrace your life and infuse every day with divinity—whatever it means to you."

—London Lucille, Yoga Teacher and Wellness Coach
  (Brooklyn, NY)

"Built to be accessible to a wide audience and written with a conversational, approachable tone, *21 Spiritual Lessons for the 21st Century* is a book that I expect will enhance and uplift anyone picking it up. Peppered with song quotations and artistic references, the book seeks to meet the readers where they are, honor them, and identify available foot-paths toward self-betterment. It is both grounded and "woo-woo" without being pretentious or assumptive.
The book is like a wizard in a business suit: improbable, compelling, and deeply multi-faceted."

—Eon, Civil Servant (Portland, OR)

"A book that speaks honestly from direct experience to a generation of hopeless, lost, and cynical young people who stand at the precipices of their lives, not knowing how to proceed. *21 Spiritual Lessons for the 21st Century* is a humorous and spirited book told in several voices – one male and one female, one older and one younger, and both from completely different worlds. Chapter by chapter, lesson by lesson, this book is packed with honesty and personal insights told straight from the heart. Suggestion: keep a journal along the way. You are in for a rollercoaster, not a carousel ride. You will not be the same "you" when you turn the last page."

—Maya, Professional World Traveler,
   College Counselor, Life Coach, and Kitchen Witch
   (Copenhagen, Denmark)

"Laxmi Dady really breaks down what it is to find your own source of spirituality while living in the distractions and stresses of the 21st century. She cuts through the noise of the "shoulds" and the naysayers and gets to the simple heart of it. She points out that our spirituality is inside of us and can look like anything we want it to. We don't have to faithfully follow a guru or purify our lives beyond recognition. She suggests very achievable exercises to help connect you with you. For anyone looking to find their way, this is a must-read."

—Rachael, Yoga Studio Owner and Massage Therapist
   (Ajijic, Mexico)

"As a millennial, unapologetically reading this book from a hot tub in the middle of the day on a Thursday, I couldn't get through the dedication page without tearing up. Prepare for unbridled realness. Prepare for openness, vulnerability, emboldened wit, fire, passion, and wisdom. This book is a gift to the collective. Thank you for your service. "

—Tess, Creator of Koiwolf, Eco Swimwear and Apparel
   (Sayulita, Ibiza, Canada)

Published by OmPoint Press, Asheville North Carolina.

ISBN 979-8-218-32558-9

No part of this book was touched by Artificial Intelligence.
Only living breathing human beings created this book.

First Edition: November 9, 2023.

Cover and book layout design by Terese Elhard.
Back cover photo by Vanessa Weichberger.

Printed in the USA by IngramSpark.

Coxist icon used with permission
of the Coexist Foundation

Photo of Meher Baba during 1927
in old Mandali Hall, at Meherabad, India
in chapter "The Avatar" is courtesy
www.msicollection.zenfolio.com and copyright
© 2023 Meher Baba MSI Photographic Collection,
used by permission.
Thank you to Christine and Martin Cook.

21

Spiritual Lessons for the 21st Century

BY

LAXMI DADY

LAURENT WEICHBERGER

OMPOINT PRESS

Contents

Dedications   ix

Acknowledgements   xii

Introduction   1

Lessons

1: **Know Thyself** by Laxmi   29

2: **Honesty** by Laurent   63

3: **Personal Power** by Laxmi   73

4: **Unshakably Centered** by Laxmi   99

5: **Relationships** by Laurent   149

6: **Finding the "I" in "We"** by Laxmi   175

7: **Oneness** by Laurent   183

8: **Love** by Laurent   109

9: **Obedience to the Divine** by Laurent   199

10: **Humility** by Laurent   207

11: **Drugs** by Laurent   223

12: **Surrender** by Laurent   253

13: **Saints and Spiritual Masters** by Laurent   259

14: **The Avatar** by Laurent   267

15: **Intuition** by Laxmi   291

16: **Listen!** by Laxmi   317

17: **Befriending My Shadow** by Laxmi   333

18: **Forgiveness** by Laxmi   361

19: **God Is Dog…Dog Is God** by Laxmi   385

20: **Sex Is God** by Laxmi   399

21: **Gotta Have Faith** by Laxmi   415

Notes   423

Dedications

"...Dedicated to all the teachers who told me I'd never amount to notin'...To everyone in the struggle. It's all good baby baby. It was all a dream."

—Notorious B.I.G., "Juicy"

Special dedication to the English teacher I had freshman year at my private, Catholic, all-girls high school; St. Mary's Academy. Molly Egland told 15-year-old me that if I left St. Mary's, I would "never see success in my life." This one's for you, Molly.

I had to look up your name in my '05 yearbook, but I will never forget how you made the "I'm going to prove you so wrong" fire I already had in me blaze even stronger.

To my fellow millennial babaaaays out there who are unsubscribing from the matrix, healing generational trauma, and creating your own realities: GO OFF!!! I believe in you. XOXO.

—Laxmi

This book is dedicated to My Girl, Aspen. She is
an incredible daughter, loving friend, tremendously
hard worker, and one of the most spiritual
millennials I know.

I have faith in you and can't wait for you
to fully actualize and know yourself.

—Laurent

Acknowledgements

"I come as one, but I stand as ten thousand."

—Dr. Maya Angelou

First and foremost, to God—universal spirit, creator, source, Buddha, Krishna, Allah, or whatever you call divinity (as the Doctor Bronner's soap label states, it is all one God)—without You, nothing exists. Thank You for this incarnation in my human meat-suit. Thank You for every breath, the birds in the sky, the worms in the dirt, and everything in between. Thank You for birthing me into my family of origin and gifting me the opportunity to love and be loved by some of the most brilliant (and challenging) people you've created.

Thank you to the numerous earth angels shepherding my experience on this spinning rock we call planet Earth. Most notably, thank you to my incredible co-author Laurent for demonstrating patience, persistence, and trust throughout this three-year book writing journey. Thank you to Meredith Evridge, editor extraordinaire, for taking what was basically a journal and making it into a book.

To the many women who held my hand and picked me up out of the spirals of self-doubt that writing this book brought to the surface. Special gratitude to Maya Luna for transmuting my spoken truth into written sentences; creatrix soul sister and hot mama, Lulu Kelly, for gifting her design brilliance; Marisa del Río for believing in this project from its inception and being its initial editor; and graphics queen, Terese Elhard, for designing the beautiful cover and layout of this book. Thank you to my mother, FionaRhea Rickford, for always encouraging my creative spirit and affirming that I can do anything.

Thank you to the countless light beings who have touched my journey and redirected me back onto God's path when I fell from grace. This includes Kris King, former owner of WINGS Seminars where I began my healing journey at seventeen. This also includes my deeply Catholic father, Charles Dady, who showed me the power of ritual and inner peace that can be felt within the cathedral walls. Gratitude to Daniel Mieses Gonzalez who acted as drill sergeant and gave me a literal space to finish writing this book.

Gratitude to my ancestors: East Indian farmers, Guyanese foresters, and German aristocrats. It is an honor to be your offspring and carry our legacy into the 21st century. May it be one of faith and love.

To my beloved chosen and blood family; your support gives me courage when I am weak, and breath when I feel as if everything is closing in around me.

You have assisted in carving me into the holy woman I am. I am eternally grateful to be witnessed by your loving gaze.

Introduction
How to Remain Focused in a World of Constant Fuckery and Distractions

"We teach best what we most need to learn."
—Richard Bach

"If you light a lamp for somebody, it will also brighten your path."   —Buddha

Does the World Really Need Another Spiritual Book?

The intention in creating this book is to make accessing the divine easy, relatable, funny, and down-to-earth; to ultimately increase the consciousness of everyone on the planet (no pressure). We are inspired people and as such, it is our duty to share the message on our hearts.

21 Spiritual Lessons for the 21st Century was born from a podcast episode I did with my co-author, Laurent Weichberger. At the peak of the pandemic, I started a video podcast called "The Conscious Hotline" (find it on IG and YouTube) with my dear friend, Altaire Cambata.[1] People really resonated with the spiritual concepts discussed on the show. It became clear that the world wanted more of what Altaire, our guests, and I had to offer. Our episode with Laurent highlighted the growing need that millennials and Gen-Zers have for access to resonant, digestible, and non-denominational spirituality.

Laurent had the brilliant idea of co-authoring a guide for young people to access the divine, and I excitedly said yes. However, I was slightly shocked that someone who has written as many books as he has, and who knows me as well as he does, would want to collaborate with me on a book of this nature. If I were asked to write a book on being a wild woman, breaking free from societal norms, or how to travel 75% of the time without spending more than $12K in a year, I could do it with my eyes closed. However, the prospect of writing a book on spirituality when I was still in the process of ascending my own spiritual awakening and transformation was a big leap. I was only comfortable taking this journey with the handholding of my dear friend, Laurent. It is an honor to write my first book with one of my spiritual mentors, who is a devout disciple of Meher Baba.

I met Laurent in Ashland, Oregon, at a restaurant called Sauce. He was attempting to impart spiritual wisdom to his then-disinterested ten-year-old son, Cyprus. I observed the juxtaposition of a wise man discussing karma and living simply so others can simply live with Cyprus responding, "Baba this, Baba that. When I grow up, I want to move to New York City and be rich and famous." It was so hysterical to me that when there was a break in the conversation, caused by Cyprus going to the bathroom, I felt compelled to walk over to their table and get to know Laurent. Similar to how we initially connected, our hope in writing this is that our varying perspectives, lived experiences, identities, and ages bring value to young folks on their spiritual journeys.

Why Read What I Have to Say?

My journey to spirituality began at birth and continues to unfold today. I turned the self-help burner all the way to "high" once I got to college. While thousands of my peers were getting blacked out at University of Oregon Ducks football games, I spent the majority of my weekends in personal growth and development workshops. If I wasn't participating in a workshop, I was either helping facilitate one or volunteering so that I could participate in the next one for free. From the age of seventeen, I have had an insatiable hunger to grow, and a burning desire to heal the generational trauma passed down to me from my immigrant parents. The shadow that this unresolved trauma cast over my family includes mental illness, addiction, child molestation, abject poverty, cultural assimilation, and death by suicide. It ends with me. The dysfunction and challenges within my family of origin, along with my inherent Libra Sun/Leo Rising astrological nature to shine, serve as infinite fuel for my self-help fire.

After watching a particularly skilled facilitator aid even the most resistant of participants to their truth, I realized that holding space for personal discovery is part of my life's purpose. I immediately asked the facilitator, "How can I be more like you?" She recommended the life coaching school she attended, New Ventures West. I said yes to my dream and enrolled in coaching school at NVW. Much to my surprise, coaching school was significantly more challenging and rigorous than my master's (I had already completed my Post-Graduate Certificate in Education and taught middle school English, which wasn't my scene). Dedicating a year of my life to my own growth so that I could support others in theirs was a powerfully transformative experience.

Shortly after turning twenty-five, I quit my job and started my first LLC. (B)Free is dedicated to supporting people's transformations, both internally through coaching and externally through organization and design. In dedicating myself to the art of coaching, I realized I'd tapped into my potential and was doing what God put me on this planet to do! Helping people from all walks of life integrate the many pieces of themselves to live joyful, aligned, connected lives was my wildest dream manifested. Finally, I'd found my stride and felt like a fairy godmother helping folks grant their own wishes. Coaching felt like a magical space where time slowed, God worked through me, and I was watching the divine unfold before my very own eyes…until I wasn't.

After over a decade in the personal growth and development game, I became jaded by the false prophets and rampant hypocrisy. I ran into snake oil salespeople in the coaching industry. One was Curtis Pipes, a "coach" who befriended me over the course of a year, finally sold me an $8,000 coaching package, and then blocked me. These fakes pollute the waters of love's message and make the coaching industry look like a bunch of quacks. I've experienced countless examples of this: the Instagram-famous sex coach who is actually a complete wallflower in person; the world-famous author and spiritual guide who screams at people in the elevator on her way to speak in front of 6,000 women at a conference; and the influencer who promotes her own herbal skincare line, while hiding her irritated skin behind makeup, photoshop, and filters. Having been behind the veil, I know without a shadow of a doubt that everyone (yes even Beyoncé) has their sh!t. No one is perfect, and it is so easy to inflate or deflate the truth in order to support a desired image. We are human, after all; perfectly imperfect.

My intention in sharing myself and what I have discovered with you, dear reader, is to pull the veil all the way back. I am showcasing the whole shabang, without filters or spiritual bypassing. I am keeping it real, raw, and honest. My aversion to so many of my peers in the coaching space and the mere premise of charging for "enlightenment," particularly during the pandemic, caused me to take on fewer coaching gigs.

I replaced my constant search to be okay, enough, rich, and not crazy with developing a relationship with my creator. Knowing God brings me a sense of love and peace beyond anything any substance ever could.

Dismantle any illusions of what you think a life coach from Portland, Oregon is or should be. Hopefully, this book leads you to the only conclusion that really matters: your own. I am not here to "should" all over you, nor do I have a particular denomination. I am as poly-religious as they come. I have spent decades searching for truth through teachers, retreats, workshops, breathwork, plant medicine, yoga, moon rituals, pagan holiday celebrations, meditation, herbs, journaling, and more. I think this quote from the Bible, in Psalm 139: 13-14, says it well: "For you created my inmost being; you knit me together in my mother's womb. I praise you because I am fearfully and wonderfully made; your works are wonderful, I know that full well."[2]

We are all made perfect and whole in the image and light of God. The more I get right with God/Creator/Source (and this is NOT exclusive to the one in the Bible! Call it what you will, folks), the happier and easier everything is.

Americans (millennials in particular) are spiritually starved, but materially, mentally, and physically overfed. We have replaced time with God for social media, and it's killing us—quite literally. Trigger warning: according to the National Institute of Mental

Health, suicide is a leading cause of death in the US, and it worsens with each generation thereafter. This is something that has touched both Laurent's family and mine. When Laurent was a teenager, his father committed suicide. I have also lost a dear childhood friend and uncle to suicide. Everyone knows someone who has been impacted by it.

Thankfully, mental health has become a national discussion and resources are rapidly growing. However, rates of addiction and ways to dissociate are increasing even quicker. We all have things we are addicted to and ways we dissociate from reality. However, it is key to be aware of them, even if they aren't overly impacting our day-to-day lives.

If you or someone you know is struggling with mental health or addiction, I suggest getting help from a trained and licensed therapist. There are many ways to sign up for therapy. Two that I have used and had positive experiences with are the Psychology Today website and the app, Better Help.

If you are in the US and are thinking of hurting yourself, or know someone who is, call the National Suicide Hotline (1-800-273-8255). You can also dial 988. The hotline is a free, confidential service that is available 24/7, 365 days a year. Another option for getting help is AA. This is a free, worldwide program that has saved millions of lives from addiction since its inception in 1935. I have sourced a lot of healing from AA. They offer many types of meetings for various struggles. The one that most changed my life is Codependents Anonymous.

Addiction: We've All Got One...or Two...or Ten

It is important to be present to and with our addictions. I average five hours a day on my phone! I'm not proud of this, but it's true: we can be addicted to anything. My best friend attended a Church of Recovery meeting where someone was addicted to New York City. Someone else was addicted to chocolate cake. It doesn't matter if it's that or methamphetamine; we're all participating in similar dissociative behavior in different ways, and to different extremes. By living in our addictions, we completely miss the juiciness and purpose of life: the present moment. The precious, tender experiences that breathe life force energy into us, make us feel alive, and command our full presence do not usually come from a screen.

Social Media:
The Slow, Painful Road to the Middle

When I start my day by grabbing my phone to turn off my alarm, it's game over. I'll sit on the toilet and spend the first forty-five minutes of my day scrolling. At times, I delete Instagram from my phone to eliminate the distraction, but I still find myself getting distracted with social media replacements. I check my Slack for work, keep an eye on my stocks, respond to emails, or learn Spanish via Duolingo ("Yo como manzanas"). Coaching clients across the globe means there is ALWAYS something to respond to on my phone, day or night. Distractions are a necessary evil of life in the 21st century.

Late 80's and early 90's millennials such as myself are uniquely positioned to have experienced childhood with *and* without smartphones and social media. Way back in the day of 2004, I joined the hip social media platform, MySpace. Remember the old top eight conundrum? MySpace has long lost its relevance, but nearly twenty years later, we are still scrolling. Now, we have newer interfaces and uncontrollably powerful algorithms. Each generation born after millennials will be unaware of a world without the internet or handheld computers. Tweens today completely skip the awkward, gawky phase of adolescence and step directly into Instagram filters. This results in them robbing themselves of their precious goofball moments in lieu of trying to look

Tik Tok, @acooz31

Millennials   Gen Z

Netflix, *Wednesday*

good for the camera. The internet is rich with hilarious TikTok videos and memes about the stark differences between my generation who didn't have social media until middle school, and our younger siblings who had to start typing their homework in the second grade. This TikTok video of a girl pictured as a millennial, then as a Gen Zer encapsulates the contrast.

The distraction is always there. We simply cannot put the genie back in the bottle. We can, however, learn to *master* it instead of being a *victim* to it. As this brilliant meme points out, millennials may have more work to do around this than our Gen-Z brethren.

Life isn't happening to us; we are creating it. Changes in my habits, like using a physical radio alarm clock and charging my phone in my office, have helped me avoid my phone until after my morning rituals are complete. Mastering your distractions does not involve ignoring social media. It means wielding it for your benefit, rather than reacting to it. This goes for anything in life. When in a state of reaction, I'm allowing things to happen to me. Actions made from a reactionary place are not intentional and will often fail to produce fruitful results. We must learn to be *with* technology, not a slave to it.

The Paradox of Choice

The constant inundation of information has exacerbated Western culture's throwaway mentality. America is a single-use society. For decades, the US has had one of the highest divorce rates in the world. It also consumes four planets' worth of resources annually, if all eight billion earthlings lived like us.[3] We have more convenience, material goods, and options for said goods than ever before, but happiness decreases when consumption goes beyond a certain threshold of basic needs. Ask any billionaire. America has long surpassed the point of more choices leading to greater joy. This is evident by the fact that we are one of the richest, fattest, most medicated, and least happy countries on the planet. Modernization has created a world wherein we have so many options. We expect perfection in the decisions we make—whether it's about finding a new pair of jeans or a job—that checks off all of our boxes. Then, we feel disappointed when our very high standards aren't met, because we know there is always something better out there.

Barry Schwartz, a professor of social theory, wrote an entire book on this called *The Paradox of Choice*.[4] Schwartz explains in his TED talk that "a significant contributor to this explosion of depression and [death by] suicide is that people have disappointing experiences. Their expectations are so high, and when they have to explain these disappointments, they think that they themselves are at fault."[5] We are quick to throw away relationships, clothes, public figures, and companies that do not align with our instant gratification desires. Why do the hard work of understanding one another? If I don't feel like continuing to get to know someone romantically, I can just click, block, and return to Tinder. I'll instantly have a dozen new options. Relationships have fallen victim to throwaway culture and are often treated with the same flippancy as ordering takeout from a restaurant. One can now get food (or oral sex) delivered to their doorstep with the touch of a screen. The Western world now has a mentality of "I can have any and everything at any time, and if I don't like it, I can block it from my life."

What's Mental Health Got to Do Wit' It?

These prevailing mindsets are contributing to the soaring rates of depression. When I reject pain or avoid discomfort, I cut myself off from gaining the tools to navigate hard things. It would be naïve of me to neglect that mental health has in the last two decades become discussed on a national level, which factors into why it is a greater issue. Surely, many 1950s housewives were experiencing suicidal ideation

and depression but didn't have the language
or understanding to express it.

The relationship between spirituality and mental
health is deeply intertwined. This book provides
insights into how they are braided together, and how
when they are united, they can create and maintain
a sense of inner peace. Mental health is not a far-off
subject for either of the authors of this book; it's up
close and personal. Learning how to navigate our
individual mental health and witnessing the untreated
mental illnesses of people in our families has greatly
shaped who we are today.

Laurent shared, "I had my first memorable nervous
breakdown in third grade. The school called my
parents and I went into therapy. So much was
revealed in therapy. Beyond that, I'm the only person
in my immediate family who is unmedicated and
hasn't been hospitalized for mental health issues in
a psychiatric hospital. How I dodged that bullet is
unbeknownst to me. However, my friends and family
attribute it to the grace of Meher Baba's presence
in my life. He has guided me out of the darkness
of mental health issues. My father's psychiatrist
responded to his mental health issues by saying,
'If this doesn't get better, we're going to have to put
you in a mental hospital.' The very next day, my
dad committed suicide. It was tough, and it was the
hammer and chisel that sculpted me. I have grown
and changed because of all the heat and pressure
of that experience."

This book seeks to highlight the relationship between positive mental health and spirituality. Most of the atheists I know don't seem particularly happy. One of Laurent's favorite jokes is, "God doesn't believe in atheists." I love that.

Spirituality Is Faithless and Simultaneously Every Faith

This book is for everyone from all walks of life. People with a strong faith, people who don't believe anything happens after you die, and everyone in between. Believe whatever you want to believe, and then look at the people following your belief system. Are they operating within a values system that you subscribe to? Do they emulate the things that are important to you or the lifestyle that you want? Both sides (atheists and believers) can be equally unhappy. Religion and spirituality won't instantly cure you of your sadness —shocking, I know.

The Power In and Of Spiritual Masters

Meher Baba, my co-author Laurent's wonderful spiritual guide of the last several decades, once said, "The less you think of yourself, the more others will think of you." He had no thought of self. He wasn't living for himself. It wasn't about him. He was there to be of service. This is the essence of how one can positively impact millions of people without ever meeting, seeing, speaking, or physically touching them. It has never, and will never be, about the individual. When we show up to be of service, magic ensues.

Another prominent spiritual leader shaking things up while living a life of service is Pope Francis; the current pope of the Catholic Church, and sovereign of the Vatican City State. Pope Francis is the first non-European pope in 1,200 years, and the first to be from the Americas. How he even became pope was unprecedented, as the prior pope stepped down and named his successor (they usually hold onto the title until death). Pope Francis has been prolific for the institution of the Catholic church. He is denouncing the child molesting that the institution has spent so much time, energy, and resources covering up.[6] He is showing support for the LGBTQIA+ community[7] and instituting women to ministries previously reserved for men.[8] Clearly, things are changing—even in archaic religious bureaucracies. We're going for progress, not perfection. The patriarchal structure is crumbling and in its wake, people's minds and hearts are opening.

Spirituality Has Been Hijacked

Nowadays, people are looking for spirituality under the giant square of ice in their whiskey glass, in the crutch of their joint, or between the likes, comments, and follows on their social media feeds. The social scientists and gambling experts that build social media algorithms manipulate our desire to belong, in order to commodify our insecurities and sell us things we don't need. The Netflix documentary, *The Social Dilemma*, affirms this evil intention and points out that "...if you are not paying for the product, then you are the product."[9] This phenomenon is only exacerbated in America, where the loudest person wins. It doesn't even matter whether what they are saying is true. Exhibit A: Donald Trump received more free airtime across all channels than all the previous presidents put together. The loudest and most unconventional person wins our attention.

Religion in America

There are countless ways to connect with spirit, be in prayer, and have a strong spiritual practice outside of church. However, organized religion builds that routine for people while simultaneously providing a community based on shared values. Over the past twenty years in the United States, fewer and fewer people gather to collectively worship. Only 50% belong to a church nationally, and a mere 42% of millennials identify with a religion at all.[10] The only churches that have grown in the last twenty years are evangelicals like Southern Baptists, Mormons, and Orthodox Jewish communities. The annual growth rate of evangelicalism in the United States is 0.8%[11] higher than the growth rate of the general population (0.5% in 2020).[12] To put that poignantly, there are more evangelicals converting every year than babies born. Churches that do not align with the mainstream open-mindedness of the 21st century are the only ones increasing in numbers. Christian denominations that welcome and accept people outside of heteronormativity, such as Lutheran, Methodist, Unitarian, Presbyterian, and Unity churches, have dying membership bases. Oftentimes, church demographics look like a bunch of people over fifty-five and millennial me.

My upbringing was as church-fluid as you can
get. We attended them all: Buddhist monasteries;
Hare Krishna, Hindu, and Jewish temples; Catholic
basilicas; hippie dippie/free love communes; Alien
worshiping and channeling circles; African drumming;
Unity churches; and non-denominational spiritual
centers. Thank you, Portland, Oregon, for having any
and every type of spiritual worship one could ask for.
Attending such a diverse range of religious spaces as
a child showed me that it is all one God cloaked in
many different names, customs, and outfits. Matthew
18:20 states, "For where two or three gather in my
name, there am I with them."[13] As an adult, I attend
temple, mass, or church on various high holidays
because I enjoy worshiping in the house of God.
Something deep in my chest grows when I worship
the divine with others.

My fellow millennial, Gen-X and Gen-Z brethren
born after 1981 are the lowest church attendees of any
recorded generation.[14] Finding one's own spiritual
practice outside of organized religion is growing.
However, we swapped God for Bravo TV. I'm not
saying you can't have both. Some people view Bravo
as their insight into the collective consciousness.
We put down the Bible, Koran, TaNaK, Bhagavad Gita,
and other such literature, and pick up remote controls,
smartphones, and gaming controllers. As a collective,
we deny God and choose technology. Technology is
constantly advertising that we need to buy a product
in order to be happy, change our bodies to be beautiful,
or live beyond our means in order to mimic rich
people. No wonder death by suicide is on the rise.

Take the Best, Leave the Rest

My eclectic spiritual background has manifested as an appreciation for attending many different places of worship. I love being in a positive community. Moving in with my very Catholic Indian father during the pandemic put me in the cathedral more often than I'd ever been (ironic, as it was supposed to be a time of complete isolation). The repetition, and finally learning the necessary call and responses of a mass, became a welcomed ritual in my week. I don't believe in or adhere to the Catholic way of life, but any activity where people gather over shared values (e.g. day drinking while playing dodgeball or speaking in tongues and flailing on the ground) builds community through camaraderie.

My Papa always says, "You want a boyfriend? Go to church. Jesus is the best man out there." If the church is so great, why don't I belong to one? Why don't I get confirmed or finally finish converting to Judaism, as I've wanted since attending Jewish summer camp as a kid (shout out to B'nai B'rith)? What I needed to join any organized religion is total alignment. Some people who attend church are so moved that they are compelled to go every week. They find the leader prophetic, follow their words, and do whatever the church or book specific to that group wants. So far, no place of worship I have attended has felt like a whole body "Yes!"

No church building could speak to my spirit greater than being on God's green earth. Nature is my favorite church and is available worldwide without any dogma. Why sit in a big room to listen to (most often) a man share about his experience with his connection with God, or read from a book written thousands of years ago, in place of tapping into my built-in eternal connection with the Creator? Wherever you best connect with the divine is your church. Good news: it can be anywhere, anytime. I often attended a Unity church as a child called The Living Enrichment Center. It was led by Mary Morrissey. At the end of each sermon, the congregation would say in unison, "The light of God surrounds me; The love of God enfolds me; The power of God protects me; The presence of God watches over me. Wherever I am, God is!"[15]

Spirit → to Reality = Spirituality

Sometimes, I want to be witness to my own internal wisdom while also hearing other perspectives. Belonging to a community (even if only a member during the mass itself) brings a different kind of spiritual connection. Particularly during the pandemic, opportunities to gather were so limited. Simply being in a room with others, even while widely spaced apart, helped ease the isolation that crept in after days spent in solitude.

Other times, I make my own church. I burn sage, light new candles with a prayer I create, call in the four directions, and pull goddess cards. The misnomer so many people have with spirituality is that it must be all or nothing. Either I'm a staunch, gun-toting, gay-hating, evangelical Christian, a devil-worshiping pagan, a vegan Hare Krishna, or an atheist. This is why the only churches growing are the extreme forms of religion. People think, "I have to do this 'God' thing all the way." My question to you is, all whose way?

It's called spirituality for a reason. It's about what resonates with your spirit. That's the whole point. So, go off with your fine self. Pray at a Catholic mass one day and howl at the full moon the next. Talk to birds and hug trees, do a Course in Miracles, or get on your hands and knees at the Wailing Wall in Jerusalem (all things I've done). Flow with your internal clock and move your feet to the heartbeat of what your spirit is resonating with that day. Don't assign labels, rules, or constricting expectations on how your spirituality needs to look—outside of being loving. Love is the universal message of all religions. Even when cloaked in outdated, sexist ideology, all religions have an underlying message of love.

Allow yourself to be with your spirituality and you will simply be spiritual. That freedom to be with your spirit in whatever way it desires from moment to moment is the greatest gift you can give yourself. It cannot be found in any institution, building, leader, or place outside of yourself and your unique connection with God. You determine what your connection with God looks like and means to you.

While living on Lago de Chapala in Ajijic, Jalisco, Mexico, I had the pleasure of participating in multiple

Temazcal ceremonies. A Temazcal can be likened to
a sweat lodge, used by Mayans, Aztecs, and other
First Nation peoples. Imagine a sauna that's built out
of clay and heated by stones that glow orange from
baking in a sacred fire all day. Throughout history,
people have bathed in the steam, cleansing their
bodies, recharging, and connecting with each other.
Not only do they feel great, but Temazcales are also
a way to connect with spirituality.

The ceremonies I was a part of were on top of a
mountain and run by an alcoholic painter who lived
in a hut with no running water. A single, exposed
lightbulb was his source of light. Even a drunk can be
a medicine man. A true person of spirit isn't a typecast.
If you're breathing, you have a spirit; in that sense,
we're all spiritual teachers in our own regard.

At the beginning of the ceremony, we open with
gratitude for the ancestors who kept the tradition
of Temazcales alive all throughout Mexico's 300-
year occupation by the Spanish conquistadors. They
deemed all indigenous spiritual practices to be "of
the devil." Those caught in indigenous practices
would have their tongues cut out so that they couldn't
verbally pass down their tradition. Still, their spirits
blazed strong. They gathered in secret at night, risking
their lives to keep their traditions alive. Now, even
tourists visiting Cancún can practice ancient, spiritual
practices previously deemed punishable by death.

I share this to shine a light on the power of spirituality. It transcends religions, cultures, and even time. Nothing and no one is powerful enough to end people's connection to their maker, or the rituals they create to get closer to them. When the essence of the practice is pure, it MUST be carried on. No amount of risk or fear can stop it. Spirit speaks to and through us. It exists with us and *is* us. It is the creator, and we co-create its continuation through our very existence.

Connection With Spirit

There is no "one-size-fits-all" for spirituality because we are all like snowflakes. Each one of us is a unique individual with our own lived experience. Spiritual practice cannot take the form of simply going to and from a building on Sunday mornings. Connecting with the divine is not a simple task to check off your daily to-do list. Spirit lives and breathes. It is ever-present and eternal. It cannot be confined to a book, necklace, or space. My co-author hasn't been to church since the year I was born (1991). He has spoken up in places of worship, inquiring deeper about concepts like universal values and all religions being based on a similar foundation of love. He would say things like, "That's an interesting interpretation of that scripture," to the Minister, while in a Bible study, "I think we all have wisdom and insight; can we share around and hear other people's interpretation of the scripture?" Ministers would reply with, "You probably shouldn't come here anymore." He was 23 years old, immediately shut down, and hasn't been back to church since. He's repeatedly felt very unwelcome, probably in part because of his straight-shooting Scorpio/New Yorker way of inquiring and deep-diving into things. He's a spiritual guy who has been following Baba since he was nineteen. He doesn't resonate with the shame and guilt that many religions attempt to rule their constituents by.

That is the downfall of religion today. The only churches that are growing are the churches that promote singular thought and acceptance of another man's word as one's personal truth. In the confines of the most conservative religions, such as Mormon or Southern Baptist, there is little freedom to question, interpret differently, or explore beyond. The evangelical and Mormon churches I have witnessed have extremely limiting beliefs around right and wrong, and no space for freedom of expression. The women consent to being held to drastically different standards within these patriarchal structures of religions. Even the men in Catholicism are oppressed in their own way by swearing to celibacy (and they haven't been very successful with that).

It is hard for me to write this. I don't want backlash from my family or loved ones and am resistant to "othering" others. I don't want to put anyone or anything down that speaks to people. If evangelical religion is serving you, that's wonderful. Keep doing it. If it isn't, look within and around. Many people were raised in religion, and as the statistics show, it's becoming less popular. I see why churches and organized religions are deeply flawed.

I want this book to be a resource for young people who reject the status quo and want to create their own definition of and experience with spirituality.

What matters is the individual experience; not what anyone else thinks about it. My eldest sister Santi has a saying: "Do whatever you want. Just don't be a d*ck to kids." If someone feels spirit when they go to Catholic mass, where the same words are spoken every time and the music is sung in Latin, go for it.

We cannot separate the introduction of technology, processed foods, reality TV, social media, and (for my "red pill" or "tin foil hat wearers") 5G with the decline in connection to one another, Pachamama and spirit. Everything is deeply interconnected, even as we attempt to elevate ourselves from the need for others with our automated lifestyles. Nothing replaces the fact that humans are pack animals who thrive in community and need connection with other beings.

Spirituality is like a precious gem. You can hold it up and appreciate its beauty from every angle. Each of these twenty-one lessons is like the facets of the precious stone you were just viewing in your mind's eye. There are countless dimensions to spirituality, and all are part of the journey to God. There are infinite ways to build, grow, and maintain your connection to spirit. Reading this book is one of them.

Journaling & Practices

21SL21C is meant to grow with you. Use this book as a guide to unearth the parts of yourself you buried long ago or never took the time to get to know. At the end of each lesson, Laurent and I have written reflective questions to help you dive deeper into the real you; the you beneath the many egoic masks we wear to protect ourselves. By taking time to ask yourself the hard questions and dig deep, you are supporting the collective upris ing. Together, we're breaking free from a world of shoulds and musts. I encourage you to dedicate a brand-new journal to answer the questions in 21SL21C. Coach tip: answer the same questions a few years apart in the same journal and read the differences. As a coach, I always recommend writing by hand. However, we live in a fast-paced world, so if what you can commit to is voice dictating the responses into a note in your phone, that works too. It's not about how you do it. It's about taking the time to be in reflection.

Feel into these questions, take your time and go deep. The examples are just to get your mind going. They are by no means complete responses.

Journaling Prompt

How do I escape my reality?
Ex: time on phone, future tripping, media

**In what ways am I creating
a reality that I want to escape?**
Ex: putting off the things that matter most to me

**What makes me feel alive or
connected to universal consciousness?**
Ex: exploring nature, lying in savasana pose at the end of
a yoga class

When do I dedicate time to do those things?
Ex: Daily dog walks

Lesson 1
'Know Thyself'
Who the H–E–Double Hockey Sticks Am I?

"To know thyself is the beginning of wisdom."
—Socrates

"Don't confuse what people say you are and
who you know you are."   —Oprah Winfrey

The very definition of "cliché" (a phrase or opinion
that is overused and betrays a lack of original thought)
means you should rarely, if ever, use one in your
writing. If ever there was an overused phrase that
betrays a lack of original thought, "Know Thyself"
has got to be in the top ten. For that reason, it's hard
to even know what the concept refers to any longer.
Yet, as the definition of a cliché points out, they
become clichés for a reason.

In one of my favorite poems by Oriah Mountain Dreamer, she writes,

> It doesn't interest me
> if the story you are telling me
> is true.
> I want to know if you can
> disappoint another
> to be true to yourself.
> If you can bear
> the accusation of betrayal
> and not betray your own soul.
> If you can be faithless
> and therefore trustworthy.
> —"The Invitation" [16]

The concept of being "faithless and therefore trustworthy" blew my mind when I first read this. Aren't these words mutually exclusive? Either I have faith and am trustworthy, or I'm faithless and therefore have nothing upon which to hold myself accountable.

Then, there are times, she writes, when we must "bear the accusation of betrayal and not betray [our] own soul." That verse made absolutely no sense to me in my teens and early twenties. Why would I be accused of betrayal if I'm simply being true to myself? And how could I even be true to myself without faith? As I've grown older, lived experience has taught me the truth of these stanzas.

Know Yourself in Order to Show Yourself

Some of the hardest decisions I have ever had to make involved doing something that felt like a betrayal to someone I love, and yet, they were a crucial part of my soul's journey. The Laxmi-defining story that I am about to share with you could easily be a book all by itself. This coming-of-age tale involves disobeying my father's wishes. Trust me, going against your father's wishes as the youngest Indian daughter in a Catholic household is a huge deal! Still, my soul kept whispering to me that I had no other choice than to follow the path I knew was mine. Anything else would have been a complete betrayal of my soul's evolution.

It all started when I learned that my paternal grandmother in India was dying. I got wind of this from an email that my aunt had sent to my father. Apparently, I was meant to take the journey of a lifetime, as a result of these particular winds. At the time, I was a sophomore in college, surviving off of my $8.25-an-hour wage earned at the University of Oregon's recycling center. I was sharing a very dirty house in Eugene, Oregon with four girls. Surviving as best as I could as a first-generation college student at a large university, I had become very resourceful. Almost daily, there was some kind of event on campus with leftover food at the end; a student union group having a cookout, or a company offering free grub in exchange for sitting through a presentation on what was surely predatory financing. The picture I'm painting is that I was young, on my own, and had learned to be scrappy.

Upon hearing that my grandmother was on death's doorstep and that her dying wish was to see my Papa before she crossed the rainbow bridge, I became determined to reunite them. Nothing could have stopped me. It felt like there were thousands upon thousands of lightning bugs inside my chest cavity, pulling me to India. It was as if an invisible energy cord had manifested out of thin air and attached itself to my heart. I could do nothing but follow it. I had to meet my grandmother before she died. This family member about whom I had heard so little and had never met; that distant relative that we never spoke of. Up until that point in my life, my Papa had never gone back to India or shown any interest in doing so. He rarely, if ever, mentions his life in his home country. Outside of his favorite Indian Restaurant, the Taj Mahal, and the occasional visits to the Hindu temple (where they offered free food and childcare), I knew very little of my East Indian heritage.

It's not my story to tell, so I'll keep it high-level. Upon the death of his father when he was ten years old, my father and several of his siblings (there were around twenty kids) were sent by his mother to live in an orphanage. Imagine growing up in a Catholic orphanage, in the same town that you were born in, but away from your family. It carved deep wounds. Papa wasn't given the skills to process or transcend his pain, and by extension, he couldn't forgive his homeland.

With that background explained, I'll turn our attention back to the story. I was dead set on getting to India before it was too late to meet my grandmother, and therefore, too late to fully understand where I come from. There were no obstacles in getting myself to India; I only saw a mission I had to carry out. My nineteen-year-old self knew this was an opportunity to understand my heritage that, if lost, would never come again. I investigated study abroad programs to explore how I could get myself to India while fulfilling the requirements for my full-ride scholarship. The majority of the programs in India were in big cities like Delhi and Mumbai, which were not close enough to Papa's hometown. Therefore, they were out of alignment with my quest. I refused to be discouraged. Instead, I found a program called Semester at Sea that happened to dock for five days in Chennai, Tamil Nadu. This port was a mere two hours away from my destination: the city of Pondicherry, located in Southern India. By the time I found this program, I had missed their deadline by two months. I needed Semester at Sea to accept me even though I was late, and I needed to attain $27,000 in scholarships to cover the cost. The fire inside of my younger self was wild and untamable. It burned so bright that it manifested exactly what I needed. Failure wasn't an option.

Papa was pissed! Like every other Indian parent, he wanted me to be studying, working towards a respectable job, and putting all of my energy towards becoming "successful." His idea of success did not include sailing around the world on a cruise ship with 600 spoiled (in his eyes), college-aged brats. He had no interest in reuniting with his mother or in healing ties with his native India.

Despite being deeply uncomfortable by the thought of causing my father pain, I knew that I had to remain true to myself. I simply had to go, even if it caused a huge rift in our relationship, or even if he could not accept that his precious baby girl was disobeying him by "dropping out of college to go party on a boat." Sometimes my path is made so glaringly obvious that all other options become mute, and all I can see is my destiny. For these moments of utter clarity, I am extremely grateful.

He told all his siblings not to give me any information about my grandmother. Without a full name, an address, or even a picture to go on, I was headed out on mission impossible, Dady style. All I had were a few stories, the name of a city in Southern India, an invisible natal-like energy cord pulling me to my grandmother, and a burning desire to find her. To somehow, by magic and miracle, locate her before she died, in one of the most populated countries in the world and with only four days to accomplish it before having to get back on the ship. Yes, I know that it sounds like madness, but I never once doubted that I would make it happen.

When I finally got to India, they wouldn't let me into the country because I hadn't gotten the right visa. This was due to the rushed nature of my application and admittance into the program. The immigration officers were blown away by my conviction to enter the country. I passionately told them that if they didn't let me off the boat, I would climb the rope to the dock, or jump overboard and swim to shore. They finally let me in. No one and nothing was going to stop me, especially after overcoming countless financial and familial obstacles to get to my father's land. In addition to that, I had to get all the vaccines necessary to travel, I didn't have money for malaria meds, I contracted scabies while on the boat, I was seasick, and I got food poisoning that led to untreated parasites in my stomach. They ate through my stomach lining and caused years of IBS issues. As if that wasn't a long enough list of health obstacles I had to overcome, we also had a rabies scare. When we were in Brazil, monkeys came onto the boat one night and bit some of the students. They were all over the boat, curious about what was in our suitcases. At that time, there was a global shortage of rabies vaccines, so we had to basically pull straws to see who would get the vaccine. I opted out because I hadn't really come in contact with a monkey, but I knew that there was no cure for rabies.

Regardless of all these hurdles, I finally arrived at this vibrant, small beach town of my father's birthplace. I FaceTimed him. I remember that conversation, plain as day. "Papa, I made it! I'm finally in India, in Pondicherry. I know you did not want me to go, and I'm sorry, but will you please help me find my grandmother?" Papa provided me with nothing, saying only, "You're not my daughter. My daughter would never leave college and disobey her father." I was in complete disbelief at what I was hearing. After everything I had gone through to get here, after literally sailing around the world for months, everything I'd done and overcome—my papa still would not budge. That was the moment I learned what it meant to bear the accusation of betrayal in order to remain true to myself. I realized that I was going to have to find her on my own. I was an American girl who didn't speak any Tamil or French (the local languages). I was wishing on a star that I'd miraculously cross paths with my grandmother and immediately recognize her based on a twenty-year-old photo that I had seen as a child.

Knowing that India is no place for a young woman to move about alone, I obeyed my father's request to not travel solo. A fellow shipmate, Elliot Dahl, agreed to accompany me on this wild and crazy adventure. I am forever grateful to him for his generosity of spirit and encouragement along the way. Elliot came with me to government buildings, telecommunication company offices, orphanages, strangers' houses, and cemeteries in search of Meme. Together, we followed every lead we could get our hands on, like Hansel and Gretel following their trail of breadcrumbs. It was to no avail. As day three began to slip away, I started to doubt myself and wonder if it was all just some silly fantasy. I was beginning to lose my sense of self-assured destiny. Had I created an unnecessary divide between my father and myself? Had I hyped up an entire ship of college students and faculty with my overly confident and enthusiastic sharing that I was on the adventure of a lifetime to find my long-lost grandmother? I had felt so sure that this was what I was meant to do. I couldn't believe it wasn't coming true. Everything had fallen so beautifully into place, all pointing to "green light, go go go."

The wildest part of this whole journey is that I did it. YAS, QUEEN! I found my grandmother on the third day. I had about 24 hours left in Pondicherry before I had to ship out to our next port. Amidst the chaos of India's tuk tuks, street dogs, a naked toddler being hosed off by his mother in the street, and the shouts of people shocked to see two white-looking people walking down their humble street, I looked up at a woman standing on a balcony. I immediately recognized my Meme looking down at me. As soon as I caught sight of her, everything around me fell silent and became blurry. All I could see was her.

She threw down, I kid you not, an antique skeleton key attached to a handkerchief. We let ourselves into her home. Having known my father married a fair-skinned woman, she knew I was Charles' daughter by the sight of me. The tears immediately flowed as we embraced, smiled, and laughed while sitting on plastic chairs in her cement house. I had trusted so deeply in myself that I had manifested, without much to go on, my long-lost relative. To read the whole story in detail, check out my travel blog from 2011, Cement Sailor (thought I was so clever with that title!).[17] Unbeknownst to me, my shipmate and fellow detective, Elliot, was surreptitiously videotaping our entire adventure. He produced a short video of our three-day search and my first-ever meeting with my grandmother.[18] It remains one of the greatest gifts I've ever gotten and reminds me that miracles happen every day. God answers every prayer, even if the answer is no—but in this case, I was blessed with a yes.

When my father saw the video and witnessed for himself how his mother welcomed me, her never-before-met granddaughter, his heart thawed and he decided to go back to India the following year. He brought all three of his daughters. We now have strong connections to our Indian family and Papa makes a practice of going back regularly since I reunited the family. It's amazing now to understand that me answering my soul's call ended up healing generations, both old and young.

It was in the listening to that quiet inner voice of my soul self (well, in this instance, she was shouting at the top of her lungs, "GO SEE YOUR MEME BEFORE SHE DIES" while waving her arms and jumping up and down) that I discovered my truth. When we give ourselves the time and space to go inward and explore who we are, away from the prescriptions, judgments, and rules of our culture, family structure, religion, and society, then we come to know ourselves. We begin to understand the utter importance of not betraying our own souls. The cost of living for others and by their rules, so as to not rock the boat (or in my case, a giant ship) is simply too great.

Life Tests How Well You "Know Thyself"

If you're reading this book, chances are you've already borne the accusation of betrayal so that you don't betray yourself. Whether it's ending a relationship while the other person is still deeply in love with you, choosing to leave your family's religion, or even going vegan in an immigrant or southern household, all can invite shame from others. Having done all of the above, I have a greater understanding of and compassion for those moments in life when it's necessary to do something that may be hurtful to another. It is sometimes what is right, and best, and of the highest purpose for self.

As Socrates put it, "The unexamined life is not worth living."[19] We've never had more reasons NOT to examine our lives with the constant influx of dings, beeps, bings, tweets, zing-zings, and endless channels of entertainment. Our modern, entertainment-filled, virtual existence has swapped the common mid-life crisis for a quarter-life crisis. Being raised on the boob tube doesn't leave much space for looking at the clouds and daydreaming, wondering if they are made of cotton candy, and imagining yourself riding a sparkly, purple, rainbow-eating dragon across the sky. It's in those whimsical, nonsensical, free-form moments to simply be that we create the space to know all those complex parts within us that comprise our authentic selves.

What "Knowing Thyself" Is (And Isn't)

A mental image that illustrates the concept of "knowing oneself," as the remainder of the aforementioned poem by Oriah Mountain Dreamer states, is the ability to stand in the fire without shrinking back.

It doesn't interest me
who you know
or how you came to be here.
I want to know if you will stand
in the center of the fire
with me
and not shrink back.
—"The Invitation" [20]

It means to stay fully present, no matter the circumstance; to be aligned with one's inner compass without running, hiding, or straying from one's inner truth, no matter the perceived cost. It means being unmoving in one's perspectives, beliefs, and values. It means fully showing up in the world as oneself and not being swayed by how other people are showing up. For example, it may be perceived as betraying one's family to be outspokenly anti-racist, if one's family subscribes to racist beliefs. However, it would be betraying that person's soul to do otherwise.

It's easy to think that knowing oneself necessitates sitting on a mountaintop alone without food or water for days or going to a ten-day Vipassana silent meditation retreat. Whereas these are paths to encounter our divine selves, truly knowing oneself is so much more nuanced and complex than those activities. I have come to believe that it's about knowing myself in all possible ways, under all possible circumstances; and remaining true to myself amidst all of them. It's easy to know myself in the context of my comfort zone, and in the context of my close friends who cherish and value me. But, do

I know myself in the many environments where
I am not known? Where no one is known to me,
or when I find myself in challenging circumstances
where I might stand alone for what I believe to be
the ethical way forward? Do I know myself in an
environment where I am persecuted, judged, belittled,
and perceived as less than? Do I know myself in those
spaces, and most importantly, do I like how I show up
in those moments? When in a heightened emotional
state or triggered space, are my actions aligned with
my highest values? If not, perhaps I recognize that
I am lying to myself about what my highest values are.

Regardless of liking how I show up, can I face it;
accept it; own it? Can I own even the ugliest sides
of myself? The "true self," who we are at our core,
often slips away when we're challenged or feeling
vulnerable. We become malleable, hampered by
wanting to fit in and needing to be loved. We abdicate
and abandon ourselves. Simply put, we sell out.
In these moments, we come face to face with the true
test of knowing ourselves and experiencing what it
takes to remain strong in our resolve to be ourselves.
That is truly knowing ourselves. That is authenticity.

What do we mean by authenticity? Put simply,
authenticity means that you're true to your own
spirit, your own personality, and your own
values, regardless of the pressures you're under.
You're honest with yourself and with others, and
you take responsibility for your choices, actions,
miscalculations, trespasses, and mistakes.

Authenticity is not being shiny, sparkly, perfect, or beautiful. Authenticity is being exactly who you are, moment by moment, day by day. An ever-evolving organism, showing up to the best of your ability, heart, mind, and soul—even on your worst days—and still being okay with being you. That's the trippy part about coming to know yourself (if you're doing it "right"—lol). You realize that you're constantly evolving and up-leveling.

Being in constant evolution means your authentic expression looks different from moment to moment, and that it is unique to you. Justin Bieber comes to mind as a perfect example of this. The Canadian sweetie pie with a mushroom haircut, discovered on YouTube, became a neck-tatted, hip-hop collaborating, Los Angeles celebrity by his teens. Tween stars have to go through the painful (and often ugly) process of finding themselves and their authentic voice, while in the face of millions of fans and thousands of cameras. They're all telling these stars who they are expected to be and who they should be, in order to maximize everyone else's personal agenda. Talk about a sh!tty way to find your authentic self; in the glaring, profit-driven lights of stardom. No wonder so many of them turn to drugs and alcohol. It's not a pretty process, even if you're doing it in the comfort of your family home. Imagine having to unwillingly share it with millions of people. Regardless, the journey of self-discovery is one we have to undertake, in order to become who we are here to be.

How Will I Know?

How will I know if I really love me?
I say a prayer with every heartbeat.
I fall in love whenever we meet.
I'm asking myself 'cause if I don't know,
no one will.
—Laxmi's remix of the late, great Whitney Houston's
classic tune "How Will I Know"

It is said that everyone and everything is a mirror for us. Wanting to know how someone else feels or what they want is an insight into our own inner world. If you find yourself desperate to understand someone's true nature, other than getting obliterated with them (you know, the kind of drunk where your souls leave your bodies and you have that dead-eye zombie walk going), there are three really good ways to get to know people's true essence:

1. Travel with them in a foreign country where you don't speak the language. Proceed to get lost.

2. Live with them—especially if you have to share a bathroom.

3. Go through some sort of large riff in the relationship that creates the kind of tension you could cut with a knife; followed by a period of not talking.

Any of these three experiences will clearly and quickly show you who someone really is (as well as who you are). Oftentimes, relationships will make it or break it in the above-mentioned circumstances. Each experience is a pressure cooker that brings emotions to a boil. Authentic selves will rise to the surface, no matter how seemingly solid the façade and the self-lies may be. You, as the receiver or perpetrator of the bubbling over, get to choose how you show up in the face of adversity in a way that's authentically you. Sometimes it's "Cool, I'm really glad I'm learning this about you and about myself," and sometimes it's "Ugh, this is really ugly and I don't want to be involved in this." Knowing oneself is being able to look at all of it: the good, the bad, the ugly, the beautiful, the judgmental, the open-hearted, the kind, the generous, the fearful, the past self, the future self, and the present self. We could get *really* meta with this and talk about past-life self, astral projection self, alien species self, or hybrid alien child self. There are infinite versions of the self, and the discoveries are equally as infinite. We really do contain multiverses!

It's crucial to recognize that knowing yourself is a constant evolution because as we unfold a lot of what was modeled to us as kids, we get to know ourselves on deeper levels. We receive the blessing of knowing things about ourselves from past lives that may shift how we show up in the present life. We may also get visions of the future that can make us think, "Wow, my life is going to be so beautiful, juicy, and exciting!" Déjà-vus come to me often. I call them "God crumbs."

Viewing déjà-vus as God's way of reminding me that I'm on my path, doing what I'm supposed to be doing, and living in alignment with universal values gets me jazzed. It's equally true that sometimes I see insights into my future and think, "Whoa, that does not look like anything I'd ever do." Fast forward to reality and I'm in that exact situation doing that thing I thought I would never do. Anytime I do something out of alignment with who I am or who I want to be, spirit course-corrects me—oftentimes very abruptly and harshly (think car accidents, dramatic breakups, and cross-country moves). It's like God has 24/7 surveillance cameras on me and whenever I'm breaking my own boundaries, a force puts me back on track, lickity-split. I'm then reminded why I have those values. Knowing yourself when you're triggered, when you're happy, and when you're sad are all equally important and constantly evolving.

Discovering Oneself Is The Song That Never Ends

Are you committed to the never-ending journey? I know it doesn't sound as glamorous as Instagram wants to make you think it is. It doesn't fit into an aesthetically pleasing infographic or color-coordinated grid post. You can't squeeze all that goes into knowing yourself into a TikTok video of a skinny, blonde twenty-something who's swinging over a valley in Bali. The journey of knowing yourself is one of the few things YouTube can't fully teach you (although there are incredible resources on there by people like Abraham Hicks and Joe Dispenza, and so many TED talks). The journey of knowing yourself comes with and from the quality of questions you ask yourself, as well as the level of presence and attention you give to this noble and sometimes daunting task of self-discovery. It's definitely not as beautiful as sitting on the top of a mountain in a white shawl, watching the sunrise spread over the misty sky, like motivational seminar advertisements want you to believe. It's kind of like selling baby products to first-time parents. Personal discovery and childbirth are messy, gritty, chaotic, and painful. Simultaneously, alongside the feelings of crazy, challenging chaos, the most rewarding, fulfilling, confidence-creating, juicy, vibe-boosting reality *imaginable* can be found.

The journey of self-discovery is much more like that clip of Charlie in *It's Always Sunny in Philadelphia* when he's losing his $hit in the mailroom, seeing ghosts, and imagining real people to be non-existent.[21]

The journey of knowing oneself is well worth the painful transformation we undergo. We're being liquified and having our known world totally vanish, because when we know ourselves, then we can *be* ourselves. And when we can be ourselves, we create space for others to be themselves too (paying it forward, y'all). Then, we free the whole planet and eradicate suffering for all beings, as many Eastern philosophies strive for.

When people feel safe to be and express all of who they are, that's when the magic happens. That's the secret sauce; the juiciness that fuels creation, fostering all manner of new thinking and powerful ideas. It sets innovation in motion. Countless incredible transformations and improvements have come from

FX, *It's Always Sunny in Philadelphia*

friends simply connecting, laughing, brainstorming, and then saying, "That's actually a really good idea. Let's do it." It typically starts in a basement or garage (often with a cash injection from a family member) and explodes from there. Magic moments like that are only possible when we know ourselves, because only then do we really understand what we're capable of. Knowing ourselves opens us up to the knowledge that we are capable of everything we really put our hearts and minds into. We are magnificent, powerful beings that are truly capable of doing anything we desire; but to do so, we must be completely clear on who we are and what that real, deep desire is.

For me, knowing myself also means knowing my family, knowing my heritage, and knowing my culture. It means understanding my past, the people

in it, and the things they've contributed so that
I can craft my life into what it is today.

Knowing my ancestors, even those I can only touch
on the energetic, spiritual plane, is part of knowing
myself. On a heroic-dose mushroom journey I did in
2022 with my best friend, I physically felt the pain
of my West Indian, Guyanese, and German female
ancestors, seven generations back. Regardless of
culture, each generation of women in my ancestry
suffered horrible treatment in the shackles of
womanhood. Both my mother and father are from
countries colonized by the British. The blood that
flows through my veins is of the colonizers, as well
as of those who weathered intense brutality at the
colonizers' hands. In contrast, my German lineage
controlled all of the wheat in East Deutschland.
There is a town named after my ancestors, Uckro and
a museum dedicated to them there. There are giant,
ornate, gold-framed portraits of them painted in
powdered wigs, living in castles. They were one of
the first families in Germany to acquire a vehicle,
outside of the government, in the early 20th century.
I give thanks for the hardships and the joys my
ancestors experienced that led to my existence
in the here and now.

Knowing yourself involves knowing your
grandmother. The seed that made you was inside
of your grandmother when she was pregnant with
your mother. Women are like Russian nesting dolls.
The seed that my mother came from was inside of

my grandmother (Mutti, as we called her) when she was a baby inside of my great-grandmother (Oma). When we look at it from this perspective, it becomes easy to see the importance of knowing your lineage and your culture. It may sound cliché, but we really are all connected. The human birthing process and aforementioned cycle of generational egg-carrying highlights and further proves that.

We are less than six degrees of separation from every single person on this planet, through a combination of biological relations, friends, and/or acquaintances. The world is so much smaller than we think it is. Read these next few sentences slowly: the more we know ourselves, the more we can know others. The more we can know others, the deeper we can love others. The deeper we can love others, the deeper we can experience love—especially love for ourselves.

Everything we see in other people is reflected back at us. If I see something in someone that I find absolutely incredible, admirable, beautiful, gorgeous, and amazing, I am actually seeing those things in myself. Otherwise, I wouldn't be able to recognize them elsewhere. That is the beauty of knowing yourself; for in knowing yourself, you come to know everything.

Mystery of the World

You already have the answers; all you have to do is tap back in. Tap back into your inner child, because you were probably never more self-aware than when you were two years old. Young children walk around vivacious and free, loud and energetic, fully present and self-expressed in every moment. They know nothing else! When raised in societies where they are unrepressed, toddlers do what they want, when they want. Little ones are a great example of what it means to be fully self-expressed. They cry when they feel like crying, scream when they feel like screaming, laugh and squeal when they feel joy, and fall asleep right where they stand, when they're tired. Clothes come on and off as they are hot or cold, food goes in when they are hungry, and so on. They simply respond to their present need without thought or judgment.

As we grow into slightly older versions of ourselves, the rules change and we become "socialized and civilized." We start judging these responses to primal needs, swapping out freedom for culturally appropriate behavior known as manners, social rules, ethics, religion, and tradition. We abandon our true selves and get lost in the capitalist, religious, patriarchal norms of Western society. As we discover the loss of ourselves, we spend a good portion of our remaining life trying to get back to that place of childlike wonder; back to that place of exploration, joy, and freedom.

You Are The One You've Been Waiting For

In the brilliant show *Insecure*, by Issa Rae and Larry Wilmore, two best friends (Molly and Issa) discuss how there are certain things you don't do with your girlfriends that you would do in a romantic relationship. One example was treating your BFF to a trip to Mexico, just because you know that they love Mexican food. Molly told Issa that she would never do something like that because they weren't dating. It made me think, "Why don't I do stuff like that with my girlfriends? Why don't I spontaneously do random, fantastical acts for my loved ones (other than sending them handwritten cards, which I often do)?"

Then I thought, "Why don't I do those things for myself?" I thought about how I love having flowers around. Fresh-cut flowers make me feel loved, rich, special, and inspired. I like smelling them. They literally remind me to stop and smell the roses. However, I rarely buy myself flowers because I can't justify the expense. The internal dialogue that I have had is, "I should be saving that money to propel my business, put it towards retirement, or donate it to a worthy cause." It wasn't until my father asked me to buy his girlfriend flowers that I decided to buy some for myself at the same time. Now, when I awake and see a gorgeous bouquet strategically placed to be the first thing I see in the morning, I feel joy.

The concept of romancing and dating oneself is lost in this world of busyness, distraction, and constant connection to technology. In reality, the more we know ourselves, the more we "date" ourselves. The more we date ourselves, the more we come to know, accept, appreciate, and love ourselves! The more we do that for ourselves, the more we can date and love others. Right now, take a pause. Breathe, and think of something you can do to get to know yourself deeper and more intimately. Treat this interaction as you would if you were getting to know someone else for the first time. It could be something as small as Googling "The 36 Questions That Make People Fall in Love," (developed in the '90s by psychologists Arthur Aron, Ph.D., and Elaine Aron, Ph.D.) and journaling about a different one each day. You could try setting a timer for five minutes and looking into your eyes in the mirror, or observing how you feel in different types of lighting.

Knowing yourself comes in many forms. Most often, it comes through self-reflection. Time being alone and quiet, and experiences just outside your comfort zone are crucial. The suffragette and former First Lady, Eleanor Roosevelt, said "Do one thing every day that scares you."[22] What is something that terrifies you? Safety permitting, go do it! While doing it, be aware of how you show up and feel during the process. How does your body react? What thoughts are going through your mind?

Everyone is a Reflection of Us

90% of what goes on in our brains—thoughts, bodily responses, actions, and more—are subconscious (meaning below our conscious, thinking mind). We're not consciously making the thoughts; they're simply happening based on patterning we developed in early childhood (0–8 years old). Unfortunately, the majority of people's subconscious patterning is set to negative internal dialogue. We tell ourselves harsh things like, "I'm not good enough. I'm fat, bad at things, ugly, and all-around terrible. Everyone is mad at me." Because we are so tough on ourselves, it is often easy to allow others to treat us like sh*t. Why? It's because, at a subconscious level, we're already telling ourselves that we aren't worth anything. We say it over and over in a variety of ways, multiple times a day. All of this negative self-talk, however subtle, undermines our self-worth and deeply embeds the limiting belief that we are not worthy of good things happening to us.

I used to be best friends with a bully. One time, after this person had berated me particularly harshly, I asked them, "Why are you so mean to me? You say the most horrible things. I would never talk to anyone like that, especially not someone I claim to love." They replied, "This is nothing. You should hear how I talk to myself inside my own head." Looking back, it's obvious that there was a lot of self-loathing going on. Conversely, if I had wholly loved myself back then, I would not have chosen that friendship. I understand now that part of me wanted to feel oppressed, controlled, stifled, belittled, and to live in fear of this person's reactivity. I co-created a relationship in which I was frequently put down and felt like $hit, because I subconsciously felt that I deserved it. I thought that this was the cost of admission to receive love. Having to tolerate extreme ups, downs, and violent outbursts in order to be loved was a message I received in adolescence. I've been unlearning it ever since.

Everyone is a reflection of us. Truly! How I treat others is how I treat myself. A violent but poignant example that illustrates this point is that the majority of mass shooters kill themselves after their heinous acts.
If you don't value others' lives, there's no way
you value your own.

As we begin to absorb this concept, it becomes easier and easier to see ourselves in everyone, and everyone in us; universal Oneness, if you will. The concept of Oneness does not negate the differences in the many unique, lived experiences that play out on this planet. Each human, on an individual level, experiences differences in access to opportunity or privilege based on their skin, wealth, nationality, education, able-bodiedness, and more. Focusing on Oneness is not a way to "spiritually bypass" the injustices many people are subjected to on a daily basis. These injustices are often based on circumstances out of their control, like their lineage or family of origin. On the contrary, spiritual Oneness shows us that there is an invisible web uniting all beings and that we are all much more alike than different.

Oneness is how we can feel the pain of others that has nothing to do with us; like when there is war halfway across the globe and it outrages those who will never see even a single bullet fly. Part of knowing yourself is knowing what is yours, what is someone else's,
and what is universal oneness.

There are times to take on and receive true feedback. There are times when what people are giving you is not yours, and merely someone else's projection of themselves onto you. When you're consciously managing your thoughts and are aware of yourself and your words, it becomes much harder for people to f*ck with you (in this case, remove you from your center and truth).

The negative feedback and screaming I received from my former friend never truly hit home for me, because it wasn't true for me. As a result of knowing myself, I knew it was their own sh*t reflecting back at them. Knowing yourself will help make you stronger, more resilient, and more spiritually aware. This comes in handy when people give you feedback. You can simultaneously be open to the feedback that's true— what you need to hear for your continued growth and unfolding—while also recognizing what is not yours, or what doesn't resonate with you. The deeper you know yourself, the deeper you can differentiate what is yours to hold, and what is other people's bullshit, karma, and/or insecurities that they're projecting. Knowing your subconscious thoughts helps you curate and manifest a life of intentionality that's really fulfilling, connected, and empowering. No bad can come from knowing yourself! Yes, you will see parts of yourself that you don't want to see. It will be uncomfortable, and you will be challenged. But remember this: if you're not being challenged, you're not living fully. You're growin' or you're dyin', right?

The Harder the Journey,
the Better the Destination

Whatever it takes for you to get to know yourself, it's worth it. At the end of the day, all you have is yourself. After all, when we die, we die alone. Many believe that we reincarnate. That would potentially make it so that the more you can uncover about yourself in this life, the less work you have to do in the next life, or the more fulfilling and free-flowing your path will be. Only *you* get to determine what that is. Only *you* get to decide how deep you go on the journey of knowing yourself because it is literally infinite. Be gentle with yourself while also challenging yourself.

As I invited you to, choose one thing every day that facilitates getting to know yourself more. Maybe it's a meditation practice, or writing down a list of things that you're afraid of and then scheduling them into your calendar once a week. Maybe learning a new skill, language, or hobby (letting yourself be "bad" at something) is a great way to get to know yourself. That way, you get to hear that subconscious internal dialogue brought to the forefront. At the beginning of the pandemic, I took Zoom voice lessons from my friend Elle Logan (I highly recommend her. Find her on IG at @the.elle.logan). What I learned about voice lessons is that they consist of very little singing and a lot of noise-making. Never before had I just twisted and curved my mouth into such odd shapes while huffing, puffing, and hoping to blow the house down with my raw talent. Somehow, I managed to feel like I was "bad" at producing obscure sounds that didn't resemble either beauty or singing by any stretch of the imagination. The sounds I was making differed greatly from those my opera-singing teacher was producing. I didn't sound as eloquent and struggled with replicating notes in the same key and pitch as I was hearing them. It was really fun being a beginner but really hard to be bad at something—especially something that sounded weird to begin with. "This is embarrassing. I sound weird, and I'm sure my family can hear me," and other unhelpful thoughts ran through my head. I came downstairs and heard the Dadys mocking me, all attempting to make the same funky noises I had been attempting. Even in the midst of my self-judging mind swirls, I laughed at myself and felt pride that I was courageous enough to try something new. Remember, we can always choose to learn a new skill. We can always choose to push ourselves outside of our comfort level, creating new goals to strive for. What are you going to choose?

Practice

Imagine you're sitting on a park bench and another version or twin of you sits beside you. Y'all engage in a pleasant conversation, as two strangers sitting beside one another might. Who is this other person? What age, gender, or part of your ancestry do they represent? What message do they have for you? Imagine an entire conversation with this person and be present with whatever they want to share with you.

Journaling Prompts

What part of myself can
I spend time with today?

What is one fun thing I can do
regularly to better learn myself?

Want To Go Deeper?

Dady's Gotcha. What are your top three values? If you don't know or want clarity, try the following:

- Play music that uplifts your spirit.

- Search for a list of values online with at least one hundred listed.

- Circle all the values that resonate.

- Do a second pass and highlight a maximum of fifty that really hit.

- Do a third pass and star your top twenty.

- And finally, draw three circles on a blank piece of paper and clump those twenty top values into three categories.

- Whichever word best describes each category becomes one of your top three values.

Still Begging for More?

Ok, teacher's pet! Here's some extra credit: Once you identify your top three values, write them in big letters on the back of a poster board. Make a vision board emulating those top three values.

Lesson 2
Honesty
Relationship Within and Without

"The words you speak become the house you live in."
—Rumi

Honesty is better than lying, and is foundational to spirituality. When I say "better than," I am referring to the fact that having to remember a web of lies one has told and living a life of deceit is incredibly stressful. Not to mention that one will rapidly fall into a reputation of being dishonest. Even in organized crime circles, the hierarchy expects honesty and loyalty to the members of the "family." In all walks of life, honesty is regarded as virtuous. The hard part is to understand what is meant by honesty in a spiritual sense, as well as what it is NOT, and how to live up to this extremely challenging aspect of spiritual life. Let's break it down.

What Honesty Is Not

Have you ever noticed how some people weaponize the truth or honesty? They say mean and hurtful things, which happen to be true, and after they decimate someone to tears and anguish, they justify this with the words, "Well, I was only being honest." From the spiritual point of view, while that may be honest and true, that is not the type of honesty we are looking for here. My spiritual guide, Meher Baba, is an ascended master (like Jesus) from the Middle East who lived in India and did not speak for the last 44 years of his life. He once said to one of his closest disciples, Eruch, "The Truth, when told, is that which uplifts another. Anything which crushes another person cannot be true."[23]

What Is Honesty?

My mentor, Don Stevens, was one of the people who helped Meher Baba create the spiritual order known as Sufism Reoriented. It was named "reoriented," because it was originally a Sufi order founded by a saint named Hazrat Inayat Khan, and then it was "remastered" by Meher Baba. Khan did great work, but when Baba took over as the head (and heart) of the order, he gave fresh instructions for how the disciples (mureeds) should live. One of the points he gave in their new rules (or "charter") was absolute honesty.

Don told me that for the Sufi mureeds, this was one of the most difficult instructions because there was tremendous confusion about what this means and how to live up to it. One fellow said to Don, "If I am totally honest with my boss, I will get fired." Naturally, Baba needed to clarify his meaning of the word honesty in this spiritual context of living in a Sufi order. Here is the gist of what Baba eventually explained to the Sufis, based on what Don explained to me (and those gathered with Don). Please forgive me for paraphrasing this explanation, I am not sure it is published anywhere else verbatim unless the Sufis have it written down in their archives.

Baba said to the Sufi mureeds that there are many factors to consider when being honest, and that what he means by honesty is basically a careful consideration before action. For example, he said, let's say you are asked by someone about something you are knowledgeable about, and you want to give an honest response.

First, he said, you have to ask yourself about what you know. How much does this individual have the right to this information? And is speaking to them about this issue going to be helpful, or useful, in some way? In general, what is your relationship to this individual, and how much of what you know is really for them to receive and know? Baba said that in some cases, they have no right whatsoever to what you know. Remaining silent is an option, and silence is not dishonest. He said that in other cases, you may have a relationship with this person which dictates they have a right to everything you know about the situation, but this is rare. Most likely, Baba continued, you will be in a conversation where you feel that that individual should be given some portion of what you know (not nothing, and not everything). Baba said to start with this consideration and become clear about this.

Okay, so next he said, one must make a determination of this situation in relation to the exact person asking about it. Naturally, some of what you know will be considered "positive" by the person asking, and some will be received as "negative." Some of what you may share may be received by another in a way that is difficult, and in other cases, what you say will be pleasing.

In any case, Baba said that if you only tell that person the positive and willfully withhold the negative (or that which is difficult for them to hear), that is not honest. On the other hand, if you only share the negative, and withhold the good or pleasing, to "spin" the sharing in some way, that also is not honest. So what is honesty? It is to share that which is present in your original understanding in the correct proportion. This doesn't mean half and half. It means the proportion you know to be present in the situation. It is not simple.

For example, let's say you are asked in conversation about your recent divorce and there is a lot to share. However, you size up the situation and decide that this particular person can know about 20% of your own direct experience of divorce. So right there, the scope of what you share has been reduced. Now, of the entire experience of your divorce, some of it was "positive" and some of it was "negative," naturally. And this is also in relation to what you feel the receiver of your sharing will deem positive and negative as well. It is a careful consideration.

Perhaps your overall experience is that divorce was 75% negative and painful and suffering, and there was 25% positive or pleasing, and growth, or whatever. So, when you share with this person that 20% of what you know, in that 20% should be reflected the 75% negative experience and the 25% positive. This means the proportion would be accurate, so as not to spin the story towards either positive or negative, but honestly state what you feel and know to be true. Whew!

I know that was a complicated definition from Baba about spiritual honesty. However, there is something quite amazing about Baba's version of honesty. Many things strike me as remarkable, actually. Let's take them one by one.

1. The first thing I notice is that Baba's process of contemplating all this before speaking slows down the mind.

2. Instead of blurting out some half-baked statement (and potentially harming someone), it becomes a real process.

3. By considering this all so carefully, I believe the ego has less ability to "weaponize" honesty.

4. We can see from what Baba has said that one can actually decide that there is nothing to say, so remaining silent may be the best option for the situation.

5. Lastly, with Baba's consideration of how useful or relevant what you know is to the receiver, it also gives you an opportunity to be of real service to the listener.

Naturally, at work, or in some cases with others it is simply not possible to remain silent. However, I have noticed that even at work, sometimes remaining silent and witnessing how things unfold may be the best option. All this requires practice, and I have been practicing. I would encourage you, the next time you feel tempted to lie about something, to practice Meher Baba's version of honesty and see what adventure unfolds. I believe that you won't be disappointed.

How To Live Honestly With Oneself, With God, and With Community

I would like to close with an experience I had around honesty, which is a great spiritual case study and close to my heart.

This is a story about my first marriage, which ended in 2011. Meher Baba said once, in response to whether spiritually we can get divorced, "If there is no love left in the marriage, why remain married?" The love was not only gone, in its place was emotionally abusive damage to myself and our children, as well as our close community of friends. In a short time, two peoples' lustful behaviors created an impact crater of anguish in my heart, and on our community landscape. It was compounded by denial, lies, and gaslighting. Furthermore, once-intimate love connections can be found to act like complete strangers once their behaviors are exposed.

I walked out the front door of my home and never returned. I rented a new house near my daughter's high school (so she would have a short drive to school), and moved out alone. I set up two bedrooms, one for each of my children, and I began a new life doing my best to keep my children as close as humanly possible. That was over ten years ago.

I can say now that while the divorce and what it did to our family was the single most painful experience of my life, so much incredible good has come from that experience. Now I am extremely happily remarried and have created a new life with my lovely wife, Vanessa. We live in North Carolina, where we continue to create new love adventures. I am also closer to my children now than I have ever been.

Thank you Baba!

Lessons

- Honesty with oneself can lead to the dissolution of denial, delusion, and self-deception and connect one more deeply with one's higher self.

- The extra effort made towards honesty leads to a more spiritual life.

- Honesty doesn't bring popularity, but it does help ensure that you're with "the right people."

- Deceptive words and behaviors are toxic, and long term loving relationships can be destroyed in just a few days.

- In spirituality, honesty is not to be weaponized by the ego but navigated with care. This ultimately contributes to the weakening of the ego.

- Honesty is a spiritual value that can be embraced by anyone at any time.

Journaling Prompt

In what ways have I struggled to become more honest on my spiritual journey?

Lesson 3
Personal Power
It's About Me, and
That's the Good News!

"You are the sky. Everything else—it's just the weather."
—Pema Chödrön

The term "personal power" is pretty much everywhere these days. Personal power is a topic that is so *hot* right now. As they say in *Zoolander*, "That damn Hansel! He's so hot right now!"[24]

What is personal power, and what does it mean to stand in one's personal power? A quick Google search brought infinite answers. I grabbed the first explanation that came up. This one is from LinkedIn: "Personal power is your own skill and ability to influence people and events, whether or not you have any formal authority."[25]

When I think of this, I think of the power that lives within us all. Whether it's dormant or engaged, we all have it. We also all have the same amount of it. I can feel you wanting to argue this point with me right now. Maybe you're thinking, "I don't have as much power as the Supreme Court Justices, the Kardashians, or the global elite (Bill Gates, Jeff Bezos, Mark Zuckerberg, and Elon Musk)." These are examples of people with positional power. You have just as much personal power as anyone else on this planet. The question to ask is not whether you have it or not. Rather, the questions to ask are: Are you aware of your personal power? Are you tapped into it? Are you consciously choosing to use it? The idea that one person has more personal power than another is a fallacy. The confusion around this comes from old social structures of power. Regardless of who you are, your personal power is always there. Always! Whether or not you are tapping into it, acting from it, and living within it, it's *right here*, right now.

Do you want to free your personal power? Are you ready to step into it and wield it wisely from a place of love? To use it in service of creating your unshakably centered and balanced self? If the answer is "yes," then keep reading. I warn you; it's going to cost you. A-ha! It's going to cost you your "poor me" mentality. You know, those delicious victim stories that give you free passes from taking any action in your life. The ones that allow you to blame what happens to you on everyone and everything else around you. The ones you can get your besties to agree with, and really feel sorry for you as you choose inaction or moping instead of creating the life you want for yourself. I'll give you one pint of Ben and Jerry's and a season of *Sex and the City*, but after binging three seasons in three days, that behavior stops being restorative and goes into the self-deprecating bucket. I believe that you are ready to transform how you see yourself and your self-agency; otherwise, you would not have picked up this book.

Back to personal power, A.K.A. your inner Princess Shuri of Wakanda (or whoever your favorite superhero is). Personal power is the amount of agency, self-respect, self-advocacy, self-knowing, self-love, self-ownership, and self-awareness that we have. In other words, it's nothing more or less than your ability to recognize yourself. This is super important. I'd even call it a superpower because we can only recognize others as deeply as we can recognize ourselves. Back I go to that spiritual view from high up on the mountain. That elevated view gives me the ability to see you as me, and me as you. If I can see the divine in myself and come to love, accept, and respect myself, I'm giving myself the power to act in the world within my known-to-me value system. I can then see the divine in you. I can see how you love, accept, and respect yourself, and give yourself power to act in the world within your known-to-you value system. If I can't find this in myself and understand that I have agency to choose and make changes for myself, then there's no way I can find it in you. I wouldn't be able to honor it in you.

Think about all the relationships you have been in, and the people that have co-created those relationships with you. Take a moment to filter them all through this new lens of personal power. I bet you will very quickly be able to identify a whole bunch of really unhealthy relationships that you have found yourself in. The ones that go, "Why doesn't (insert someone's name) love me? What's wrong with me? I've done everything I could to change myself so that they will love me, and they still act like a jerk half the time. I just want to be loved." It's just like that stereotypical quote. "They can't love you because they don't know how to love themselves," said a bunch of girls to their heartbroken friend. Relationships like these are rampant, and they are rooted in victim stories; old trauma, helplessness, and neediness. The opposite of this approach is trying to act in a way that makes changes for the better in our own lives. Maybe you leave that sorry-a$$ lover behind and set out on your own hero's journey of self-discovery and self-empowerment. Sadly, we must go through our own version of hell to get there, and we always come out stronger and wiser for it. The prolific American author, Joseph Campbell, spoke to this often when comparing mythology across cultures and mythic creatures. Another great philosopher who speaks of the hell we must endure is the Italian poet, writer and philosopher from 13th century Florence; Dante Alighieri. Most famous for writing *The Divine Comedy,* Dante "traces the journey…from darkness and error to the revelation of the divine light."[26]

This also works in reverse, in the realm of that which we perceive as negative. I can't spew hate and shame onto you if I don't have hate and shame in me. Shadow work, people…shadow work. I cannot stress enough the importance of this in coming to know ourselves, accepting ourselves, healing ourselves, and empowering ourselves. We'll explore our shadow much more, a little further on. Searching through the depths of who we really are is actually like mining for precious gems. I think of myself as a beautiful diamond still in the rough. Ever wonder how diamonds are formed? I thought I did, but as it turns out, I didn't. I had just adopted the explanation I had been fed once upon a time. Turns out that the old story of coal being squeezed under high pressure is just that: old! And erroneous (like most of America's education system!) Diamond creation is actually much more exciting than just applying pressure. Dr. Evan M. Smith says,

Diamonds are exotic because they originate from so deep inside the earth. The diamonds we find have been transported close to the earth's surface by special magmatic eruptions, forming the rocks known as kimberlite, and occasionally lamproite. This magma rises quickly from the mantle up to the surface, sometimes whisking diamonds along for the ride as accidental passengers. Most natural diamonds, say 98%, come from a depth of about 150 to 200 kilometers, in the base of the thickest and oldest parts of continents. Some rare kinds of natural diamonds are formed at even greater depths, estimated to be as deep as 800 kilometers and perhaps more. This information alone draws an important distinction around diamonds. Almost all minerals, including most gemstones, we can access or mine at the earth's surface where they're formed within the crust, at comparatively shallow depths less than 30 to 50 kilometers.[27]

Wild, ain't it!? This process is no different for us humans. The deeper we dare to dig into the oldest parts of ourselves, and the more we dare to excavate and unearth, the more we come to understand our unique preciousness and our immense power. Our true inner diamond qualities. Diamonds are not only extremely exquisite and precious, but they are also the hardest, toughest substance on earth. Marianne Williamson, a phenomenal woman and student of the Course in Miracles (read her writings if you are not familiar), wrote about our "diamond-precious-gem-light." In her book, *A Return to Love*, Williamson writes a quote that is often misattributed to Nelson Mandela.

> Our deepest fear is not that we are inadequate. Our deepest fear is that we are powerful beyond measure. It is our light, not our darkness that most frightens us. We ask ourselves, 'Who am I to be brilliant, gorgeous, talented, fabulous?' Actually, who are you not to be? You are a child of God. Your playing small does not serve the world. There is nothing enlightened about shrinking so that other people won't feel insecure around you. We are all meant to shine, as children do. We were born to make manifest the glory of God that is within us. It's not just in some of us; it's in everyone.

> And as we let our own light shine, we unconsciously give other people permission to do the same. As we are liberated from our own fear, our presence automatically liberates others.[28]

Think about it this way: "I'm rubber, you're glue. Whatever you say bounces off me and sticks to you." It's really that simple. We know it as children before we become polluted by socialization and dragged away from our innocent, divinely-connected selves.

If someone sees something that they don't like in you and points it out to you in an abrasive or unloving way, it means that they're seeing parts of themselves that they have repressed. Our judgments, prejudices, and criticisms of others are our best mirrors of what we actually think about and suppress within ourselves. This is where personal power comes in. The power to truly know ourselves!

In the first *Matrix* movie, we watch the scene where the little boy in the Oracle's waiting room shows Neo how to bend the spoon by simply changing his perspective. This young, innocent-looking, monk-like boy holding the spoon and bending it purely by his intent instructs Neo to "not try and bend the spoon; that's impossible. Instead, only try to realize the truth… there is no spoon. Then you'll see that it is not the spoon that bends, it is only yourself."[29] We all have power. I've seen it demonstrated in ways I cannot explain; ways I would have thought impossible if I hadn't experienced it firsthand. For example, the day after finding my Meme in India, I watched someone levitate. I never would

have believed that someone could do that. I watched
this man, with a beard down to his knees, levitate
off of the floor of an ancient, Sanskrit-carved, stone
temple. There were no strings, lights, special effects,
or illusions at all. After effectively blowing my mind,
he stood up and walked out of the temple with us
as if nothing out of the ordinary had happened. His
movement from sitting to floating, and then walking
with us on the grounds, further confirmed to me
that he wasn't attached to anything. There was no
levitating platform or any trick to it. It was just the
power of his mind and the fact that he had trained
himself (probably for decades) to access his inner
power and outer agency.

You may not be a yogic guru or tai chi master, and
neither am I. Just like I'm not the President of the
United States or Beyoncé. Regardless, we all have that
same level of power within us, allowing us to live
according to our personal values. We get to choose
how we think, feel, respond, act, react, and proact.
As Viktor E. Frankl wrote in *Man's Search for Meaning*,
a 1946 book chronicling his experiences as a prisoner
in Nazi concentration camps during World War II,
"Everything can be taken from a man but one thing:
the last of the human freedoms—to choose one's
attitude in any given set of circumstances, to choose
one's own way."[30]

We are always, always, always at choice, no matter
the circumstance. It is always up to us how we choose
to exercise our personal powers of grace, kindness,

love, integrity, acceptance, respect, understanding, and curiosity. It means we are always at the steering wheels of our lives and can choose to change, walk away, respond, take wise action, or take no action.

Personal power is the ability to act and to choose, moment by moment. It's the mentality of getting up at 5:45 AM every day, going to the gym, working hard at your job, and being an excellent dog parent. It's also our ability to slow down, take big breaths, and exhale with big audible sighs. It's our ability to be able to take no action and simply be. Personal power is every choice in every moment because it lives within our person, always and forever. It goes with us wherever we go. We can make it act for us or against us. It literally does whatever we tell it to; loving us or hating us, keeping us stuck or moving us forward. It is on our side, whether we instruct it to create or destroy. The more we step into our personal power, grab our rudders and start steering our ships, the more miracles we can manifest. We can bring in more abundance and create more amazingness. Remember, it's not about power in terms of how much wealth I've amassed for myself, how many pounds I can lift, or how much status I can amass. Personal power is a deep, honest, vulnerable knowingness of self. It's a deep connection to source, and an undeniable, unshakable, insatiable connection to that continuous discovery of self.

Maybe you have even more questions now, being the curious human that you are. Where in my body does personal power live? What does it feel like?

How do I know if I have accessed it? When I am aligned and in my power, I feel a very vibrant energy line that travels from my red root chakra (the place between my reproductive organs, connecting me to the earth), up through my body, to my indigo-purple crown chakra (located at the top of my head, connecting me to the heavens). It roots me solidly into the earth and simultaneously connects me deeply with my spirituality. In that place, I feel grounded, centered, and aligned. I feel whole, capable, and clear; mentally, emotionally, and physically. If someone tried to knock me over physically or push me around emotionally, mentally, or spiritually, they would not be able to, because I am grounded and standing in my personal power. No one can take it away from me. No one can diminish it! No one can stop it, weaken it, deplete it, or lower it, just like Viktor Frankl wrote. Ooooohhh, would I love to see a world where we're all stepping into our personal power more and more.
Imagine *that* world!

So, what's the next step, now that you have read about this and have possibly created a small crack in your old power structure belief system? Where do you begin your journey of unearthing and reclaiming your personal power? What does it mean and what does it look like for you? The journeys are different for each of us because we are each as unique as snowflakes in a snowstorm. We are also similar, for we are all in the same storm. It all starts with awareness, externally (how we react in the world), internally (what we think, feel, and believe in the now), and spiritually (learning about our deeper belief systems, limiting and expanding beliefs, and core wounds). It can be tough initially, but really, it all starts with just one tiny little step—as all journeys do. That first step is embodied in the choice to change your belief that you are a victim and that life is being done to you. A step that says "I am born to be the star of my life." It starts with the practice of awareness. From there, everything flows. You can start to create the life you really want to be living. I use a great technique every day to see how aligned and centered I am. It's called a body scan. Give it a try! It's a simple and easy way to practice awareness.

Practice

Body Scan Technique

Lie down comfortably or sit very supported in a chair. Lighting a candle is always a great way to tell your internal self that you are stepping out of consensus reality for a few moments, and off the treadmill of life. If you want, you can use a few drops of your favorite essential oil in your diffuser or on your pulse points (sides of your neck, wrists, and insides of your ankles). I like to lie on my Biomat (therapeutic bed of amethyst and tourmaline crystals) or on top of my sheepskin rug. Some relaxation experts and meditation teachers will recommend that you do not choose your bed as a surface to sit upon, as the feel of your bed will signal to your consciousness that it is time to go to sleep. Sleep is not what you are trying to achieve here. You are here to observe yourself from a higher perspective and figure out this self-awareness thing. Wherever you are called to practice, trust that it is right for you. If it does not work, then course-correct and choose something else.

Now, get comfortable, close your eyes, and start by focusing on your breath. Become aware that you are breathing. Take some deep breaths.

LAXMI

Inhale through the nose, Exhale through the mouth.
Hold for a count of three and again...Inhale and Exhale,
reaching all the way down deep into your belly.

Slow yourself down. Inhale, Exhale, Inhale, Exhale...
belly rising, belly falling.

With your internal sight, watch your belly. Inhale and it
expands like a balloon. Exhale and it empties and falls.

Hmmmmmm, slow yourself down...nowhere to be and
nothing to do. Feel the yumminess of a deep breath.

Bring your awareness and attention to your feet. Wiggle
or spread your toes. Feel into your feet and focus all your
attention on them. Feel if your feet have any messages
for you.

Using your imagination, pretend you are a blood cell
traveling around inside of one of your major arteries,
and that the blood is going from your feet up into
your ankles.

Feel your ankles. If it sounds good, do some ankle rolls.
If you really want to get fancy, draw the letters of your
name with your feet, or spell the alphabet.

Bring your awareness up to your calves and shins.

Feel your shins. Maybe you have scars from soccer
or skiing on them. Thank your scars for the necessary
lessons they have taught you.

Take a moment to thank your body for all the things it's
done for you and all the ways in which it's helped you
accomplish your dreams and goals.

Next, feel into your calves. A light calf stretch is always a good thing. Flex and point your feet. Feel into each of your calves individually.

Now, bring your awareness and attention to your knees. If it feels right, massage your kneecaps in a gentle, circular movement.

Thank your knees, one of the most complex and vulnerable joints in our bodies. Knees make it so that you can run, sit, jump, stand, walk, and do all the other amazing things you do. We would be able to do very little without our knees, so take a moment to thank your knees.

Bend and straighten them if that feels good to you. See if you can hear any pops, creaks, or cracks.

Moving our awareness up into our thighs, send big breaths into your thighs.

If you're anything like me, take a moment to thank those stretchmarks (or as I like to call them, tiger stripes) for existing and for being a part of your miraculous self.

Try engaging and relaxing one of the larger muscles in your body; your quadriceps.

Continue upward. Bring your awareness up into your buttocks, or your gluteus maximus. The largest muscle in the human body has the job of keeping the trunk of the body in an erect posture. It is the chief antigravity muscle that aids in walking up stairs.

Again, engage the muscles and relax. Engage, and relax, and again, engage and relax. Really squeeze them tight (sometimes scrunching up my face helps in the practice of tightening my butt cheeks). And then, let it go completely. Ahhhhhhhhh.

LAXMI

Moving further upward into your reproductive organs,
bring your awareness into your sacred, red root chakra.
This is our first embodied chakra according to many
energy healing traditions.

I like to envision drawing a spiral with my mind's
eye directly onto each chakra. This spiral consists of
seven circles, one for each chakra, and I'm mentally
drawing the spiral on my root chakra. I am feeling into it,
sensing it.

The root chakra is the source of all raw, unformed
universal energy; the source of all beginnings, of creation,
abundance, and manifestation.

Now, move your attention up from your root chakra
to the space two inches or so below your navel. Right
between your reproductive organs and your navel is your
second chakra, your orange center of creativity. Let your
red, raw energy flow upward into your orange center
of creativity and let the two mingle. Your raw energy is
ready to be sculpted into creation. In Tai Chi, they call it
the Quhai center; the lower of the three Dantians, our
three power centers.

Bring your attention through your intestines and further
up into your solar plexus. The third chakra; your inner sun
and power center. In yogic teachings, it is believed to be
the source of your personal power. Your centering force.
The place from which all action emanates.

Breathe a deep, big, clearing breath into your belly.
Audibly sigh out the breath. Big, loud sigh. Again, deep
breaths into the belly, into the solar plexus, and deep, full,
emptying releases, letting it all go.

Yesssssss...letting it all go.

Remember to draw the spiral in your mind's eye at each chakra point. Seven circles for seven embodied chakra points and energy power centers.

Moving up into your heart space now.

Feel into your heart space. Scan for any blockages, both literally and metaphorically. The heart's health is our health.

Return yourself to that imagined blood cell, becoming once more that blood cell inside of your body. You're being pumped by the heart throughout your body. Feel yourself on this journey of exploration, going in through one side of your heart chamber and exiting out on the other side.

Explore all four heart chambers. The two upper chambers, the right and left atria, are receiving incoming, oxygenated blood. The two lower chambers, the more muscular right and left ventricles, are pumping blood out of the heart.

The heart valves, which keep blood flowing in the right direction, are the gates at the chamber openings. As you traverse through your own heart, release any fear, doubt, shame, emotional blockages, negativity, and past aches. Let them all simply flow away. Let it be easy. Be grace.

Let anything that is holding you back from the present moment—anything that keeps you stuck in the past or worried about the future—leave your system and disappear.

Journeying up into your throat now.

The throat chakra is located between the collarbones. Find your attention at the base of the neck; that really sensitive area just below the Adam's apple.

Again, draw the spiral if it feels good to you. You can use your finger to draw the spiral on your throat chakra. Gently and slowly, breathe in and out, in and out. Feel the air pass beneath your fingertips, gently circling the skin above your larynx.

Moving into your third eye, the space in between your eyebrows; this is your true sight. The third eye allows for clear thought, spiritual contemplation, and self-reflection. It is considered to be the highest chakra in the physical body, allowing it to provide a visionary perspective. The third eye helps determine your reality and beliefs based on what you choose to see in the world.

Release any tension you feel here and behind your eyes. Release anything that is not serving you. Stress, worry, fear, anxiety, story, limiting beliefs, and false sight told through victim stories—release anything from the past. Anything that you want to let go of, let it simply flow away on the out breath.

Release anything that isn't of the highest love vibration; anything that does not support you in becoming the You that you dream of being.

Breathe in new perspectives and exhale old worldviews. With your imagination, draw that spiral directly on your third eye. See that beautiful spiral moving. Watch it spiral inward on itself. Ajna is the Sanskrit name for the third eye. If it feels good, draw the spiral with your fingertip seven times, round and round, making circles on this point.

Bring your focus all the way to the top of the body, to the crown of your head. Take a BIG chakra-clearing breath here and audibly exhale. Bring your awareness up to the crown of your head. I like to give my temples and ears a quick pass with the metaphorical relaxation wand as I move to this point.

The crown chakra is known as "the bridge to the cosmos." It is the most spiritual in nature of all seven chakras, located just above the crown of the head in your energy field.

The crown chakra is your center of spirit, enlightenment, wisdom, universal consciousness, and connection to higher guidance. In a sense, the crown chakra is your highest potential. It governs interaction and communication with the universe. It is your sense of inspiration and devotion, union with the higher self and the divine, of a deeper understanding. It is also responsible for a healthy spiritual life. And again, spiraling, spiraling...you know it well by now.

Resting here, breathe and take this moment to be still with yourself. To tune into anything that may have come up for you during the body scan. Lie in savasana (or corpse pose, as Western yoga has renamed it) and simply be, after this process of taking in and being with each nook and cranny of your body. Only when you feel good and ready (and not a moment sooner), start coming back into the present moment.

Slowly move your body, beginning with your feet and ankles. Try gently swaying your legs from side to side.

Circle your hands and wrists, wriggling your arms.

Move your head slowly from side to side, stretching your fingers, bringing the awakened awareness with you as you sit up and reach for a drink of water.

Perhaps there is something you want to write down; feelings, thoughts, insights, an image you want to draw. Whatever comes to you, let it flow. Be water.

This is the end of our body scan.

A Few Notes About the Body Scan:

It is important to note that the body scan often starts in the feet and works its way up to the top of the head, going just beyond it into the crown chakra. The reason to start at your feet is because we often live in our heads. Bringing our attention to the opposite end of our bodies helps shift perspective and focus, which is the whole point of meditation. I like to loop my body scan from the feet to the head and then back down again. It's amazing how different it can feel to scan the same body part a second time after the initial energy clearing. This can help to clarify and release even further. It can grow your breath awareness even deeper and re-ground you in the earth before you return to your consensus reality tasks. You will find your own rhythm with it. Some days you may go from feet to head, while other days may find you going from feet to head and back down to feet. Sometimes you may travel up and down two or three times, or maybe you'll fall asleep at the knees and never even make it up to the top of your head. That's great, too. Allowing ourselves to be exactly where we are is the greatest practice of them all: the practice of radical self-acceptance. Wherever you are is exactly where you are meant to be.

Part of understanding and stepping into your personal power is the knowing of that feeling of centeredness in your body. The Right use of Power, a Buddhist concept like Right Speech and Right Action, lives within us. Our bodies are the houses of our spirit; our very own temples. We have to be aware of and take care of our bodies. Otherwise, where will our spirit live?

The body scan is a great tool that helps us to be present in our bodies, cleaning up and clearing out. It's like a good, old-fashioned spring cleaning, assisting us in making space for our personal power to show up. When first introduced to the body scan as a teenager, I was skeptical. Now, after practicing and leading it for more than a decade, I can attest that a body scan is a great practice in gaining awareness of what personal power feels like. Then, you can know what it feels like to be unshakably centered and calm in your body. When things come up, you can navigate them with more grace and ease, from a point of self-awareness that is in line with your own values and physical body.

While recording my former podcast, The Conscious Hotline, my co-host (Altaire Cambata-Turner) told me a story about operating from her own personal power. A dear friend of hers accused her of owing him money. At first, she was really resistant to the accusation. She felt so confused. She did not want to pay money that she didn't owe. Before responding to him, she stopped, scanned her body, and realized that she was in full reactive mode. She had an impulse to either rush over to his house and defend herself, or just ghost him entirely. This told her that she wasn't coming from a centered and grounded place.

Instead, she found her way into her truth. Her reactivity subsided and she wasn't being driven by old, limiting belief patterns. She stood unshakably centered in her own personal power. She then put on her leather jacket and a motorcycle helmet, rode out into the night, and had a calm conversation with her friend. They were able to resolve matters and create what we call a win/win: that beautiful situation where everyone gets heard and no one is on opposing sides of a battlefield. You know, the one we imagine there to be when in conflict, with a whole army of demon enemies on the other side ready to demolish us…then we get out the full arsenal of atom bombs. A-ha, yes. We all know that illusion. When we're in our personal power, we can choose to burst our illusions and instead do things the way Altaire did. She operated from an aligned and centered place. Riding a motorcycle is also a bada$$ ritual for getting into an empowered state.

When we're not in our personal power, we don't have the strength to calmly enter into a conflict space with another person. This often means that we end up navigating it in a way that feels out of alignment with how we want to be treated and how we actually want to treat others. Start figuring out what feels like to be rooted and self-aware. Understand your own personal value system and act from it, instead of reacting to outside forces that constantly yank on your chain. They can cause you to feel like the blow-up doll in a used car lot, which symbolizes the opposite of personal power.

You may have read the wise old book, *The Body Keeps the Score*, by Bessel Van Der Kolk M.D.[31] Before I share thoughts from his book, let the record show that

Mr. Van Der Kolk was a massive hypocrite and treated his staff very poorly. However, I didn't throw the baby away with the bathwater on this one. His book has a lot of golden nuggets. For example, it says that if you have trauma in your body, there will be places where it doesn't feel safe to go. There will be parts of yourself that you are not ready to visit.

Respect that. Learn how to acknowledge and be with those parts of ourselves, like the little girl within who was molested in childhood, or the young, troubled boy who ran away from home because he felt misunderstood by his father. We have so many different parts of ourselves, and they're not all going to be ready to undertake the deep journey within at the same time. Nothing is black or white, as we normally think of this concept of duality. An example of duality in parts work is that part of myself is an environmentalist empath. I really care about climate change. Simultaneously, another part of me wants to drive a white leather interior Mercedez G-Wagon right into the climate apocalypse. I also love to travel so much that I fly every month. Similarly, thoughts like "This is who I am" and "This is who I am not" are oversimplifying the situation. Life is nuanced. There is always a wide and vast spectrum; so many ways that all the different parts within us can show up at any given time, and so many different combinations that these parts can show up in.

It's paramount to be really aware of what parts are showing up in certain moments. We need to be very careful with our most tender parts when we start growing our self-awareness. Changing how we show up for ourselves in those early phases of our self-discovery personal power journey is so important. Self-care can be adjusted based on how our needs fluctuate. Different parts of us may have different views of what it means to be powerful. It is important that we listen to and honor them all so that we can begin to step into our self-empowered center in a healthy, self-loving, radically honest way. One step at a time, we are inviting more and more of our parts to join with us and work towards wholeness and integration.

Years and years of downloading your family's belief systems and society's messaging around what is expected got you to this place. Do not expect to be able to wave your magical body-scanning wand and have your personal power instantly installed. Life is not a video game (it's also not *not* a video game, but that's more of a Matrix/Ram Dass/"Everything is an illusion" conversation). Mindfulness practices like the body scan, yoga, and meditation are called practice for a reason. On the self-discovery path, we travel step by step and slowly begin to change. Anyone who wants to sell you a quick and easy one-pill solution is, in my experience, a "snake oil" salesperson. Run as fast as you can in the other direction and do not give them a penny. Definitely don't give them any of your time or personal power.

A huge part of the first step of being wholly and fully in our personal power is knowing and understanding who we are. From there, we can come to truly know what our personal power is. That is the magnificent, delightful, and joyous journey of self-discovery that you are already on by reading this book. By the way, making it this far in the book means you are already on your way. I commend you wholeheartedly, for it is challenging work. It's not for the faint of heart and often comes without accolades, trophies, or any other kind of recognition. It is the quiet work of self-discovery that often goes unseen and unheard.

You might be thinking, "You want me to do this horribly uncomfortable, painful thing, and I don't even receive any external rewards from it? *And* it's a lifelong journey!!? Hell no!" To this, I pass wisdom onto you from one of my teachers: "The freedom you will experience, the unshakable inner peace that comes from doing this hard work, there is nothing like it elsewhere in our universe! Nothing like the freedom you will feel on the other side of liberating yourself, of coming home to yourself, of simply allowing yourself to be your full and unique self! Nothing else!"

Imagine yourself being able to navigate the world from such an empowered, confident, trusting place that you're unshakable. No one can f*ck with you! Nothing can knock you over! It's like that silly Chumbawamba song from the '90s: "I get knocked down, but I get up again, you are never gonna keep me down."[32]
No matter what life throws at you (a pandemic,

bankruptcy, a murder, a death, a life-threatening illness, a lost loved one, a mental health crisis, or whatever it is), we can become less phased by external factors and instead be masters of our own reality.

Of course, being in your personal power is going to come and go like waves on the shore. Knowing your personal power doesn't mean that you always choose to mindfully operate from that place. Lord knows, I am no puritan. Sometimes I look back at texts I've sent and think "Ohhh, I wasn't in my personal power at *that* moment." I lose my cool and have strong reactions. I don't always show up in ways I want to. I am human; messy, imperfect, and real. Part of knowing your personal power is also knowing how to get back into integrity, into wholeness, into alignment with yourself.

So, dear reader, personal power is not a place of extreme force. We are not breaking wooden boards with our foreheads or arm wrestling alligators. Instead, we observe that everything flows more naturally, organically, and easily when we're in a state of personal power. It feels right, good, and natural because this is where we are supposed to be.

Journaling Prompts

What does my personal power
physically feel like in my body?

As I step into my unshakably centered self,
what is the next step to remain there?

How do I live in and from
this beautiful, new place?

How do I act from this centered place,
especially in challenging moments
when I could so easily be knocked down?

When I get knocked off course, how do
I get back home to myself; into alignment
with my personal value system, into my
grounded wholeness, in a way that works
for me?

Lesson 4
Unshakably Centered

Unfuckable With
vs. Unshakably Centered

"Freedom doesn't mean the absence of all restrictions.
It means possessing unshakable conviction
in the face of any obstacle."—Daisaku Ikeda

After proclaiming that I wanted to be an "unf*ckable with" woman, a wise woman once told me, "Be careful what you say. The universe is very literal and always listening! You still want to be f*cked; just not f*cked with."

As crass as that analogy may be, truer words were never spoken. I kept the aspiring title of "unf*ckable with" woman for a while. While holding the title,

I continued to have an extraordinarily wild and fun sex life, which unfortunately also included being "f*cked with' a few dozen times—but that's the nature of the beast.

After co-creating a series of deeply codependent relationships throughout my twenties—all of which left me with my head bowed and my spirit lowered— I set out to be an "unf*ckable with" woman. I aspired to be like my eldest sister, Santi, who used to be President of the National "Men Are Trash" Club. Santi spread her gospel truth far and wide for years, until one fine day in her early thirties, she fell madly in love with a wonderful man. This person proved her M.A.T. theory wrong, and thus, the man-loathing baton was passed onto her next single kin: me.

I fiercely launched my own M.A.T. crusade as if my life and the future of womankind depended on it. Due to my faithful and steady belief that men were only bad news, I was attracting nothing but (you guessed it!) trash men. This affirms a very necessary and simple principle: the benevolent universe, always on our side, gives us what we tell it to give us. We get back what we put into it. Abraham Hicks has a powerful video on this wherein she repeatedly states, "Everything is working out for me. Even when I don't feel like things are working out for me, everything is working out for me."[33] Such is the principle of manifestation. Quite simply, we are in charge of our experience and are in constant co-creation with the universe!

An M.A.T. Story (Or Two, Or Five)

In thinking about which comical "men are trash" story to share with you, a montage of epic fails races through my mind. Before I launch into the storytelling, I'm going to pause for a moment to share that I do not actually believe there is such a thing as failure. Rather, I believe that events we refer to as failure are actually learning experiences that the universe is constantly and generously giving to us so that we can see ourselves. The universe is a constant stream of feedback that guides us in learning, growing, and correcting our charted courses. We have all had the experience of looking back at a seemingly devastating event (like being fired from a job or tanking out of school) and realizing that it was exactly what we needed to happen. We can even feel gratitude for something that was extremely distressing at one time.

Back to my epic failures, or epic learnings. Skimming through my little black book provided ample reminders of the slew of low-quality dudes I had allowed into my space. Some bullet points are included below for a quick illustration:

- Married, Raw Foodist Spiritual Dude:
  I met Effervescent Skin at a personal growth and development workshop. Immediately thereafter, we had a whirlwind week at my house. The following week, one of my professors was extremely rude to me, and when I asked why, she informed me that she'd seen me holding hands with her best friend's husband.

She'd been the maid of honor at their wedding *ten years prior* and had been the one consoling her during his unexplained disappearance. He had told me that he was divorced and was in his 30's…both lies.

- Red-Headed Childhood Friend and Liar: I've known Freckles since I can remember. We used to hook up in college. Four years after graduation, I was visiting from out of town and he offered to host me. The day I got to town, he ghosted me, spontaneously leaving me houseless for the night without an explanation. Months later, he guiltily admitted that he was engaged at the time and wanted to host me, but he couldn't bring himself to ask his fiancé to host a childhood friend with a past such as ours. He texted me and said that he needed to "avoid the temptation of my presence." Until he left me stranded, he had been a loving force in my life; one of the gentlest, most loving men I had ever met. He was someone who held me while I cried and stood up for me when he discovered that I had been sexually assaulted. He even painted a wildly intricate and fierce painting of me wearing a sari in college that I've since thrown out.

- $180K Tesla-Driving 23-Year-Old Who Ghosted Me: I met Baby Boy at a Bone Thugs n' Harmony cover band concert in Minneapolis, Minnesota. We had a steamy week breaking in his new Tessie. Months later, he randomly showed up in Boulder, Colorado during a period when I was

between places, crashing on a friend's couch.
I went out of my way to rearrange my schedule
to hang out with him and rented a friend's tiny
home to accommodate him. Another steamy,
multi-day hang took place, this time at the base
of the Rocky Mountains. We exchanged the
occasional friendly text after he left and then
a few months later, he returned to Boulder.
He notified me the day of by texting me a
picture of the oxygen bar I'd taken him to,
with the words "I'm back." When I followed up
wanting to connect, it was clear that he was with
someone. He never had the courage to be honest
about that or call me back. Why tell me you
were in town at all, if only to ghost me?
The disrespect. SMH.

- Double-Timing, D-List Celebrity Musician:
I met Self-Deprecating Artist at a birthday
potluck without any idea who he was or
anything about his singer/songwriter career.
He seemed grateful to meet someone who
connected with him before knowing he had
any sort of a stage presence; albeit a small one.
After laying it on thick all summer, attempting
to woo me, we finally made plans to link up at
High Sierra Music Festival. Upon confiding to
one of my dearest friends from college camped
beside me at the festival that I was meeting up
with one of the main performers, I discovered
that she had already been dating him seriously.
She wasn't aware that she was one of many.
Awkward…

- Twenty-Year-Old Security Guard Thief:
  Immediately following the musician scandal,
  I opted for someone seven years my junior
  who'd never seen so many hippies. Wide-eyed
  by the amount of nudity and psychedelics,
  tatted Toto was a long way from central Cali.
  After five flirty days, I allowed him into my
  temple. He commented on not having a towel
  and needing a shower. I lent him mine and then
  he ghosted me, towel and all. He might as well
  have stolen my entire tent's contents; a towel
  is one of the most crucial things for festivaling,
  especially in Northern California in July!

- Publicly Indecent Tech CEO: This Tinderoni
  begged for a second date after I said, "This was
  fun, see you never." He'd consistently break his
  word on meeting up or communicating. He had
  a habit of calling me while drunk driving his
  parents' red BMW to their Rhode Island beach
  house. While I was out of the country, my father,
  who'd only met him once, invited him over for
  a spiritual dinner. My father was impressed that
  he'd gone to rabbinical school and could recite
  the Torah expertly. He brought another girl to
  my father's house for dinner! I only learned of
  this by seeing an Instagram video of her dancing
  in *my* traditional Indian clothes, in *my* house,
  with *my* father and uncle. Idiot. When I returned
  from Mexico, he was intent on reconnecting.
  I reluctantly allowed him to take me to a
  Mediterranean spot for lunch. After lunch, he
  wound up attempting to very publicly f*ck me
  in my car. When I told him that he was the CEO

of what would become a big company, and that he has shareholders and should be protecting the company's reputation, he said "I'm acting *exactly* as a CEO does." That was the most honest thing he ever said to me.

The list of jabronis goes on and on. These stories are somewhat comical, but they are also painful to share. They illuminate why it was so easy for me to write men off as selfish, unaware, therapy-needing dinguses.

Puppy Love

The crème de la crème of my M.A.T. stories involves a man who literally calls himself "Junk King." He collects roadside finds, random scrap metal, and remaining materials from handyman jobs. The Junk King's home was an old tool shed behind a mobile home, sketchily converted to be "livable". He'd made the double wide into a "vintage store". The shop, A.K.A. decrepit mobile home, was rented out to two individuals willing to live in a junk store without a kitchen. Tenants brought his monthly rent down to a whopping $0, leaving him the shed as his own living quarters. His shanty home had electricity via an extension cord that ran from the "store," over a small creek, and through the backyard. A hot plate was his only means of cooking food, and a picnic table outside (in the mountains of Colorado, mind you) was the only chopping or eating surface.

Having spent the majority of my twenties attaining
two post-graduate certificates while building multiple
businesses and dating a very successful serial
entrepreneur, this sort of primitive living, vagabond,
bohemian lifestyle was oddly alluring to me. I didn't
know that it was possible for me to feel excited about
an extraordinarily scrappy, long-haired, bearded,
white guy who walked around with an eyebrow
piercing and a tattoo that read "f*ck racism." He
rarely wore a shirt or shoes. I looked right past his
outrageous Facebook profile picture of him in an
'80s tracksuit with Jesus hair, riding a bright orange,
tricked-out, lowrider bicycle and I dove in headfirst.
At the time, he was a can-do, "Mr. Fix-It" type with
washboard abs, a gorgeous dog, and the desire to
date me. I was trying to break free of my pattern of
dating rich dudes and CEOs, and he couldn't have
been more different.

We met at a recycling center. Junk King was walking
around with a beautiful German shepherd, off-leash.
I was instantly attracted to the wolf-dog because of his
striking looks and immense fluff. I was curious how
he trusted the dog to be off-leash in such a bustling,
heavy machinery-filled place (warning sign #1).
Before I knew it, I was asking to pet Chuck (the dog)
and exchanging information with his owner,
Junk King.

He owned a truck, was self-employed, was a former
Eagle Scout (I've dated three of those and they're
delightfully handy), and wanted to build a stronger

network in his new state of Colorado. I offered him a gig with the reusable sticky jewelry company I was co-founding at the time, Artemis Wild. We were going to be at an upcoming four-day music and art festival called Arise. During the long weekend, Junk King helped load, set up, and tear down our massive bedazzling den and diva glamp-ground. Spending that amount of time together while immersing him in my thriving social circle based around music and fun quickly accelerated our relationship.

A month into hot and heavy dating, he had to go back East for a few weeks. He asked if I would watch Chuck, the German Shepherd wolf-dog who had brought us together in the first place, while he was away. Not only did Junk King live in a shack without a bathroom or kitchen, but he also hated his family, came from a long line of racist blue bloods, and was from New Jersey, which as a kid who partly grew up in NYC, felt like treason. Those red flags should have been enough to send me running. If I said no, Chuck would be kept in Junk King's shed of a house, and the hard-drug-addicted roommates would occasionally let him out to pee. Beautiful Chuck in such poor care?! That wouldn't do. I had every reason to say no. I was working 24/7, building a fashion and beauty company. Chuck shed his gorgeous coat like a motherf*cker, and I was living in a carpeted, pet-free rental with three roommates. I wasn't even a dog person.

After checking in with my roomies, who were all stoked to have a puppy around, I agreed to watch

Chuck. I am a firm believer that how we do one thing is how we do everything. My agreeing to care for this wolf puppy when I was not even a dog person speaks volumes of the lengths I used to go to be needed; to receive love, to feel wanted, and to be owed a favor (owning up here to my manipulative shadow side). Trust me, writing this now from my current perspective while looking back makes me cringe.

A deal was struck. In exchange for ten days of dog-sitting, Junk King agreed to replace my car's brake pads. If the yard full of old, rusting vehicles next to his junk store was any indicator, he was obviously a master mechanic. Chuckleberry Finn, as we sweetly referred to him, arrived at my house with the cheapest food in existence, which resulted in terrible diarrhea. He was without a single toy, treat, or even a food bowl. His "leash" was a piece of rope that was nearly chewed through. He had never been formally trained, was just shy of being two years old, and was literally part wolf. They say that dogs are a reflection of their owners, and I very quickly learned what a sh!tshow the guy I'd been dating for the last month was. The list of grievances against Chuck in just the first week included:

- Jumping out of the car window and nearly getting picked up by animal control

- Getting into very intense dog fights anytime he was on leash, ending with me picking him up and/or dragging his 100 pound body away by his back legs

- Liquid pooping all over my bedroom and sliding glass door

- Attacking a skunk, then being sprayed by it

- Learning to jump the fence and constantly escaping the backyard

- Chasing anything that moved with the strength of a pack of Alaskan sled dogs

Days turned into weeks. By the time we passed the month mark, Chuckleberry Finn felt like my dog. Despite all his chaos and poor behavior, he showed me the depth of love that flows between animals and humans in a way I'd never experienced. I went from reluctant dog sitter to full-blown, deranged dog mom. I turned down social activities he couldn't attend, left events and work every two hours to let him out, sent guys home because the three of us couldn't fit in the bed, and bought him all the bells and whistles. I knew the names of the local PETCO employees and my neighborhood learned where to return the "wolf dog" when he got out.

Chuck turned out to be one of the best things that ever happened to me. He taught me about unconditional love in ways I am still unearthing and opened my heart in ways I am still exploring. He turned me into a dog lover. As a kid, I rejected the family dog, not wanting his golden retriever/lab hair all over my mostly black clothes. I hated the burden of picking up his poop. Prior to Chuckleberry, I was disgusted by dogs licking humans' faces. I never wanted to

share my food with an animal, and didn't approve
of inviting large creatures onto the bed. I wouldn't
be caught dead lying in the dirt, snuggling a giant
hairball. I most certainly would not turn down
concerts, social plans, and dinner dates (you know
it's serious when I turn down free food) to spend
time with a four-legged creature.

Within the first two weeks of being with Chuck, I had
broken every rule in my former, non-dog-obsessed
mind. I went from being laissez-faire about dogs to
not wanting to leave Chuck alone for more than a
few hours. I became the very kind of person I used to
make fun of. I never understood how people could
center their lives around a dog and put its needs
above their own. God has the best sense of humor
and finds the most comical ways to remind me that
all judgment is self-judgment. I re-learned that what
I see in others, I see in myself. Now, not only did I
understand dog lovers, I felt like there was literally
no one I'd rather spend time with other than this
damn dog.

As they say, what goes up must come down. After
Junk King witnessed how phenomenally I cared
for his pup, he recognized that he was an unfit dog
owner. He knew that he was without the required
resources to truly care for this dog's wellbeing. He
told me I should just keep Chuck. The way he was
so quick to hand over this regal creature blew my
mind and solidified my growing belief that this dude
was TRASH. My business partner at the time told me

it was either Chuck or our business. Though it was an outlandish ultimatum, I was distracted from the business by hyperfocusing on the dog. I chose the business and proceeded to find Chuck a new loving home. His adoptive doggie parents had jobs that even provided pet insurance; a tech company perk.

True love, the sages say, is non-attachment and wanting what's best for another—even if that's not you. That was how I felt about Chuck. I loved him so unconditionally that I understood that this new couple was exactly what he needed. I prepared myself to say goodbye when Junk King decided he didn't want Chuck with anyone except me or him. Thus, the adoption fell through. Even though it fell through, it was a powerful process of immediately manifesting the best possible outcome I could have envisioned. The experience reminded me to trust in my abilities to create what is of the highest service for the greatest good.

I had cared for Junk King's dog like it was my own newborn baby for nearly two months—when he was originally only going to be gone for ten days. At this point, I had spent double the amount of time with his dog as I had with him. It was clear that I wanted nothing to do with the dude beyond this and absolutely LOVED his dog. Junk King was embarrassed by his "dog dad" inadequacies and the work I'd had to put in to compensate for them. Instead of facing me, he sent a friend over to my house to pick up Chuck.

Ashamed, he did what wounded people often do: lashed out. In the end, this man I'd been dating and sharing my mind, body, and social circle with had the "caucacity" to cuss me out. He also refused to complete his end of our bargain. Another nail in the M.A.T. coffin!

Chuck's fluffy love spell never wore off of me. His ever-loving, puppy-like wonder and playful essence permeated my soul, leaving an indelible paw print on my heart. He inspired me to get my first dog, two years later! Our most profound teachers often come in interesting packaging.

Chuck was my first deep love with a non-human. Tears of joy filled my eyes many times when we were together, as I felt the depth and purity of his unconditional love. It was a love I had sought in the wrong places; a love I needed to experience for my evolution. It was a love that began to heal parts of myself that I did not even understand were crying out for care. I am still in absolute awe that it was possible for me to transform into a dog lover overnight. The only thing Chuck did was be a pain in my ass, and I loved him unconditionally for it. I cared so deeply for another being who didn't give back to me the way I gave to him. It was an extremely heart-opening experience. I learned so much from Chuck about what I want in a partner and what I deserve. From his owner, the Junk King, I received total trash. The *lessons learned* from knowing him ended up giving me total treasure. No regrets!

"I am whatever you say I am."—Eminem[34]

Bottom line: if I believe that men are trash, then my experience of them will be. I manifest my own reality. I find what I expect to find because that is what I will be concentrating on. If I believe that men are incredible, loving, wonderful, good-natured human beings who are often culturally and emotionally repressed, I will see the world differently. I will be able to hold a lot more compassion for the men in my life and for all men in general.

Men have within them the skills and tools necessary to be the fullest expression of themselves, even though socialization and cultural norms keep them from understanding this. In the name of manhood, boys are sent to "Be a Man" school. Because of this education, their natural inclinations towards love are often twisted into what expresses itself as toxic masculinity. When I remember this, I can begin to feel compassion for men, even when I am caught in the crosshairs of their emotional unintelligence. From this more holistic perspective, I can honor the ways in which I want men to be better and different while holding space for and understanding why they are the way that they are.

When I rid myself of my negative beliefs and expectations about men, I open myself up to manifesting and attracting men who are incredible, emotionally available, and self-aware. I understand now, as I reflect on my younger self who craved being unf*ckable with, that my true, everlasting desire was for an unshakable sense of self.

Unshakably Centered: What It Is and Isn't

My understanding of what it means to be unshakably centered is to be in the presence of adversity without allowing it to impact how I feel, how I show up, and what choices I make. In more poetic terms, it's the ability to sit in the eye of the storm, observant and unattached, and meditate. Maybe you are thinking, "F#ck meditation! I don't have time for it. That's for people on mountaintops. I have a business to run, a career to build, a degree to finish, and a kid to raise. Furthermore, what does it even mean to be unaffected by all the life stuff that comes up? Demands, deadlines, disappointments, disasters!" If this resonates with you, then trust me; I know where you are right now. That was my outlook at one time. That was what I would have said too, if I had read my own writing ten years ago. However, it is actually possible to live from a place of unshakable centeredness, once you find your way back into your core. Hang in there and keep reading. You know you picked up this book for a reason.

Let me tell you about Vipassana meditation; a specific style of meditation originally taught by Buddha himself, and then onward through his lineage of teachers for thousands of years to find us in the Western world today. Angelica, a wise Mexican Mama, encouraged me to take the Vipassana course for ten years before I had the courage. These teachings taught me how to become and remain unshakably centered; how to become and remain who I really am.

Vipassana meditation, as I am beginning to understand, is the practice of being completely present in the moment without craving, avoiding, needing, or resisting. To simply be; no doing, no distractions, no demands; and to remain aware of only the body and breath the entire time. The practice is taught in ten-day retreats all over the world, with silence, sobriety, and vegetarian food. These simple teachings and the mere practice of this form of meditation can create the outcome of being unshakably centered. It can also rattle a person to their core and make them feel like they are losing their mind. That is exactly what happened to me during my first go-round. Had I not trusted my wise friend Angelica and known that there was something here for me, I would not have tortured myself through the first one. I most certainly wouldn't have jumped from my first ten-day retreat right into a second one. Now, on the back end of this choice, I am so grateful I trusted older, wiser, more life-worn women, in addition to my own intuition. Without these retreats and this practice, I could not be sharing this authentically with you right now. Also, you might have figured out by now that I am an extreme goal-setter and achiever. A current goal of mine is to be so centered in my practice that I can do an hour-long Vipassana sit in the middle of Times Square. With the world now reopened post-pandemic, I'll attempt this at some point and report back via my social media.

Now, when I am presented with opportunities that fall outside of my values system, my steady, guiding, unshakable sense of self guides me to choose the high road. Who knew?! Definitely not my younger, twenty-something, Junk King dating self. Without her courage to jump right into the maelstrom of life, it might have been years and years of attachment to co-dependent and toxic patterns before I came to realize who I really was. Shoutout to the old me for all her fearless, false starts and heinous hiccups.

To me, being unshakably centered means that I always make the "right-for-me" decision, according to my internal compass. It also means that when the right decision isn't clear, I find a way to be still enough to hear my spirit, my angel, and my ancestral higher power guide me. As an unshakably centered person, I am fully aligned with my values from moment to moment.

My journey of wanting to become an "unf#ckable with" woman was a result of feeling that I had been f#cked with by men my whole life. Talk about a victim story. In addition to multiple, overt experiences of sexual assault that I went through, I used to allow my state of being to "billow in the winds" of the men I dated, as well as of the people in my innermost circle. "Boundaries," "internal compass," and "personal values" were all terms that had no practical application in my life. Fifteen years of personal growth and development work later, the simple, universal truths are now clear to me: only *I* can allow myself to be f*cked with. Only *I* can give my power away. Only *I* can choose how I act and react. Only *I* can choose what I hear, see, feel, think, and believe.

Only *I* choose how I will interpret something. When I act outside of my value system, that is my choice. It is also a direct result of misplacing my power to external factors and/or feeding into the illusion that it's even possible for my power to lie in another's hands. No one and nothing can make me feel or do anything. In every moment, I have a choice. Therefore, I am the creator of my life. As we have learned, everything is made in cocreation with the universe. The universe is benevolent and always on my side. I take ownership because I am 100% responsible for my life, 100% of the time.

Again, for the people in the back! Stick with me here because whether you believe it right now or not, this can set you free:

I am 100% responsible for my life,

100% of the time.

Repeat it out loud three times right now!
Even if it feels like you are lying to yourself.

I am 100% responsible for my life, 100% of the time.

I am 100% responsible for my life, 100% of the time.

I am 100% responsible for my life, 100% of the time.

And that's the good news!

Because, from that center point of 100% ownership, I can act on my own behalf and make whatever changes to my life that I wish.

When I was younger, my unconscious and often rebellious quest to become an "unf^ckable with" woman led me through a series of wild adventures that I wouldn't take back for anything. I thought that having a tough exterior, a heart that was "cold, black, and deadened" (as I jokingly said), and a complete lack of attachment to men would make me "unf#ckable with." I prided myself on being able to have sex without emotional attachment or commitment. This falsely gave me the notion that I was a liberated woman who was in charge of her own destiny. I now recognize that encouraging reckless abandon with our bodies as a means of self-empowerment is further shackling us, and is a complete trap created by modern-day feminism to further oppress us—but that's a rant for a different book.

I was sitting in a Codependents Anonymous (CoDA) meeting, feeling armored and proud of my liberated, cold, black, dead heart. I heard someone say that they were accepting sex when they really wanted love. I had never heard this statement before and felt as if a quiver of arrows had struck the center of my chest. I burst into tears. I had given my body away freely, hoping to get love in return. I'd lied to myself by saying "Sex is fun! I am in charge of my body, and I am a free, American woman. I do what I want!"

Equating sex with love has become a trademark for
many of us young, "liberated" women. Sitting in that
CoDA circle with newly lodged arrows vibrating in
my chest and tears flowing freely, sex and love began
to take on new meanings.

I began practicing one of CoDA's mantras: "I forgive
myself for the times I accepted sex when I wanted
love." I said it to myself, over and over and over. I said
it again and again until every cell in my body began
to hear, understand, and forgive. I could choose sex
anytime I wanted to, but it would never fill my innate
need of wanting to love and be loved.

My failed attempts to show up as a liberated woman
by mimicking the stereotypical male approach
(a hypersexual and emotionally unavailable mentality)
had left me feeling empty, drained, and powerless.
I was wasting my time chasing what others had,
instead of creating that which I truly craved. During
my stint as President of the National M.A.T. Club,
I realized that I had become closed off from life's
betrayals, instead of cracked wide open by them.
The goal of being unaffected by my environment
and blocked off from the whispers and cries of my
heart is exactly the reverse of "The Invitation;" Oriah
Mountain Dreamer's poem shared in the intro
of this book.

As a result of my diligent efforts to be someone I was
not, A.K.A. a cold-hearted, sexually reckless, out-
of-control woman, I spent years and a lot of my life

force energy masking my true Queen essence. I'm no fu*kboi. I am a Libra goddess, born to love. A bougie hippie from the Pacific Northwest who howls at the moon, jumps naked into the lake, befriends anyone within a five-foot radius, and thinks she's naturally psychic because of her East Indian heritage.

As a gratefully recovering codependent (thanks to CoDA's 12-step program), I now understand that if I want to dance the toxic dance of "victim, perpetrator, rescuer," I will always be able to find someone or something (like a job or community) willing to play out the full cycle of abuse with me. There will always be something outside of myself that I can blame for why things are not the way I want them to be. The moment I stop participating in the malignant blame game is the moment I take 100% ownership of my own life. That is the moment I step into my truly unshakable sense of self.

Vipassana meditation has taught me that building a strong sense of self can be a long, hard, and sometimes terrifying road. While hysterically weeping at the end of my first ten-day silent meditation retreat, I said to a volunteer checking in on me, "I can't hear anything over the deafening cries of my own sadness." Never had I experienced silence to be so overwhelmingly loud. This is where I learned that the path to spiritual ascension can only be walked alone. No guru, teacher, superfood, plant medicine, breathwork, or reading can truly lead us to life outside of the matrix. We have to set ourselves free from the low vibrational fear patterns ingrained in us by society from birth.

My practice of silent meditation gradually rids me of attachments to how I want things to be, how I think society should operate, and my endless cravings and aversions.

Vipassana is the daily practice of taking some of the trash out of the dump that is my brain. Post-meditation, I feel more spaciousness in my being, more clarity in my mind, and more ability to be gentle with myself. Some days, the amount of garbage in there seems like endless landfills collected over generations and passed down to me through my ancestors. On these days, it feels like the only thing that the hour-long session accomplished was removing one grocery bag full of trash from an infinite heap. As encouraging as that may (not) sound, a meditation practice remains my path to wholeness. It may not be the path to yours, but there is no harm in trying it. Regardless, I can assure you that there is a path for you. It could be art, cooking, dance/movement, meditation, poetry or other writing, yoga, swimming, outdoor adventures, or something else. The paths up this mountain are infinite and the view from the top is the same for us all, no matter how we get there. No path is "wrong" or "less than," except for the path that runs around the base of the mountain. It's trodden by those who will tell you that you are not doing it right. There is a path and a practice for you; one that will bring you into the flow of your unshakably centered wholeness. Whatever you find, I want to hear about it. Contact me on IG at @21SL21C or use #21SL21C to share stories of what has worked for you to reach your unshakable centered self.

Bring Shadow To Light

As you begin your practice, you will discover that an unshakable sense of self can take many forms. One powerful element of any unshakable centering practice is the ability to stare deeply and steadily into your own eyes. In the mirror, take a long, deep look at not just the physical parts of you, but at all parts of yourself. Look into your eyes, smile at yourself, and say, "I love you! You can do anything! I believe in you. You are smart, capable, whole, magnificent, loved and loving, and you have everything you need to create anything you want!" Channel your best Issa Rae impression (I'm once again referencing the HBO masterpiece, *Insecure*) and have the type of honest conversations that she has with herself in the mirror. You get bonus points if you break into song or rap like she does. There's also nothing like a Broadway ballad to pump yourself up. My go-to is "Take Me or Leave Me" from the hit 1996 musical, *Rent*.

Then, there's the deeper look inside yourself; beyond the surface, beyond the eyes and skin to the real sh*t below: the shadow self. Thank you to Carl Jung for this great concept and insight. This has been written about by many brilliant people, so if this topic interests you, I invite you to go deeper. I'll share a quick overview of the shadow self: these are the parts of yourself that you have suppressed deep inside your unconscious since birth. They include things that make you cringe, things that make you feel shameful, and things that you feel like you need to run away from. They can involve messages about you being too loud, too happy, too outgoing, too shy, too outspoken, too girly, too needy, and so much more. All those messages you have received since birth about how you should be, and how you should not be, have caused you to strategically hide parts of yourself.

Avenues you can take to explore your shadow self include dream work, re/birthing work, the North Node in your horoscope, Human Design, Enneagram, Akashic Records, and the Myers-Briggs Type Indicator (MBTI) test (or any other personality test that resonates with you). For a deep dive into shadow work, find yourself some Jung books and settle in for a mind-blowing experience. We all carry shadows! No one is exempt. According to Jung, we cannot ever look at them directly. We can only come to know parts of them through our prejudice (all judgment is self-judgment), through our dreams, through listening to how others perceive us, and through working with the unconscious part of ourselves. There are clues everywhere, once we begin to look.

If you have your hidden parts buried so deeply under your pageant queen "the show must go on" persona like I thought I had, just ask your family or close friends. They'll probably have a laundry list of feedback for you. When I react strongly to feedback with comments like, "I don't do that," or "That's not me, I'm just hungry," these are usually red flags that indicate that I am operating from my shadow self.

When one has an unshakable sense of self, one can take all kinds of feedback without allowing it to change one's relationship with oneself. I will argue that there is no such thing as positive or negative feedback. Everything is inherently neutral. Things just are what they are. Our attachments to desired outcomes and perceptions of value are what make thoughts, feelings, situations, relationships, and basically everything we experience either "good" or "bad." This is the human experience of living in a dualistic universe. Putting philosophy and metaphysics aside, and for the sake of easy comprehension, I will stick to blanketing concepts under the flawed black-and-white lens of "good/bad" and "positive/negative."

When I receive what seems like negative feedback, and I pause instead of reacting, I am demonstrating an unshakable sense of self. In the small but mighty act of pausing, I am able to look at it without allowing it to impact how I see or value myself. I am instead able to examine the feedback and understand that it is simply someone's subjective experience that actually has nothing to do with me. I can take from it what rings true and leave the rest behind. Being unshakable is being able to look at it all—your greatest qualities, the things you dislike greatly about yourself, the things you do not want others to know, the things you hide, and the ones you lie about. Often, when I judge someone for something, God puts me in that very same position. Voilà! There I am, being taught the lessons of the experience firsthand. It is so easy to judge another, but so much harder to walk a mile in their shoes. It brings to mind the age-old saying, "For every finger I point, there are three pointing back at me." God continues to remind me of this each time I place blame or judgment on another. From the shadow perspective, each judgment we harbor is a clue to something we have suppressed in our own shadow.

The unshakably centered sense of self includes being able to look at the attributes and qualities of yourself that make you the special, magnetic, loving, wonderful, incredible, conscious, intelligent, and beautiful human being that you are, while also looking at the challenging, traumatized, and wounded aspects of your being. The unshakably centered sense of self is radically accepting of every part of you, all the time. It's not telling stories about why it is that you act the way you do. It's not whining, or lying, or doing any of those other defense mechanisms we all know so well. The key to the unshakably centered sense of self is holding the whole kit and caboodle without allowing any single part to take over.

Living in Alignment

How do you know when you are or aren't in alignment? An excellent example of people who are not living in alignment is the average American politician. Elected officials often acquiesce to corporations' wants in exchange for whatever advantage lobbyists have to offer. Guiding their decisions from ego and capitalistic gains instead of from an unwavering moral compass results in living out of alignment.

Some believe that being in alignment has to include
reaching some or all of these milestones: having
a great job, living in a beautiful house, being in a
relationship with one's soulmate, or having a picture-
perfect family. However, life will still throw surprises
at us, and our roots have to grow deep in order for us
to stand tall and unmoveable in a storm. I love to think
of trees and mountains as examples of an unshakeable
sense of self. A favorite quote of mine from the Disney
movie Mulan illustrates this sentiment very simply:
"No matter how the wind howls, the mountain cannot
bow to it."[35] Nature is one of our greatest teachers.

Of course, there are always going to be those seismic
shifts that take place; the ones that shake even the
most fundamental and solid things on our planet.
The ones that upend our world as we know it, totally
changing our reality. However, mountains and giant
trees are what they are regardless of who or what
is around them – and because of who and what is
around them. They couldn't change their shapes
even if they wanted to. They are exactly how they are
meant to be. They stand where they stand, and that
unshakeable sense of self is our natural, true, and right
state of being. It's also the only place from which we
can create an abundant and loving life and world.

When we stand in our power, conscious, centered,
and in love with ourselves, no "wrong" decisions
can be made. When tapped into the divine, allowing
ourselves to be guided by God (which is our ultimate
highest self, personified), there is no way that we will

make choices with negative impacts. When everyone is in their power, things like polluting the planet, hoarding wealth, or neglecting the needs of others will become a thing of the past.

The way forward is not as hard as we think it is, because it really begins with each one of us individually. One unshakably centered, self-embracing, awakened person at a time, making conscious, individual life choices. Being able to stand in the face of the good, the bad, and the ugly without allowing it to change us is the ultimate goal.

Be Like Water

Human beings are about 60% water. No matter what kind of container water is in, it assumes the shape of that container. If water is put on the floor, it will spread. Water in a lake is lake water, and once that water is fed into the ocean, it becomes the ocean. Put water in a stream that flows down a waterfall, and it turns into a waterfall. You get the gist. Our bodies are no different than water. We take the form of whatever environment or container we are in. Living in a clean, functioning environment, surrounded by positive, curious, open-minded humans with healthy living habits tends to produce even more positive, healthy lifestyles. Invert all of that and you end up with unhealthy living. Little by little, our out-of-alignment life choices take us off-course and we begin to shape ourselves to the container we are in. Our thoughts, feelings, habits, and beliefs morph. Therefore, part of living our unshakeable sense of self is being in a container that is reflective of who we want to be.

The containers we live in are our human meat suits.
I like to call them our body temples. We are spirit
beings first, having a human-embodied experience.
These temporary suits of flesh and bone are our
containers; our water vessels. Like water assumes
the shape of its container, we assume the shape of
our meat suits. So, an unhealthy diet (I'm thinking
here of the Takis and Popeyes' spicy chicken
sandwiches I treat myself to once a quarter) pollutes
our vessels, as well as the "waters" within. Drugs
of all kinds (including prescription drugs), media
binging, processed foods, unhappy and depressive
thought patterns, lack of exercise, and other unhealthy
behaviors all make for undernourished, run-down
vessels full of sickness and seriously polluted waters.

I love hearing stories of people who go through
great adversity while maintaining an unshakable
sense of self. I know someone who was orchestrating
a marathon and got in an awful accident. He was
flagging off one of the streets on the route when
he was suddenly pinned between a passing car
and a building. His medical acumen and physical
attunement kept him alive until the ambulance
arrived. Incredibly, he stayed centered and was able
to instruct others around him on how to stop the
bleeding. His sense of self was so unshakable that he
was able to advocate for himself during a traumatic
event. In the wake of becoming amputated at the
knee, he was enlivened to continue his passion for
health and fitness to an even greater degree. This
story reinforces for me the idea that our bodies are the
physical container that our spirit waters are held in.

It doesn't matter what the container looks like as long as we care for it and keep it strong and healthy.

As I think of what affects our bodies and minds, I'm reminded of Doctor Emoto; a Japanese man who "talks to" and photographs water. He conducts research projects photographing water molecules that change, depending on what kinds of thoughts and words are put into them. He found that water molecules turned from beautifully formed, snowflake-like crystals to fragmented, ugly, and cancerous molecules when he screamed at the water or wrote something negative on the container holding it. I use this example here to help you tune into the idea that every thought we think, every belief we ascribe to, every value we hold and override, every choice we make, every action we take, every bite of food we eat, every sip we drink, everything we inhale, snort, and put on our skin, and everything we allow into our body temples ALL impacts our spirit waters inside our human vessels. It might sound like I'm getting a little preachy here, but I share this because I battle with this myself on the regular. Remember my affinity for Popeyes' spicy chicken sandwiches? I'm no Puritan. We are all wanting to change how we experience ourselves and our lives in some way. We are all trying to heal from physical, mental, and emotional wounds. If we want to have more joy, happiness, and energy, then we have to treat our vessels with respect. We are given only one precious body temple that houses our spirits and souls. It is sacred and holy.

Alignment

Looking around, it would be easy to think that spirituality is just another commodity ready to be sold at a sky-high price. None of the fear-based rhetoric that BIG government (like the military and prison industrial complexes), BIG agriculture (for those of us who grew up closer to freeways than corn fields), and BIG pharma (including Western medicine) are spewing is in alignment with the values of a spiritual belief system. When I am considering inviting something into my body, it is helpful for me to think, "Would God put this in my sacred temple?" God wouldn't fill our cups with oxys or pesticides that make us infertile! He wouldn't fill it with methamphetamine, or with so much alcohol that we're throwing up or pissing the bed. God didn't make GMOs or processed foods.

We are each made in the image and light of God. In this sense, we are a part of God. We are here to maintain, nurture, and grow the light of God that lives in us. We are here to create beauty, not destroy it. I'd like to state that I am not here to convert you or anyone else to living the mostly sober and celibate life I experimented with while writing this book. I am only sharing my own awakening journey. Your job is to take only what rings true for you. Get curious, do your own research, read more books, question, dig, and excavate your own internal landscape. Don't take my word for anything; instead, wake up and make your own path with your own, uniquely-shaped experiences. If you're reading this while on your own

journey of finding your unshakable self, I hope
that I am sparking your curiosity and giving you
a place to start.

The saying "What would Jesus do?" is something
I regularly ponder. It's kind of like a shortcut to my
internal compass. It's a way for me to check in and
engage my spiritual self in a dialogue. Jesus is one
of my guides that I call in before I do something that
may cause me to abandon myself. I have come to
believe that everything we do should be a reflection of
God, because we are made from the divine, and to the
divine we shall return. It is in our best interest to treat
ourselves as holy as we treat God, because God made
us, and we are whole, holy, and perfectly imperfect.

It took me a long time to find my own language
around spirituality and to make peace with a lot of the
concepts that are out there. My childhood involved
so many different forms of spirituality. The concept of
God living in us was one of many reasons I struggle a
lot with evangelical religions of any kind. A lot of what
happens in such organizations, and what is taught
to be the truth, simply does not make sense to me.
The last time I went to one of those strict, evangelical
establishments, it was one of those churches in a
wealthy suburb of Minneapolis, Minnesota called Edin
Prairie. The congregation and pastor were friendly
and neighborly, preaching love and kindness to all—
only to jump abruptly into messages involving killing
the gays and smiting people who think differently
from them. After this particularly negative and

gruesome sermon, they served beverages to hundreds of people out of styrofoam cups. Five years working at the recycling center during my undergrad made me a fierce environmentalist. I started twitching at the sight of so much waste. My fiery, confrontational self walked straight to the pastor and asked, "Do you believe that God created everything on Earth?" His response was "Of course!" I asked, "Did God create styrofoam?" The pastor replied, somewhat confused, "Well, no…man created styrofoam." I went in for the kill: "Then, why would someone who loves God, all of his creations, and the earth choose to serve beverages out of styrofoam cups? These cups will never, ever biodegrade. They will continue to pollute God's green earth for eternity." He had no response. That sort of total misalignment deters me, and it is what many organized religions are serving up hot every Sunday. Can you really love God while actively destroying God's creation and smiting those who do not think like you—in the name of God?

In my view, this establishment is deeply out of touch and out of integrity. Not doing better when you don't know better is one thing. Consciously doing it anyway is another. This takes us back to our exploration of an unshakable sense of self. If you have an unshakable sense of self, all your decisions, choices, and actions are going to be in complete alignment with your highest, best self; which is your God self; which is God. If God would not do it, why would you? If Jesus would not do it, why would you? If Buddha would not do it, why would you? If your seventh-grade art teacher, who is the most unshakable person you know, wouldn't do it, why would you? If your internal compass is telling you no, then why do it? We must see ourselves as one with God. It is only in our separateness that sin exists. We lose sight of our inherent divinity when we see ourselves as separate from God, or as separate from the whole. It took me a long time to understand that I am perfect and whole, exactly as I am. You are, as well.

Our world is rapidly changing, more so than at any other time in human history. It is no wonder that we feel slightly crazy all the time and that we collectively reach for things to help us feel better (meaning more steady, more relaxed, or simply numb). It is, therefore, more imperative than ever that we begin to step into this changed world with unshakable senses of ourselves. Otherwise, we don't have sh!t! We are surrounded by the ever-present forces of advertising, social media, capitalism, fascism, patriarchy, oligarchy, and other forms of low vibration that are deeply embedded into us from birth. One must have an unshakable sense of self to withstand the constant storm. A deeply aligned sense of self isn't formed by listening to a man at the pulpit who is power-washing you with a sermon on killing the gays and then drinking instant coffee out of styrofoam cups. Someone, start asking some questions here!

Alignment doesn't come from simply sitting on a cushion for twenty minutes, twice a day. Nor does it come from wearing a necklace with 108 beads on it that you move between your fingers while repeating a mantra. Having an unshakable sense of self comes from exactly that; the Self, which is ultimately God (spirit, energy, universe, the aliens that seeded earth billions of years ago—remember, you are 100% at choice 100% of the time, so choose what works for you). Whatever God tells you directly brings you to your unshakable sense of self. It could be a hike, a bike ride, raising a family, baking bread or sculpting that brings you back into contact with your unshakeable sense of self. For some, dance is prayer, meditation is singing, painting is their contemplation, and playing basketball is a holy communion with the divine. That is their path up the mountain.

For me, a multitude of things brings me up the mountain. Some of my favorites are meditation, time in nature, long baths, breathwork, dancing wildly under a full moon, and pulling goddess or tarot cards. The significance and importance of my different centering practices change because I am constantly evolving. The important thing is to carve out space to be present with the divine (which can also be seen as yourself) every day. Spend time with spirit (which can also be seen as the self), preferably in silence, every day. When I am actively engaging in centering practices regularly, everything unfolds. Everything manifests in that still space. Whatever it is that gets you out of your head, out of your sad story, out of the past with all its regrets, out of your trauma, and into your bright, beautiful, and present self is what you are here to do.

Unshakable Travel Bug

- Think about what activities or interactions bring you inner peace.

- Think about the physical characteristics (like body posture, language, calm breath, and eye contact) that come with the above activities and interactions.

- Come up with exercises to support that unfolding or growing inside you.

An example: While I was at coaching school at New Ventures West, I was tasked with sitting in a chair with my feet on the ground, my neck level, and my eyes open, staring at one point for three minutes. Those few minutes felt like hell! My instructors then had me stand still for five minutes and imagine roots coming out of the bottoms of my feet, grounding me into this earth (a particularly necessary and challenging activity for an air sun Libra like me).

Through perseverance and a belief that this meditation crap actually works, I have worked to stretch my meditation time. I used to be able to do it for just a few minutes, but gradually, I worked up to an hour. However, some days get skipped and I'll opt for dancing, biking, yoga, or a hike, in place of my evening "sit." Sometimes, I opt for a walking meditation (which Thich Nhat Hahn wrote an excellent book about). Whatever you discover is bringing you back to center is perfect, because it works for you (mic drop!).

Bear in mind that the center has to exist in order for you to be able to return to it. In order for you to be as strong, tall, grounded, and centered as the mountain, you must *be* like the mountain; unmoving, observing, and without the need to speak, be seen, or be heard. Witness it all without judgment or attachment. From centeredness comes ascension. You will have peaks, just like a mountain. You will have beautiful views and you will also discover cavernous valleys. When I am like the mountain, grounded and centered within myself, I can be of the highest level of service.

Finding and re-finding my center has been a lifetime of trial and error. At 23, I didn't even feel like I had a center. My lifestyle was literally blowing in the wind, living out of the back of my manual, hippie version of "Pimp My Ride." A swooped-up, '96 extended cab Toyota Tacoma was my home while I camped all over the United States. After a heart-wrenching breakup with my former fiancé, the wind blew me to the edge of the Grand Canyon. There was an insane thunderstorm taking place as I arrived. It was so bad that they closed the park after I entered. While watching lightning illuminate that vast pit of land, I held out my arms as if being crucified. I threw my head back to taste the polluted rain and asked God to show me my way (drama queen).

The breakup winds blew me to Israel where I cried in the Sea of Galilee, visited a home Jesus had lived in, and walked the streets of Jerusalem. This was all while praying that my engagement ring tan line and the pain I felt when going to twirl it and realizing nothing was there would fade. The search for self through accolades was not bringing me any closer to lasting inner peace, so I tried sacred abandon. As the heroine from my favorite childhood Disney movie, *Pocahontas*, so beautifully puts it,

> You can own the Earth and still
> All you'll own is Earth until
> You can paint with all the colors of the wind.[36]

For me, learning to paint with the colors of the wind looked like traveling nonstop for months on end. My quest to know my purpose and learn about myself in deeper ways took the form of a road trip that started with $2,000. It miraculously lasted for nine months, spanning five countries and seven states!

My white truck, lovingly named Talicia (after my amazing massage therapist in college), brought me from miracle to miracle. One example of the countless miracles that took place on that road trip occurred in the land of the beautiful, tan people, A.K.A. Los Angeles. One fine morning, in a nice neighborhood, I climbed out of my humble abode to find a discreet place to pee. As I looked for a squat spot in this palm tree-lined neighborhood, a woman walking her dog started chatting me up and we strolled together for a while. She asked me what I was up to, and I shared that I was on a road trip, finding myself and living in the back of my truck. Her next question was, "Do you want to take a shower at my Airbnb?" I'd swam in a saltwater pool the day before, so I know I wasn't stinky, but there was nothing I wanted more than a hot shower and a private bathroom. As our walk came to an end, we realized that I had serendipitously parked Talicia directly in front of her rental house the night before. I was supposed to be in L.A. for a few days, but instead, I wound up staying in this woman's guest home for a few months!

She became one of my first organizing clients outside of my family, giving my miniscule bank account a serious boost. While living in her guesthouse that was next to a saltwater pool and across from a meditation yurt (!), I organized her garage and consolidated her storage units. I learned that she had married into Hollywood royalty, and I had the honor of holding their actual Golden Globe and Oscar awards while with them. We are still friends after the months we spent helping one another.

This is just one of many stories I could share with you of the countless blessings and opportunities that opened for me, as I stepped directly into the eye of my emotional storm. I said "Yes" to what the universe presented to me. My wholehearted answer did not come from my socialized brain that held limiting beliefs; it came from the unshakable center of my heart and soul. The winds of change blew me far and wide to places previously unknown, and many adventures during my time living in my car opened me up. They became precious building blocks in my foundation; the place upon which my unshakable sense of self securely rests. I experienced luxuries and fun I'd never imagined possible. While finding my lost self after the hardest year of my life to date (teaching at a Title One, low-income school, healing from an abortion, and ending a codependent relationship with an alcoholic), I could hear the praise and support of my ancestors in the winds. They were cheering me on every step of the way, saying, "Yes, girl! We see you. This is the life we worked hard for you to have. Enjoy it. Find yourself. You're not just moving and healing for yourself; you're moving and healing for those of us who came before, as well as those that are to come." Although I was having an absolutely amazing adventure, I was avoiding the tough questions of what to do next with my life, now that I had left teaching as an industry and left my fiance. I was houseless, jobless, and having a blast living for the moment. I was hakkuna mattataing it.

After months on the road, and just two days before my return to Colorado, my trip literally came to a crashing halt. On what should have been just another drive from California to Colorado, I hit black ice and spun out. Talicia fishtailed and began to flip over and over. Just like in the movies, the crash happened in slow motion. As the glass shattered, I reminded myself to go limp, relax my body, breathe deeply, and close my eyes so I didn't get shards in them.

Once I realized that I couldn't course correct and was out of control of the vehicle, I became keenly aware of all the times God had whispered, "Don't drive tonight. It's icy and dangerous. Pull over and get a hotel."

But I was listening to an audiobook (*The Ethical Slut*) instead of my inner God voice. Determined to get to my friend's house in Reno, with only two more hours to go, I didn't want to spend money on a hotel and was too busy to listen to God's repeated warnings. Pushing all intuitions aside, I instead choose to total my beloved Talicia and endanger the life of my passenger and me. Looking at Talicia in the daylight the following day, it was clear that my passenger and I were both very lucky to be alive. The middle of the roof was pushed down almost to the seat from where it had tangoed with the road. Had this dent been a mere six inches to either side of the car, it would have completely crushed one of our bodies. This was my first wake-up call to what I now know as the spiritual practice of listening within; a cornerstone of being centered.

When we landed upside down, dangling from our seatbelts, I heard the booming voice of God in my head. Loud and clear, he said, "It's time to go home and take care of your little brother." After kicking out what remained of the windshield to exit the vehicle and picking the glass out of my scalp, I followed my God voice and headed home. Big shoutout to my Auntie Debbie, a nurse who instilled in me the practice of wearing a seatbelt. Growing up, she wouldn't even move the car until everyone was buckled up.

God works in mysterious ways. If I choose to ignore the early, gentle, small nods and prods from the divine, I will get hit by a cosmic two-by-four. God answers every prayer, even if the answer comes in the form

of a car accident. It put me back on my path.
Apparently, I needed a near-death experience to go
back to basics, reground, and heal in my hometown.
When I started that road trip, I had a minuscule
amount of money, a totally broken heart, and no idea
where I was going or why. The "escape your reality"
adventure train had been going full speed for nine
months strong. Looking back, if I hadn't crashed that
car and received my cosmic wake-up call to step into
my unshakably centered self, I think I would have
been blowing in the wind for much longer.

An overused, yet poignant quote by the 19th century
poet Ludwig Jacobowski says, "Nicht weinen, weil
sie vorüber! Lächeln, weil sie gewesen!" This loosely
translates to "Don't cry because it's over. Smile
because it happened!"[37] This is how I felt about losing
my car to black ice. I'm deeply grateful for each
experience I went through while living in the back of
my beloved Talicia. Simultaneously, I'm also grateful
it ended. What I discovered is that it is most important
to take good care of myself. Self-care is much easier for
me when I'm grounded and centered within myself.
That chapter of my life was spent running, blowing
in the wind, and looking for anything, anyone, or
any reason to keep me from being still. I didn't want
to feel all the emotions I had suppressed. Stillness
felt like a trap. It felt like putting on a heavy cloak
of darkness, like a big, scary, energetic claw that
wrapped its talons around my neck, making it so that
I couldn't speak, feel, breathe, or even be alive. Now,
I realize that perpetual motion (the moving every
four to six months, the commitment phobia, and the

changing of jobs) was my intense fear of self at its core. I now know that I feared the blinding light of my own brilliance. I dimmed my brilliance so I could not see myself reflected in the people around me, or experience the blooming of the seeds I planted in my community. I never stayed long enough to enjoy the fruit of my labor. I kept myself small by staying in either survival mode or adventure mode.

During the car crash, I felt like Simba in *The Lion King*. I had to return to pride. I had to go back to the place I'd run from at the age of fifteen. I needed to go back to the home that I had deemed to be an unhappy place so that I could heal my relationship with my mother and support my little brother. I wanted to be on his team so that he could finish high school strong with a post-graduation plan.

When God crashes your car and then speaks to you because you're just not getting the message, there is no other choice than to listen. After one more adventure (Jam Cruise—a five-day music festival cruise with jam and funk bands), I wound down the vagabond lifestyle and moved back to my childhood neighborhood in Portland, Oregon. It was the first time I'd returned since graduating high school. Returning as an adult to the place that shaped me was an important part of my journey to find my center and build my unshakable sense of self.

Gotta Get Down To Get Up!

Fact: There is no greater insight into the strength of our spirits than when we are at our weakest. Here's another fact: The mind cannot tell the difference between a curated breakdown and an actual one. Whether we are experiencing stress from watching a horror movie or being involved in a real-life car accident, the same chemicals are released into our bloodstream and hitting our brains. We have only a few options to respond with: fight, flight, freeze, or fawn. It is often in this vulnerable state of complete surrender that breakthroughs and break-opens occur. Hidden truths and lies we tell ourselves rise to the surface.

Practice

Goal-Setting and Facing Fears

Make a list of five activities or experiences that seem unfathomable or impossible for you to accomplish. Brainstorm things that are so outside of your comfort zone that it makes your heart rate go up simply by imagining them.

Examples to get your inspiration going:

1. A large physical feat.

    E.g. marathon, mud race, military boot camp, body competition, attaining a six-pack.

2. Extreme temperature.

    E.g. sweat lodge/temazcal, hot yoga, ice bath, swimming in the ocean in the Pacific Northwest.

3. Participating in an intensive personal growth and development workshop or retreat.

    E.g. WINGS Seminars (this is where I got my healing start. They offer online workshops, too!) or Vipassana (a ten-day silent meditation retreat that is located worldwide and is donation-based).

4. Changing your physical appearance in a drastic or very noticeable way.

    E.g. shaving your head, dyeing your hair green, wearing contacts that take the color out of your pupils, gender-bending if that's out of character for you (like painting your nails bright pink as a man).

5. Stripping yourself of common luxuries for thirty days.

    E.g. not spending money on anything other than bills and groceries, not eating or drinking out, abstaining from using a vehicle (rideshares/apps included), and having to bus, walk, or bike everywhere.

6. Learning a new skill and allowing yourself to be "bad" at it in public. Brownie points if you do it with people much younger than you.

    E.g. joining a musical group, doing improv, joining a chess club. When I was nineteen, I took a tumbling class with my ten-year-old brother. Everyone else in class was backflipping around me in circles while I worked on perfecting my roundoff. It was embarrassing, but hilariously humbling.

Choose one! When reviewing your list, notice which ones make your heart rate go up the most; the ones that your naysaying mind shouts, "We could never!" after reading it. Consider what is safe given your unique background and lived experience, what is financially responsible, and what is currently on your plate. Choose one just outside of your comfort zone, and not in the danger zone. This is where learning occurs.

Goals are best when they are SMART:

- Specific

- Measurable

- Achievable

- Relevant

- Time-bound

Make sure that whatever you choose to do to further your unshakable centeredness can be broken down into smaller action steps. A coaching client once told me that I helped them break down the overwhelming aspects of life into attainable, bite-sized pieces. It is vital to break larger goals down in order to make them more accessible.

Some unshakably centered practices are easier than others. For example, facing a fear of heights at an amusement park can happen much faster than sculpting one's body to look like Michelangelo's "David" statue. When you notice your face getting hot with frustration, tears swelling in your eyes, or the sensation of wanting to give up gnawing at you, remember who you really are: a radiant, bada$$ light being who can literally do anything you set your mind to.

I believe in you.
Now, go forth and prosper.

Journaling Prompts

When was the last time someone or a situation encouraged me to break my own boundaries or act outside of my values?

How did I respond?

If I crossed my own boundaries, how did it make me feel? Choose one word (for example, curious, confused, shocked, or regretful).

If I did not cross my boundaries, what did I do instead?

How did that outcome make me feel? Again, choose one word (some examples are proud, challenged, joyous, or confident).

Lesson 5
Relationships
Spiritual Beings Having A Human Experience

"Make every effort to rediscover your friends of past incarnations, whom you may recognize through familiar physical, mental, and spiritual qualities.

One lifetime is not always sufficient to achieve the perfection of unconditional divine love between friends.

Try to resume such friendships, begun in a preceding incarnation, and perfect them into divine friendship."
—Paramahansa Yogananda

As a human being, relationships with other people and creatures great and small are more important than one might think. It is these relationships that create Karma, and impressions. It all has to balance in the end. This brings up the need for the right values and understanding Maya. Meher Baba explained Maya in depth, but even he agreed that it is beyond words to understand this force. In simple terms, he said that Maya is the creator of illusion and ignorance. What is that illusion? It is the illusion that we are separate beings when in reality, we are all one.

He went on to explain "The principle of ignorance, meaning Maya, can only be transcended when the spiritual aspirant is able to realize that Maya is God's shadow and as such is nothing. The enigma of Maya solves itself only after Self-Realization."

Thomas Merton was a twentieth-century monk and a great writer who lived over fifty years ago. One of the lessons we learned from him was, "No man is an island." Naturally, this points to the fact of the need for relationships and the way we walk in society with people. As he so eloquently said, "The beginning of love is the will to let those we love be perfectly themselves, the resolution not to twist them to fit our own image. If in loving them we do not love what they are, but only their potential likeness to ourselves, then we do not love them: we only love the reflection of ourselves we find in them."[38]

But this is now the 21ˢᵗ century and still our relationships are valuable. In the spiritual context, we can say that all relationships are important. Naturally, some are more important to us than others. For example, I love my daughter more than I love my boss at work. Nonetheless, there is a spiritual opportunity in each relationship, including non-human relationships with pets, or beings in the natural world. The Native American (Lakota) saying, Mitákuye Oyás'iŋ, which can be translated as "all my relations," is not limited to only human beings as relations. It can indeed be a relationship with any aspect of Creation itself. Gases (as in the sun), or stones, metals or plants, insects and lizards (as in a horny toad, or turtle), or a fish, some birds, animals, and even angelic beings we may encounter in our life. There is no limit to these possible relations, and indeed all can be made sacred.

Once, I was sitting with a new friend in Meherabad, India, where Meher Baba's Samadhi is located. We were drinking some freshly made chai, just enjoying being alive, and chatting away on the front porch of the spiritual center where we stayed. Suddenly, a gorgeous Praying Mantis flew over and landed gently on my knee. I received this as a great blessing.

However, the young Indian woman I was speaking with tried to shoo it away with a pen she was holding in her hand. I stopped her, firmly saying "No, leave it." A few seconds later, it flew again, this time landing

right on my chest and facing up towards me.
I took this as a deepening of the blessing. I stopped
speaking entirely. We sat in silence, the three of us,
and after some time, it simply jumped up and flew
slowly away. If you have never seen a mantis flying,
it is astonishing to witness. This remains one of the
great blessings I have received in this life. That mantis
is now one of my relatives.

Family Members and Ancestors

Reading through my draft of this chapter,
I see that I left this section unwritten. Why is that?

If I am vulnerable, I will say it is because my family
of origin and the story of my ancestors are full of
anguish and suffering. Naturally, there was love and
joy as well. However, my legacy is one of having to
overcome many obstacles to arrive at the place where
I find myself today.

My father was a German artist, and wildly unfaithful
to my mother. My mother was the practical one and
had to work constantly to hold the family together
financially. I had two siblings, one a half-brother in
Paris whom I never met and who committed suicide
when I was young. And my sister, with whom I grew
up in Manhattan during the 1970s and '80s. Ultimately,
the whole family was emotionally shattered in 1985
when my father jumped off the roof of our apartment
building, to his untimely death. Losing a parent when
young is difficult. Adding the dimension of death by
suicide when I was only sixteen was too much for me

to bear. I felt completely helpless to navigate this turn of events and turned to spirituality to help me become emotionally "unstuck." That's how I found Meher Baba, or perhaps more accurately, how Baba found me searching for Truth.

My family, outside of my nuclear family, was present in various ways. Aside from my grandmother Elizabeth (my mother's mother), I didn't have much of a resonance with them, as we seemed to be living parallel lives, and rarely intersected. I am sure I was "part of the problem," as I felt distant, and I am certain I acted aloof and difficult. Of my cousins, I connected with Andrea the most. However, when I "came to Baba," I could sense her disapproval, even if not spoken. Awakening on the spiritual path can be difficult for family and friends to understand, and for better or worse, my personality isn't big on explaining myself. If they can appreciate my path, great, and if not, I keep moving. Maybe they didn't like that. Of all the friends and family I had from the 1980s, almost none of them are in my current life with Meher Baba. And that's fine.

Pets

My first experience with a pet was my turtle whom I named "Ernie," when I was about ten years old. I have always liked turtles; I don't know why. I originally wanted a pet dog, but when I asked my father for a dog, he said no. I asked why not, and he said, "It is unkind to the dog to keep it in the city." I thought to myself, "If it is unkind to have a dog in the city, then why is he raising me as a child in the city?"

In any case, he said yes to a turtle. So, we bought an aquarium and a heat lamp to go over it. I was told to keep it clean and change the water frequently. It was supposed to be half water and half land, so the turtle could spend time in both elements. Ernie was what was known as a "painted turtle," which spends a lot of time in water. This is much different than a tortoise, which is a land creature.

When I asked what to feed Ernie, the man at the pet shop said, "Fish." I thought, "Okay, where am I going to get fish?" So, I asked him, "What kind of fish?" He disappeared and came back with a little goldfish that was swimming around inside a clear plastic bag of water, which had been tied carefully at the top. He said, "This kind." I was stunned. I looked at Ernie and thought to myself, "How will he ever be able to catch that fish? He will starve?!" Then I asked the man, "How will he be able to catch the fish?" He responded simply, "Watch him!"

So, I got the whole thing set up in my bedroom in our Manhattan apartment. I used rocks to make the "land" for Ernie and tap water to make the pond which was the rest of the aquarium. I made the water not too deep and put him in there, turning on the light to make it warmer. I put him in, and he explored his new home, in our home. I loved him.

Then I looked at the goldfish. I waited until the right time, but honestly, I still had doubts about how this feeding would work. Ernie was so slow, I just couldn't imagine how he could catch a fish, ever. At some point, I untied the bag and just poured the entire bag of water with the fish into the aquarium. I watched intently. Would Ernie swim faster and faster until he finally found and wore out the escaping goldfish? No. That is not at all what Ernie did. The goldfish swam around exploring.

At first, Ernie wasn't even aware of the fish in his environment. Then he saw the goldfish and what I couldn't imagine unfolded right before my eyes. Ernie stopped swimming and just rested beneath the surface of the water. He pulled his head back more deeply into his shell, and sort of floated, motionless. His eyes were open and his nose was right at the edge of his shell. He waited patiently for the goldfish to swim in front of his head and then, whoosh! In a sudden, fierce motion, his head shot out of his shell. With his mouth open, he grabbed that goldfish in a flash. It was over as soon as it started. Ernie tore the fish apart and ate it all within a minute.

I was stunned.

Naturally, I had to clean the tank again after all that, so I did. I would take Ernie up to the living room and set him free to walk around and explore. It was going great, and I looked forward each day to my time spent with Ernie. One sad day, I came home from school and found Ernie in his aquarium, not resting but not moving. Ernie had died.

I had no idea why, and I didn't ask. It was my first experience with death. I knew I needed to give him a proper sendoff, so I took an old, round cookie tin that still had the original lid and cleaned it out. I gathered some earth from somewhere and put Ernie in the tin, surrounding him with the earth. I sealed the tin and went down to the Hudson River, next to our home. I walked out to the end of an old wooden pier, Ernie in hand (in his tin coffin).

I don't remember what I said. I am sure I was crying, but I don't know about that either. I do remember I threw the tin high up and into the river, saying goodbye to Ernie in my own way. Love and loss, I learned that day, go together. I had my first grief cycle which resulted in my eventually getting another turtle. But after a few days, I brought turtle two back to the pet store. I rapidly realized I wanted to repeat the love, but I couldn't bear to repeat the loss.

When I became an adult, I moved out of New York City. I spent some time in Georgia in my mid-twenties before moving out west. While in Georgia, I got my first dog. I had set the intention to get a dog when one day I was speaking about it at a coffee shop and a woman who was sitting at the next table spoke up. She said, "Excuse me, but I couldn't help overhearing you speaking about looking for a dog…"

Everyone is so nice in Georgia, and I was both surprised and happy when she told me a tragic rescue story. She had recently rescued a beautiful, black puppy who was thrown out of a speeding pickup truck that was driving down the road in front of her car! She stopped and rescued the pup, who had landed on his back and suffered a road rash that scraped the skin off his back on that spot. She said she oiled it regularly and that he was a lovely dog. She asked if I wanted to meet him. I said yes.

I followed her car to her home, where I met a most handsome, young, black puppy dog. He looked like a Labrador mixed with something. He was friendly and came right to me. I didn't want to let him go, so I didn't. I told her I wanted him, and brought him to my car. However, he refused to enter the car on his own. I realized at once that his recent, deep trauma was associated with a vehicle and being thrown out of the moving pickup truck. I told him that I understood, gently picking him up and assuring him that it would be alright. I carried him into my car and drove home immediately. I found some olive oil and oiled his now healed back scar, and the fur around the scar. She must have sent me home with some food for the puppy, so I fed him and thought of a name. What should I call him? I landed on "Degas," after the French impressionist painter, Edgar Degas.

Degas and I became extremely close. He was fast, strong, and smart, but he was also the new addition to the neighborhood dog pack. It was made of some

strays and some family dogs who were allowed to
roam freely. We lived in a tiny town, at the edge of
a 300+ acre cow pasture. Degas had to prove himself
to the other dogs, but he first had to submit to the
current top dog, which was a rottweiler. I watched as
he rolled onto his back and exposed his belly to the
rottweiler in front of the other dogs. The rottweiler
was pleased with Degas' submission.

As time went by, however, Degas rapidly became more
popular. While the rottweiler was certainly stronger,
Degas was lightning fast and also strong. One fateful
day, Degas challenged the rottweiler to a fight.
I watched this unfold in a field next to our log cabin,
with all the neighborhood dogs in attendance. Degas
was so smart, he had a strategy and tactics. He ran
around the rottweiler in circles and then would run
directly away from him, turn, and then run full speed
right at that big rottweiler. He would strike fiercely
with a bite, and then run away again. He would then
turn around again, run back full speed, and repeat the
whole series of fierce bites until the rottweiler yielded.

I saw that big dog roll onto his back and present his
belly to Degas, who accepted his submission. It was
impressive, and a big day for us both. After that,
Degas started to sire puppies from what seemed like
all the female dogs in the neighborhood. One of his
female companions was a stray, and I named her
Bamboo. She was stocky with a deep, rusty, short-
haired coat. It took weeks of my offering Bamboo
food before she would eventually eat from my hand.
Eventually came Bamboo's litter; about five or six

stocky jet-black pups. I knew I had to give them away immediately.

I gave away all but two on the first day. But what to do with the last two? I had heard there was some sort of weekend festival at a park near our home, so I made a plan. I would create a sign and bring the puppies to the festival. I thought that someone would surely want them! I got paper and a pen, and a long piece of string, and I wrote on the paper: [I NEED A HOME]. Then, I used the string to turn the paper sign into a sort of awkward necklace. I drove with the puppies to the park and found a stately tree at the entrance to the festival. Sitting down under its shade, I placed the sign around the neck of one of those puppies. About a minute later, that one was adopted. I moved the sign to the neck of the last remaining puppy.

Two little girls came over and said, "Aww, can we have him? I said, "Sure!" They responded, "Can we take him to show our parents first and ask them?" I agreed, "Go ahead." I took the sign off the puppy and placed it on the ground, watching them carry the puppy to their father, about a hundred feet away. They pointed at me, and he gave me a sort of long-distance scowl as if to say, "Now look what you've done!"

Just then, a young woman around my age (or maybe a bit older) walked into the festival, and as she passed where I was sitting beneath the giant tree, she looked down at the grass in front of me and the sign resting there, which read "I need a home." She said to me lovingly, "Well, I have a tree in my backyard, you can live there." I said, "What?!" And then I started to laugh long and hard, reading my own sign.

Khadija

My current pet is our Korat cat breed named Khadija. She is amazingly affectionate, surprisingly independent, and loves to be outside. She loves to sleep with us in our bed and can also be outside so late that we have to call for her from the front porch at night, to come back inside. Her claws are untrimmed, so they are long and sharp. It used to be that when she wanted attention, like petting, she would reach out her paw and try to grab a hand or arm, or even my face in the morning. We had to train her to not do that since it was painful. Now she sort of comes over and stares deeply into our eyes. Lastly, we recently moved into a new home in Asheville, North Carolina, and there were plenty of cats already living in this neighborhood. When we got here, the neighbor cats would face off with her and invariably end up chasing Khadija. She would run up a tree for safety, so I helped her get down from some trees. By now, it's been six months and she is doing much better with those cats. If I hear some cat sounds and go outside to see what is happening, as soon as Khadija sees me by her side, she seems to feel empowered and chases the other cat away. I am proud of her.

Friends

They say we can't choose our family, but we can choose our friends. They also say, "Enemies are made of steel, and friendships are made of glass." I have many stories after fifty years of this life, about friends, and what that means in a relationship. What is a friend? Obviously, it is someone you want to be near, to get closer to, to spend time with, and to communicate with in some way. Some friends may be more activity friends, as in, "We hike together, but the conversation is not great." Some friends may be more intellectual, and the conversations are incredible, but we don't do a whole lot other than meet and have a beverage and discuss things. Other friends may be the kind where there is always some type of tension; sexual, competitive, or otherwise. Some friends, in my experience, are instant (as if we were close friends in our previous lifetime and I immediately recognize them in this lifetime). This reminds me of a good friend story:

I remember sitting with Nick, one of my close, intellectual friends. Nick and I can talk for hours. We were sitting in a coffee shop doing our thing, when in walked a young woman wearing a baseball cap. As soon as I saw her, I said to Nick, "Now that is a woman I would like to meet." He turned to me, and said, "Shelly? I can introduce you to Shelly!" After she ordered coffee, Nick called her over, and Shelly and I met. We became friends instantly, and we are still friends now over twenty years later. We didn't have to make an effort to be friends, but we did make an effort to schedule time to spend with each other as friends.

Some friends start as "enemies," and after much effort become friends. Some friends become enemies because of some betrayal, wound, or irreparable schism. Whatever the case may be, it seems to be a universal need of human beings to cultivate friendship. To be honest, some people may have a closer relationship with friends who are not human, like horses, dogs, cats, or plants. And that is fine too.

Meher Baba, as a spiritual master, frequently used to say, "Make me your constant companion." It is a bit like having an imaginary friend who happens to be a spiritual guide and much more. Friendship, in whatever form, can be a rich and fertile area of life to explore the spiritual aspect of human love because it involves a give and take. We give to our friends, and we receive from our friends. So many great lessons come with friendship.

One of my best friends is Christian O'Neil. In 2006, I was visiting the Gila Cliff Dwellings near Silver City, New Mexico with my family. I had my baby son, Cyprus, in a front carrier on my chest since we literally had to climb up and down wooden ladders to get around the cliff dwellings. I had a Native American flute with me, made by Aaron White in Flagstaff. I played it in one of the more sacred spots in the cliffs. After I played, I asked my wife to carry the flute (it had a case and shoulder strap), since I had to have my hands free to navigate the ladder.

As we walked from the cliff dwelling back towards our car, there was a bridge over a river. Someone who was at the cliff dwellings at the same time as us approached my wife who was still carrying my flute, and asked if she was the flute player he had heard in the cliffs. She said, "No, that was my husband, Laurent." When I caught up with them, they were standing by the river's edge talking, and that man was Christian. That was about twelve years ago. He now calls me by his made-up nickname, "Soul Candy." I asked Christian about our friendship, and he said:

> Later that same day, we were both in the hot spring. You invited me to join you and your family for lunch, and that was when your daughter Aspen said to me, "Just say yes." While the story is fun to remember, the sturdy friendship that began that day has been built on by consciously making time for each other, the sharing of our spiritual journeys, supporting each other through the ups and downs of relationship, and laughter. Lots of laughter.

Sometimes friendship evolves into a more romantic expression of love. Sometimes friends can become mentors or teachers. I feel more love for and from some of my friends than some of my blood relatives. We will tackle these subjects later in this lesson.

Work

Relationships include work colleagues. These are not the same, naturally, as those who you choose to have as friends. However, you can decide whether you want to join a job (and the people who work there), and you can decide to resign. But while you are there, the nature of these relationships is vastly different in nature from other connections you form, and therefore the lessons are quite dramatically varied as well. Anytime you have people telling you what to do, or you get to tell others what to do, or you are on a team and are building that team together, you have many opportunities for spiritual growth. Some of the many lessons are connected to trust and betrayal, clear or confused communications, power struggles, politics, praise and shame, blame and guilt, pride of ownership, honesty, and much more.

Romance

Meher Baba said, "Most persons enter into married life as a matter of course, but marriage will become a help or a hindrance according to the manner in which it is handled. There is no doubt that some of the immense spiritual possibilities are accessible through married life, but all this depends upon having the right attitude. From the spiritual point of view, married life will be a success only if it is thoroughly determined by the vision of Truth. It cannot offer much if it is based upon nothing more than the limited motives of mere sex, or if it is inspired by considerations which usually prevail in business partnership. It has to be undertaken as *a real spiritual enterprise which is intended to discover what life can be at its best.*"[39]

I have been married twice. My first marriage lasted eighteen years, from 1993 until 2011. It ended suddenly and tragically with a major betrayal. In 2016, I remarried, and I can honestly say, "I have never been happier in my life." In all my romantic relationships —and I could count them on two hands and still have fingers left over—I learned spiritual lessons.

Vanessa wanted me to include what Thích Nhât Hạnh shared about relationships, in a YouTube video we watched of his interview with Oprah. Thinking more deeply on this, I decided not to quote him. It is more important to share with you what I take away from his wisdom on this subject. The essence of it is simply this:

1. We will hurt each other, unconsciously, in a relationship.

2. When this happens, the hardest thing to do is to remain present and practice our spiritual path.

3. This means not running away when triggered, not fighting, and not freezing.

4. Fight, flight, and freeze are the primal behaviors we have inherited from ages of evolution, but now as spiritual beings in human form, we can aspire to higher responses.

5. He suggested a set of responses, which all basically rest in love, and to ask for help in

> continuing to practice our loving spiritual presence with our partner, in spite of our suffering.

Let me add something important here. If your partner is harming you consciously (not unconsciously, as described above), then you should probably end the relationship and move on. Abuse is a real thing, and many have remained in abusive relationships long past the expiration date. Don't be a martyr, and don't become a victim which requires rescuing. This is what Stephen Karpman teaches us in the "drama triangle;" to stay far away from the roles of Abuser, Victim, and Savior. Cultivate less drama.

Mentors and Advisors (Including Therapists)

I had a therapist named Asha, in Ashland, Oregon. That relationship was purely professional, as I paid for her services as a psychotherapist. She helped me navigate and process challenging circumstances, and work through my feelings and thoughts at a critical time in my life. This is also a type of relationship which is quite valuable. One thing that is important here is to recognize the dangers of psychological transference and countertransference. When this happens, the patient can unconsciously transfer their feelings about either past or present relationships onto the therapist. If the therapist is not properly grounded and aware, the countertransference can be the therapist projecting back onto the client.

Other profound relationships can occur when one finds a true mentor in life, from whom one learns a great deal. I have had, in my own life experience, a number of mentors. The first mentor was Vincent McGee, Jr. for whom I worked at the Hunt Alternatives Fund, and later the Aaron Diamond Foundation; both in New York City. My most recent, and I believe my "last mentor," was Don Stevens. Don was one of the preeminent American disciples of Meher Baba. In the case of my relationship with Don, it was reciprocal, as I helped him with many of his projects for Meher Baba.

I worked with Don for nine years, from 2002 until his passing in 2011, and learned a tremendous amount about the realities of the spiritual path from him, and with him. One of the greatest lessons I learned from him was the spiritual importance of balancing the mind and the heart. One of Baba's most famous sayings is, "The book that I shall make people read is the book of the heart, which holds the key to the mystery of life."[40]

Relationship With Self
(Including the Inner Child)

When thinking of my relationship to myself,
I realize I know multiple selves:

1. There is my highest self, which in some groups is known as a higher power—or my Real Self.

2. There is what is known as the lower self of desires (such as lust, greed, and expressions of anger).

3. There is the inner child, or the wounded self in psychology.

4. There are other self-identifications as well, such as the limited false ego.

Whatever one may choose to believe, it is important to get to know oneself more and more, and that the goal of enlightenment remains what Baba called "Arriving at Self Knowledge." This is not new, as the ancient Greeks had carved at the temple of Apollo at Delphi the primary motto; "Know Thyself." What does this really mean? It means, at least in part, that when seeking Truth, one may find hints of it here or there. One may discover sayings and writings that resonate, or music and art that inspires. However, at the end of the day, the Truth can only really be found within you.

Another version of the same is from Yeshua (Jesus), when he shared, "...the Kingdom of God is within you."[41] What he meant was that you might believe that Heaven, or the Kingdom of God, is a place you need to travel to or find somewhere, but the reality is that it is all to be found within you. According to Meher Baba, once you find it, you will have the experience of God-realization, union with God, or Oneness. As Jesus said, "I and the Father are one."[42] What he meant is that when you see him as the Christ, you see him as the manifestation of God.

In 1929 in India, Avatar Meher Baba wrote out in his own handwriting (before he completely stopped writing, due to his silence) this saying of the great Sufi Master Al-Hallaj: "I am He whom I love, and He whom I love is I. We are two spirits dwelling in one body. If thou seest me, thou seest Him, And if thou seest Him, thou seest us both!"[43]

The meaning of this is the same as the scripture of Jesus: if we see him, we are seeing God, the Father. If we see God, we are seeing Jesus as well.

Relationship With Spiritual or Divine Beings (Including Angels and the Departed)

Throughout the ages, people have had contact with departed spirits (such as relatives who have passed away), or divine beings (angels, or devas), and this is also an aspect of relationship. We can think of this as the "unseen world," but some people with psychic abilities may see into this realm. They may even describe it for us here in the material world in great detail. They may clearly hear or see beings of the astral or subtle world (hearing these beings is clairaudience while seeing them is clairvoyance). They may know, for example, what an angel looks like and what they're saying or doing. Or, they may be able to convey a message from a departed ancestor (ghost) who is trying to communicate with a living person. From this point of view, both the ghost and the material person are "living," it is just that one has a physical form, and the other is between forms. This adds a twist to the meaning of life and death.

Spiritual Masters and the Avatar

We can be in relationship with a Spiritual Master such as St. Francis through reading about him, his life and work, and his writings, including "The Canticle of the Creatures."

We can be in personal contact with a Spiritual Master, such as those who personally met Meher Baba. We can also have an inner, mystical experience of the Master, or Avatar, such as those who enjoy communication with Jesus, or Krishna, or any other Master or Avatar from the past. This is, after all, a mystical journey of the soul returning to Oneness. In my own life, I have had inner contact which resulted in communications with Meher Baba. This has occurred in many dreams of Baba, and rarely in my awake experiences, wherein I "heard" him communicate to me more than once. To share that would become a book unto itself, but suffice it to say that the relationship with the Master, or the Avatar, is the ultimate relationship into which one can enter; as it is a relationship based on Divine Love.

Lessons

- While it is easy to perceive duality (manyness), the deeper truth is that all souls are one.

- Before this Oneness is experienced, and based on this spiritual belief, I can behave as if it is true.

- Whatever I do to another being, if all is one, I am actually doing the same to myself.

Journaling Prompt

In what ways have my relationships been important to me on my spiritual journey?

Lesson 6
Finding the "I" in "We"
There Is No "I" in "We"

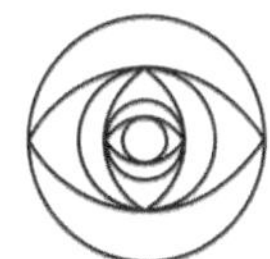

"You and I are not we, but one."—Meher Baba

It's no coincidence that during the final read of this book, prior to publishing, it became apparent that this chapter had mysteriously gone missing. My editor and I searched our hard drives and backups only to conclude that Lesson Six had vanished. At the time of writing it, I was coming out of a codependent best friendship of ten years. Whatever I had written about maintaining a sense of self in the presence of another was colored by that heart-wrenching (and gut-wrenching) experience. As I rewrite this chapter, I'm in a committed romantic relationship after five intentional years of singledom. How maintaining an "I" in the face of "we" pertains to me at this current juncture is that I'm floundering and have no f*cking clue how to do it.

Whatever I previously wrote was total bull$hit.
I think the universe made it disappear because it
wasn't written from lived experience, as the rest
of 21SL21C is.

Often, new love feels as if I'm lost out at sea in
dangerous, uncharted waters. Unable to establish or
maintain consistent, healthy boundaries with myself,
I see why I experience strife in my closest relationships.
Riding the ol' anxious-avoidant roller coaster that
is insecure attachment, I am in no position to write
about maintaining an "I" in the face of "we." When my
partner shows up as anxiously attached, I respond with
avoidance; repelled by their neediness and wrongfully
misconstruing their needs as traps that are inhibiting
my freedom. At the slightest hint of feeling controlled,
I plan my escape. Whether it's a few days in New York
City or busying myself in our home to the point of
being utterly unavailable, I physically, mentally, and
emotionally distance myself from my partner.

Au contraire, when my partner acts avoidantly,
I respond anxiously. I send twenty texts without a
response, letting my fantasy brain sprint to the future
—only to come back with terrible news that often
results in panic attacks, nightmares, and diarrhea.
When anxious, I have demanded more of their physical
affection than they want to give or acted out in protest
behavior. I'll withhold quality time, eye contact, and
authentic communication until my anxiety quells. Both
sides of the anxious-avoidant attachment coin have yet
to produce the kind of healthy relationship that I want.

Though I have never maintained an "I" in the face of "we," I have discovered roughly 101 ways to completely lose yourself in another person. I know how to center my life around someone, abandoning myself and living for their needs until the crushing weight of codependency feels like it's going to bury me alive. I bolt just before being crushed to death. As Thomas Edison said, "I have not failed. I've just found 10,000 ways that won't work." From that perspective, I may actually be an expert in this subject matter. I'm constantly beta-testing ways to nurture my anxious codependent so she doesn't need to headline the show every time sh#t hits the fan.

Something that has quelled the self-sabotaging, anxious-avoidant codependent living inside of me is the use of non-violent communication created by Dr. Marshall Rosenberg. This modality of speaking with my significant other includes:

- Speaking and reinforcing my boundaries

- Being transparent on my non-negotiables

- Speaking up when "ouch" or cringe moments occur

- Asking for what I want

- Asking if my partner is available to give me what I want

The week before re-writing this, I was in my place of origin, searching for answers in the faces of those who raised me. Both blood and chosen family didn't have much wisdom to impart to me on this subject matter, which I think speaks to how we are not taught how to relate to one another. One of my oldest friends, Patrick Seeley, said, "Finding the "I" in "we" isn't real. It's a fallacy." Another friend told me, "It's about honesty." As I trip over the limbs of the tree of life, I cannot say with certainty how someone can maintain autonomy while melding with another person. However, from what little success I have found in this area, I know that maintaining my boundaries with myself is the only way to freedom.

Somewhere on Instagram, I read, "Boundaries are not rules I get to impose on others like a benevolent dictator. They are guidelines by which I hold myself accountable." Someone can't break my philosophical or emotional boundaries; my boundaries are for me. For example, I have a boundary that abrasive name-calling is off-limits. Therefore, I must adhere to my own boundary. If someone is being verbally abusive, it is on me to remove myself from the situation and eliminate people who cannot honor that boundary from my life. I am not supposed to make others change their behavior.

This speaks to ownership and the amazing book,
The Four Agreements: A Practical Guide to Personal
Freedom by Don Miguel Ruiz.[44] If everyone on this
planet were to live by these codes of conduct, the
world would be a much more peaceful place. One of
the agreements is to never take anything personally.
I can't take it personally if someone doesn't adhere to
my boundaries. Much of life's suffering comes from
comparing ourselves to others or wanting things to
be different from how they are. To maintain a sense of
self in the face of another by releasing attachment and
control seems like a great first step.

Journaling Prompt

What boundaries do I need to maintain for myself to be able to connect with another safely and deeply?

Lesson 7
Oneness
Greater Than Equality and Unity is Oneness

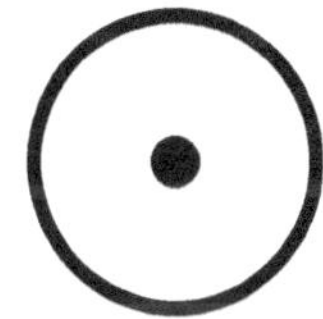

"Truth is One, but the approach to it is essentially individual."—Meher Baba

Oneness means that all that is living is one soul, expressing itself through multifarious forms in Creation. Not all forms are "equal." However, the soul within each being is the one Divine Being manifesting. What this means, according to Meher Baba and other masters, is that whatever you do to another soul (human or otherwise), you are really doing to yourself. If what occurs creates any type of imbalance, this must be worked out, or rebalanced. This is the essence of the law of Karma. Oneness is a foundational truth of the nature of God. Some new-age people throw around the term "oneness" without grasping the deeper meaning of this concept on a soul level.

It can be difficult to understand how a stone may be alive, or how it might be one with a flower, or that the tree is essentially one with an earthworm. If we take Meher Baba's explanation about evolution at face value, the entire Creation was created by God unconsciously, in order for the Divine Being to know itself consciously. The journey of God in the Creation goes from unconscious, unformed "oversoul" into the ensouled forms of gases, stones and metals, and then the various forms of vegetation, worms, fish, birds, and animals. Lastly, the soul is associated with human beings. The soul level is what is one, because it is obvious that the human and the tomato are not "equal." The souls of every living thing are essentially all divine, and this is the meaning of spiritual oneness.

When one embraces this oneness, it becomes more difficult to judge others. One's attitude towards others may start to gradually shift. This can bring one to recognize the importance of love, forgiveness, and surrender. It is easier to love when one realizes that all is a manifestation of One God. It goes further with the realization that all faiths are essentially loving and worshiping aspects of One God. Some focus on the impersonal aspects, and others focus on the personal manifestations such as The Avatar, or prophets and masters.

It becomes easier to forgive when this love inspires.
And one can more frequently surrender to the Divine
when the nature of the journey back to Oneness is
perceived. All souls are destined to consciously realize
this state of oneness with God, according to Meher
Baba. What is required is that we make an effort,
and then Divine Grace will descend when we are ripe.

Meher Baba expounds upon this in his *Discourses*:

Through unification with the higher self, man
perceives the Infinite Self in all selves. He becomes
free by outgrowing and discarding the limitations
of the ego-life. *The individual soul has to realize with
full consciousness its identity with the Universal Soul.*
Men shall reorient life in the light of this ancient
Truth, and they will readjust their attitude towards
their neighbors in everyday life. To perceive the
spiritual value of *oneness* is to promote real unity
and cooperation. Brotherhood then becomes
a spontaneous outcome of true perception.
*The new life which is based upon spiritual
understanding is an affirmation of the Truth.*[45]

Lessons

- While it is easy to perceive duality
  (manyness), the deeper truth is that
  all souls are one.

- Before this Oneness is experienced, and
  based on this spiritual belief, I can behave
  as if it is true.

- Whatever I do to another being, if all is one,
  I am actually doing the same to myself.

In what ways can I live a life more grounded in the spiritual truth of Oneness?

Lesson 8
Love
The Divine Force

"I have decided to stick with love.
 Hate is too great a burden to bear."

—Martin Luther King, Jr.

"The dawn of love facilitates the death of selfishness.
 Being is dying by loving".   —Meher Baba

"Love is a verb."   —Anonymous

What Is Love?

Meher Baba eloquently contrasts love and lust when he said, "In lust, there is reliance upon a sensual object and consequent spiritual subordination of oneself to it; whereas love puts one into direct and coordinate relation with the reality behind form. Therefore, lust is experienced as being heavy, and love is experienced as being light. In lust, there is a narrowing down of life, and in love, there is an expansion of being."

What Is Meaningful With the Experiences of Millennial Culture?

Everyone relates to love differently. We know there are different love languages (eg. acts of service, loving words, touch, etc.), and there are different love speeds (eg. some people prefer to take it slow). There are also different ways that each heart processes feelings and emotions. Given all these variables, it is not for me to say how the millennial culture experiences love. I was not raised in that culture, but I can share my observations.

It is clear to me that, like each generation before, this new generation is experimenting with love and lust, as well as boundaries and agreements (or lack thereof). It is ultimately up to each individual soul—not any culture – to decide what is best and right for them around love. I also observe the most gender fluidity in this millenial group, and the people even younger. This has been fascinating to witness. My own experience is that I don't personally need alternative gender labels, but view it as part of the current love experiment, which I understand as a creative sexual movement. I do believe that ultimately, love will prevail, and that we don't yet know how this will look and feel for people of the future.

When I was a teenager, I used to have coffee with my best friend Carl Haacke, in the West Village of Manhattan. One time, we discussed love. It was supremely intellectual and divorced from any deep life experience. My only experience with love at that point, besides my neurotic, atomic family, was my middle school girlfriend, Nisi. Over thirty years later, I can say that at that time, I really knew nothing about love.

Intellect with its logic and reason are useful tools, but they are not capable of sounding the depths of the heart, or navigating the waters of deep feeling and emotion. What's more, love is not limited to an emotional experience, but can best be understood as a verb; to be loving. There is the noun, of course— love as the experience of feeling love. However, after many life experiences, I am now certain that loving is more important than the personal feeling of love. To be a loving person means getting outside of oneself, stepping out of self-centered behaviors such as lust and greed. Questions such as, "How am I feeling?" and, "Where is the love I seek?" can be transformed by real love. Then, the questions become, "How can I be more loving today?" and, "Who can I love?" and, "How can I be loving in a way that they can best receive it?"

Ultimately, finding someone to love may
be much more important than feeling loved.

Meher Baba speaks extensively about love in
Discourses, explaining in depth the different types
of love. He explores love from the most crude or
unevolved, such as gravity, all the way up to the
highest form of Divine Love. He explains that
these lower forms of love have mixed into selfish
considerations. He then moves into the purer states
when he says,

> Pure love arises in the heart of the aspirant in
> response to the descent of grace from the Master.
> When pure love is first received as a gift of the
> Master, it becomes lodged in the consciousness
> of the aspirant like a seed in favorable soil. In the
> course of time, the seed develops into a plant and
> then into a full-grown tree…

> The descent of the grace of the Master is
> conditioned, however, by the preliminary spiritual
> preparation of the aspirant. This preliminary
> spiritual preparation for grace is never complete
> until the aspirant has built into his psychic make-
> up some divine attributes. When a person avoids
> backbiting and thinks more of the good points in
> others than of their bad points, and when he can
> practice supreme tolerance, and desires the good
> of others even at the cost of his own self, he is
> ready to receive the grace of the Master. One of
> the greatest obstacles hindering this spiritual

preparation of the aspirant is worry. When, with supreme effort, this obstacle of worry is overcome, a way is paved for the cultivation of the divine attributes which constitute the spiritual preparation of the disciple.[46]

As I am writing this, Sade Adu came on my Pandora station, singing her song "Skin." One of her lines is, "Sometimes love has to let go…"[47] This is a good reminder. Baba has explained that on the spiritual path, some things are more important than others. "The three most important things on the path to God-realization are love, obedience, and surrender. There is no possibility of compromise about these three."[48]

When we speak about love and letting go, we can easily see how love can progress in wisdom. It grows from human love between lovers and friends, to a more mature and spiritual love where one wishes to obey the spiritual master. Finally, one wishes to surrender all to God and the master. Forgiveness and compassion can be included in love. From my point of view, forgiveness is compassion in action.

My Personal Experience of Love

My love must be active for it to be real. In other words, words of love, if not lived up to, are hollow or hypocritical. The fact that I feel love in my heart as an emotion doesn't mean that I am properly putting that into action in a way that is well-received by others. It is on me to find the love language that will reach the person I wish to love.

In other words, with God, my love may be put into action completely differently than with my wife. And with my son, it may be manifested completely differently than with my daughter. And that is okay. It's beyond okay; it's healthy. Knowing what is best in a relationship and doing it (or not doing what is not healthy) is half the battle, and acting on that knowing with loving action is the other half.

Baba was silent for the last forty-four years of his life, and his life was an amazing journey of love and service to humanity. He said he would break his silence and speak one word. There are many statements from him about this; one of which I will share here:

> I must break my silence soon. And when I do, all will come to know of it. Those who have come in contact with me will have a glimpse of Me. Some will have a little, some a little more, and some still more. When the 'Power House' is switched on, there will be Light wherever the electric bulbs are connected with it; provided these bulbs are not fused. Where the bulbs are of small candle power, the light will be little; where the bulbs are of high candle power, the light will be considerable. Where a bulb is fused, there will be no light. Love me whole-heartedly.

> The time for the Power House to be switched on is so near that the only thing which will count now is Love.[49]

Lessons

- Love can be a passive noun, as in a felt feeling of love. It can be active, as in loving behavior, which reaches out towards another heart.

- At the end of the day, it is not how much we understand or how much money we have that is truly important, but rather how loving we are.

- Love can be expressed and received in millions of ways. Discover the ways that work best for you and your loved ones.

- Love can show up dressed in clothes that may not be immediately recognizable. Forgiveness is a type of love, and so is listening.

- Socially, we can say that truth and justice provide a structure which helps to keep love pure.

What is my relationship with
Love on my spiritual path?

In what ways has love shown up in my life?

How many types of love are there?

Lesson 9
Obedience to the Divine
Not My Will, But Thine Be Done

"Greater than love is obedience.
Greater than obedience is surrender.
All three arise out of, and remain contained in,
the Ocean of divine Love."—Meher Baba

This type of obedience is part of the path back to the Divine source. This obedience is not meant to be a contraction, but rather an expansive opportunity to come back into complete alignment with what is wholesome, true, and real. Arjuna experienced this with Lord Krishna, and as a result, we have the Bhagavad-Gita (a Hindu scripture). Spiritual obedience is not part of the distant past; it is only in the present moment.

What about obedience today, in daily practical life? What does that mean for those who have no living incarnation of a Master instructing them? Here, we can see that intuition can be a source of direction for the disciple, and not only heard but obeyed.

Meher Baba says, "Karma Yoga or the Path of Action consists in acting up to the best intuitions of the heart without fear or hesitation."[50] This means that while not having a living master, one can still tune in to the voice of God (or the Master) within the heart. It can be the voice of guiding intuition and inspiration, and we can learn to trust this inner guidance more and more. This is what Meher Baba named "Karma Yoga" in the quote above. It is important when living this way to surrender the results of action back to God. Otherwise, there is a risk of the ego becoming quite attached to the results and spoiling the whole endeavor.

Baba goes on to explain the importance of spiritual obedience in his profound statement:

Love is a gift from God to man.

Obedience is a gift from Master to man.

Surrender is a gift from man to Master.

One who loves desires the will of the Beloved.

One who obeys does the will of the Beloved.

One who surrenders knows nothing but the will of the Beloved.

Love seeks union with the Beloved.

Obedience seeks the pleasure of the Beloved.

Surrender seeks nothing.

One who loves is the lover of the Beloved.

One who obeys is the beloved of the Beloved.

One who surrenders has no existence other than the Beloved.

Greater than love is obedience.

Greater than obedience is surrender.

All three arise out of, and remain contained in, the Ocean of divine Love. [51]

We also have a tremendous amount of communication from the various advents of the Avatar, and the always present saints and masters gently guiding us about what is best. We can start by obeying those graceful and loving instructions. This reminds me of another message from Beloved Baba, about work:

> Do whatever needs to be done, but do it as a spiritual being; as one who knows he is divine by nature and united with the whole of life in essence.
>
> Do it as if you were doing it for Me or for God.
>
> Do it with equal consideration for the interest for all concerned, for God is equally in each.
>
> Do it with the utmost concentration, yet with utter detachment from the result of action.
> Leave the fruits of action to Me or to God.
>
> Do it as if it were the most important thing in the universe, yet let it be destroyed, or ignored, or ridiculed without concern; or let it be praised without elation.
> Leave the response to Me or to God.
>
> Do it, in short, as if you were not doing it at all, but as if I or God were doing it through you.[52]

Lessons

- Coming into tune with the wishes of God or the Master, as intuited by oneself, is not a chore to be performed, but more of an opportunity to become more and more spiritually free.

- Meher Baba said that obedience is a gift from the Master. All the love and guidance is embodied in the spiritual instruction to help one to become less entangled in Maya, and move closer to Truth: the Real Infinite Self within.

- Throughout time, all saints, masters and avatars have given their spiritual wisdom to the world. It is now time to live it.

- It is one's personal work to learn all the ways to become more obedient and strive to live that spiritual life.

In what ways do I struggle with becoming more spiritually obedient?

Lesson 10
Humility
Strength Freed From All Weakness

"If you have the humility of the earth
which can be molded into any shape,
then you will know me."—Meher Baba

In Baba's beautiful image above, we can see that he is making an analogy of molding the earth or clay into a form, and that there is no resistance to this creation.[53] We know that many human beings deny, resist, and even fight against being shaped and molded by another, or by God. Perhaps on a deeper level, this spiritual humility can be seen as an aspect of surrender to the divine. This is the role which the compassionate Master plays, which seeks to shape you into the best version of yourself—for you and with you. The Master has nothing left to gain.

Let's see what the world says about all this. The Webster's dictionary defines humility as "freedom from pride or arrogance."[54] It is fascinating that we learn only what humility is not, instead of what it is. Let's dig deeper and see what else we can find on the origins of this word, in the etymology on humility:

> Humility (noun) … from Old French *umelite* 'humility, modesty, sweetness' (Modern French *humilité*), from Latin *humilitatem* (nominative *humilitas*) 'lowness, small stature; insignificance; baseness, littleness of mind,' in Church Latin 'meekness,' from *humilis* 'lowly, humble," literally "on the ground,' from *humus* "earth…[55]

Do you see the word "earth" in the root of this word? Meher Baba starts his sentence with, "If you have the humility of the earth…" which seems to be a direct correlation to the roots of this word. Amazing.
My daughter Aspen once told me, "Remember that humility is not self-effacement. It is not thinking, 'I deserve to suffer.' That isn't humility.
That's internalized abuse."

Being born and raised in Manhattan during the 1970s was a wild time with lots of art and experimentation. The city culture where I lived was extremely intellectual. I don't remember ever thinking about humility as a value, or finding exemplars of humility until I started my spiritual search in 1985. I was a teenager seeking spiritual values. The first real encounter I had with humility was in Jesus Christ.

I was not really raised with any religion, and we were what you might call "C&E Christians" because we celebrated Christmas and Easter only—and we did that quite poorly as well. It wasn't until after my father died that I found out we were, in fact, Jewish. My mother's side of the family were German Jews, most recently from Berlin. They had narrowly escaped the Holocaust and come to America on a boat.

I began my voluntary research into spirituality with the Unity Church in Manhattan. Through them, I enrolled in a pre-internet correspondence course with Unity in Lee's Summit, Missouri. They sent me a spiritual workbook with exercises I would mail back to them and they'd respond with letters. How the times have changed! I found the Unity group to contain a real humility regarding how they embraced and lived Christian values, in a way I found lacking in many other religious groups. For example, they had a prayer service where anyone could call them or write a letter, asking for a prayer. It could be a prayer about anything, and they would hold that request with no questions asked. I also felt a kinship to their mystical interpretation of Christ's message. Here is the best example of this time:

At my first Unity guided meditation, in the heart of midtown Manhattan, a female African-American pastor guided us with great humility. She always used the phrase "God in you as you…" when making a reference to God, and I had a spiritual experience as a result.

When the meditation was finished, she simply walked away from the microphone and podium without any fuss or parting words. She just silently moved away and allowed us to slowly return from the depths of wherever each of us had gone during the meditation. As a teenager in the city, this was a fantastic new experience which I never imagined I would have. The one person in my life who exemplified humility to me, prior to this experience, was a mentor named Vinny McGee, Jr., who was a deeply spiritual man. He chose to put his vocation into action by giving away millions of dollars to various causes as the director of two different grant foundations. His was an elusive spirituality; rarely spoken, always lived.

Shortly after this I "came to Baba," and naturally had the experience of Meher Baba's humility. I also became aware of the humility present in his masters, and his own disciples as well. It seemed I was entering some new parallel universe of spirituality which I hadn't even known existed. Baba introduced me to the spirituality of St. Francis of Assisi and other great mystics, each of which embodied aspects of humility. I read about other saints, such as St. Teresa of Avila (Spain), and St. Catherine of Siena (Italy). I read St. Augustine's confessions and realized with Baba's guidance that the spiritual history of Earth was completely filled with amazing lives lived for God, and with God, from all faiths.Lord Rama lived a life of humility when he was falsely accused and exiled to the forest for fourteen years. He didn't argue about this, or fight, or appeal. He bravely entered his new life with his beloved wife Sita and loyal brother Lakshman by his side.

Lord Krishna embraced humility when he offered himself to Arjuna in the war against the Kauravas, and became Arjua's chariot driver. Together, they helped lead the Pandavas to victory. I was told by an Indian man that at the time of that great war, Arjuna would have been sitting high upon a seat over the chariot, and would have literally used his feet to tell Krishna which way to drive. He would do this by putting pressure on the sides of Krishna's temples, and turning his head in the direction they were supposed to go.

Lord Buddha's humility was in leaving his princely life in the palace for the life of a wandering sadhu seeking enlightenment. Once becoming the Buddha, fully enlightened, he continued the life of a wandering monk, begging for food and renouncing worldly pleasures.

Jesus Christ showed humility when, in the Garden of Gethsemane, he was approached by a mob. It was led by his disciple Judas, who betrayed him with a kiss. Instead of fighting, Jesus held back his divine power and allowed himself to be arrested and then crucified. And what was his crime against humanity, for which he was so violently punished? Loving and healing those with whom he came in contact.

Lord Meher Baba embraced humility in various ways, not the least of which was remaining silent from 1925 until the end of his life. He also lived a phase known as his New Life period, where he wandered India, begging for food and sleeping wherever they could find a place to lay down and rest.

Baba had close disciples ("Mandali") and many followers worldwide. Lyn Ott was a great painter and a follower of Meher Baba. He was a friend of mine, and I offered to help him travel from Myrtle Beach to India in 1990. He told me many stories about Baba and the conversations they shared. Here is one of them:

> Lyn was a painter with retinitis pigmentosa. This is a degenerative eye disease that results in complete blindness. Since Lyn was a painter, this was a particularly devastating disease for him to endure. His vision was being reduced, little by little. He told me that the final painting he made of Meher Baba required help from an assistant, as his own vision range was reduced to about the size of a coin. Prior to that, he created many beautiful paintings of Meher Baba. There is a book of his artwork called *In Quest of the Face of God.*[56]

Baba once said to him, "Lyn, you should be proud of your paintings." Lyn, being honest and natural, replied, "But Baba, isn't that ego?" Baba in his compassion explained, "That which you do for Baba is not ego."

Paramahansa Yogananda spoke about the proper spiritual attitude regarding pride. "Humility comes from realizing that God is the Doer; not you. When you see that, how can you be proud of any accomplishment? Think constantly that whatever work you are performing is being done by the Lord through you."

It would seem at this juncture that we have a lot of important words to consider and contrast when contemplating the nature of humility, such as modesty, self-effacement, pride, and self-esteem. Webster defines them as follows:

Self-effacement:
"The placing or keeping of oneself in an inconspicuous role or position, especially due to modesty or shyness."[57]

Modesty:
"The quality of not being too proud or confident about yourself or your abilities."[58]

Pride:
"Inordinate self-esteem: conceit."[59]

Self-esteem:
"A confidence and satisfaction in oneself: self-respect."[60]

It seems obvious that pride is to be avoided if it is a toxic characteristic. A healthy amount of self-esteem is a good thing, and when it goes over the limit (becoming inordinate), we land in pride, or someone can be experienced as being conceited. Self-effacement and modesty are a little more slippery. We do have a notion of self-effacement in spirituality. Like anything else, these qualities can be present in a healthy way, in a deficient way, or in a toxic way. I think of self-respect, self-love and boundaries as healthy.

When visiting my daughter in Maryland, I met a young woman who was 28. I asked her to share her feelings about humility. I wanted to honor her generation's voice on the subject matter. She stated,

> I think that humility is shunned. I don't think that humility is a characteristic that people know how to define anymore, or represent as a positive attribute. In the context of the social justice movement, if we forgive other people and take humility or self-improvement on ourselves, then we are forgiving all these unconscious or even conscious biases and saying: 'I forgive you, I'll clean up the mess.' For me to say that I can be accountable for a situation that needs improvement makes me a doormat, because I'm not holding the previous generation accountable for setting the stage for said situation.

Her comments highlight the juxtaposition and challenge of applying humility on a spiritual plane versus a three-dimensional, "reality as it is" plane.

What Is Humility?

Given all these explanations, what exactly is spiritual humility? Like love, humility must also be a verb and a way of being in the world. That way is a subtle statement of presence. In martial arts, we learn that there are three basic ways of showing up: to advance, to retreat, and to hold your ground. Humility is most like holding your ground and staying where you are.

Humility In Daily Life

When confronted with so many decisions and opportunities, one can allow another person to have their way. I am practicing humility if I am less assertive of my desires and wishes, not always imposing my way. That doesn't mean I no longer get my needs met; however, it does mean allowing others to express themselves, and get their wishes and needs met in a way that is not driven by me. There is a saying I read once on a sign in a café: "Half my suffering comes from wanting things my way, and the other half comes from getting them my way."

In many ways, we can see that self-assertion can be an ego expression, while sometimes a simple "yes" or silence is the best response. Another aspect of humility is not in judging one another but living a life of love and tolerance for all. I personally find this to be extremely challenging, as I have to be extra mindful that I am, in fact, not better than anyone else.

Meher Baba eloquently spoke to all of this when he said,

> Live not in ignorance. Do not waste your precious lifespan in differentiating and judging your fellow-men, but learn to long for the love of God. Even in the midst of your worldly activities, live only to find and realize your true Identity with your Beloved God. Be pure and simple, and love all because all are one. Live a sincere life; be natural and be honest with yourself.

> Honesty will guard you against false modesty and
> will give you the strength of true humility. Spare no
> pains to help others. Seek no other reward than the
> gift of Divine Love. Yearn for this gift sincerely and
> intensely, and I promise in the name of my Divine
> Honesty that I will give you much more than
> you yearn for.[61]

To me, humility is exemplified in all the great masters
and saints. There are so many stories. The overall
theme of humility has to do with being present and
allowing for everything to unfold in the best way for
all concerned. There is an aspect to healthy humility
and not accepting abuse; not being taken advantage
of, but also not defending oneself from criticism or
slander, or explaining oneself. It is more of an attitude.
Let people think and do what they want, for I know
who I am and where I am going with God.

I once had a dream. I was walking a narrow path in a
desert. There were small shrubs and almost nothing
was alive. It was dusk and I was not alone. About
five feet behind me, Lord Jesus was following me and
walking silently. I was taking him somewhere. At last,
we arrived at a small building, which had walls made
of arches all the way around in a rectangular floor
plan. The arches reached about ten feet high and held
up a flat roof. There were some shrubs around the
base of the aches as well. The place was long forgotten,
and I had no idea who had built it or why. I had a thin,
reed mat rolled out for sleeping in one corner. I turned
and said to Jesus, "I like it here." He responded, "I like

it too." I laid down on the mat, and he laid down next to me about a foot away, and we rested together there.

What I remembered upon waking from this dream was his incredible humility, presence, and naturalness. He had no airs about him, and he was neither meek nor arrogant. He was truly a humble, yet strong man; what I would call a real "man's man."

In another dream, I was on a small airplane with one row of seats on each side of the aisle. I was walking up the aisle towards the cockpit, past the passengers. There was no door on the cockpit, so I walked right in. In the pilot's seat, flying the plane was Meher Baba. He was focused and intent on flying the plane. He turned quickly as I entered and gave me a giant smile, beaming love at me, and then immediately turned back towards the controls. I turned to look in the co-pilot seat, and there was Jesus.

He wasn't doing anything; he was just being. He turned to me as well, and I held my hand out towards him, to shake his hand in greeting. He shook my hand, silently, and warmly. As I held his hand, I had an overwhelming urge to kiss the back of his hand, so I gently and slowly pulled his hand up towards my mouth and simultaneously bowed towards him. As his hand came closer to my mouth, he provided a tiny bit of resistance to my pull—just enough that I could interpret it as a message for me.

It was as if he was gently signaling me in true humility, "You don't have to do that." And yet, he allowed me to kiss his hand. I woke up.

We can see from all of this that humility is to be aspired for on the spiritual path. For whatever reason, it is always possible to behave with more humility. I have been practicing this while trying to serve Baba for many years, and still there is more to learn about how best to live in humility.

Meher Baba once explained, "One of the most difficult things to learn is to render service without bossing, without making a fuss about it and without any consciousness of high and low. In the world of spirituality, humility counts at least as much as utility."[62]

Lessons

- There is a difference between authentic humility, and modesty or self-effacement.

- Pride comes in many forms.

- One doesn't need to be enlightened to express less pride and more humility. This can be a practice in daily life and expressed in little things.

How can I practice humility in my daily life?

Lesson 11
Drugs
Some Paths Are Self-Destructive

"The experiences which drugs induce are as far removed from Reality as is a mirage from water. No matter how much you pursue the mirage, you will never quench your thirst, and the search for Truth through drugs must end in disillusionment."—Meher Baba

"Research and development" is the phrase I use for what I have learned in my first fifty years of life. Of the many lessons learned, one is most definitely that drugs don't help anyone get closer to Truth. Addictions are a major obstacle on the spiritual path. One of my favorite sayings from Meher Baba is, "Obstacles are meant to be overcome." I have relied upon this, especially in difficult life circumstances.

In relation to drugs, I feel it means that we cannot arrive at true Self-knowledge if we are still relying upon any external substances, period. All addictions must be overcome. However, for the scope of this lesson, I will just focus on drugs.

For the sake of clarity, I define "drugs" in this chapter as any substance which was not prescribed by a doctor for medical reasons. This includes marijuana (THC), psilocybin (psychedelic mushrooms), other plants like Ayahuasca (a form of DMT), alcohol, and tobacco. In other words, it is obvious that the substance is being relied upon to give the user some type of experience. Some people abuse prescription drugs (such as benzodiazepines), and that is also an addiction. The same drug, when supervised and monitored by an ethical doctor to treat a specific illness, is naturally not in the same category here as drugs and addiction.

I had a few experiences with drugs when I was younger. I started to follow my Spiritual Master, Meher Baba, in 1986 when I was seventeen years old. Because he said, "No drugs," I can only relate what I experienced prior to that time, when I did some experimenting. At that time, I was in eighth grade at Village Community School, in Manhattan's West Village. The psychedelic drug, Lysergic acid diethylamide ("LSD" or "acid"), was very popular. One of my close friends liked to use it regularly, and she would offer it to me. I remember what I felt in my heart as her hand would reach toward me with this drug offering. It was a mix of two primal feelings.

The first was a type of curiosity and excitement at the possibility of the drug experience, and the second which was tremendously strong and clear was an intuitive command: "Do not ingest that drug."
It was coming from some internal loudspeaker of feeling-knowing that this drug was not for me. I would surprise myself each time she offered and lovingly decline, so she would use it without me.
I am reminded to share that in my entire life, I never purchased any drugs, as they were being offered freely by friends quite frequently.

Growing up in the 1970s, I remember a friend passing me a joint. I don't remember the exact experience, or the setting it occurred in. I do remember that I accepted it, and I enjoyed it. Marijuana was the most frequently offered drug when I lived in Manhattan.

The only drug I ever used, other than tobacco, alcohol, and marijuana, was during 1982. I was in the eighth grade. It was a pill known at that time as "speed," which was the street name for Amphetamine. This drug is a powerful nervous system stimulant. My sister and her boyfriend were in high school and he was a drug dealer, so she had easy access to all sorts of drugs. I was going to a school dance one night and she gave me this pill. I think it was light blue and in an oval shape. I remember it had a line down it, like I could break it in two. It wasn't time-released; it was a solid blue pill. I remember I was scared to take it, so I broke it in two. I decided that if I liked the first half of it, I would take the other half. Otherwise, I would

just bail out of the idea. I took it on my way to the
dance, and I liked it. It was a tremendous high for me,
and I ended up taking the second half at some point,
probably at the dance. In the school auditorium,
I danced so much and so fast that it got a lot of
attention. One of the kids told one of the teachers
who was a chaperone.

The next day, the school called my parents about the
report that I had used a drug. I was summoned by my
parents to the living room of our tenth-floor apartment
for a conversation with them. I knew I was awaiting
my trial. I was asked if it was true what the school said
about my using a drug, and I said it was true.
My father was furious.

He said to me with lightning in his eyes, "If you ever
use drugs again, I will come down on you like God!"
That certainly made an impression on my teenage
psyche. I don't remember my mother saying anything.
I responded, "Well, I have come home and smelled
you smoking marijuana and seen you throw it out the
window when I arrived." He didn't say anything since
I had caught him in his hypocrisy. He just seemed
angry. I never used an amphetamine or any other drug
besides marijuana, after that day.

My father was an alcoholic. I don't remember him
drunk, as he went cold turkey when I was quite young.
My mother remembers him drunk, and my older
sister said she does too. I heard enough stories from
my father and my mother to know that alcoholism is

extraordinarily destructive. My personal experience of his destructive nature was in his other behaviors, such as infidelity to my mother, and food addiction. I believe my father was also a narcissist and bipolar, but I am not certain. Needless to say, it was not an easy childhood for me, emotionally. However, on the surface and from the physical perspective, I always had all I needed, and I didn't complain much.

At one point when I was about fifteen, I told my father I wanted to run away. I wished to leave New York City and go live in the woods. He discouraged me from doing that with cool, logical reasoning, and said that running away would mean him having to look for me with the police—and where would I be going, anyway? I didn't end up running away, but I did start drinking alcohol. This could be phrased as "running away emotionally." I don't remember when I started drinking hard alcohol, but it was vodka that I would choose. Sometime during the period when my sister was still in high school, I would go out with her and her friends and we found bars where they served underaged kids like us.

When I came to Baba in 1986, I put aside the hard alcohol and decided to have more discipline. I limited myself to only beer and wine and decided to have fewer drinks so as not to get drunk. Part of me wanted to give up alcohol cold turkey, the way my father had, but another part of me felt that I should channel that fear as motivation. I was afraid of becoming my father, but also wanted to show myself and Baba that I could drink responsibly. In any case, it has been a long journey with alcohol and alcoholism in my life and family.

I have been to Adult Children of Alcoholics (ACoA), Al-Anon (the twelve-step group for family and friends of alcoholics), and even been to an Alcoholics Anonymous (AA) meeting to see what it is all about. While I don't self-identify as an alcoholic, I believe that my family and genetics put me at risk of being an alcoholic. I am mindful of this as I walk my spiritual path with Baba. I still drink socially and in the evenings, and I haven't yet had the feeling that I need to stop drinking entirely. Maybe that day will dawn.

Everyone in my home smoked. It seemed like the whole world was smoking in the 1970s. There were even ashtrays built into the seat armrests of airplanes and buses. Yes, you could smoke on airplanes and inside offices when I was a kid. I started smoking before I went to high school. I didn't like cigarettes, but I did enjoy picking out special tobacco and smoking a pipe. The way my meerschaum pipe became physically hot in my hands, the scent of the smoke, and the taste of the pipe tobacco were all pleasing to me. There is nicotine in pipe smoke, but instead of inhaling it, it's absorbed through the mouth. I smoked my pipe until I moved from New York to Myrtle Beach in 1991. My roommate at that time said she felt my addiction to my pipe was distracting me on my spiritual path with Baba. One day I took my tobacco and my pipe and threw it into a garbage can outside of the post office. I don't know why I chose that garbage can. Maybe I was subconsciously sending it back to Baba. There was no ceremony; just a sort of grunting, "Okay, I'm done."

Tricycle Magazine

During the autumn of 1996, someone handed me a Buddhist magazine titled *Tricycle*.[63] This particular issue was dedicated to "Buddhism & Psychedelics." I knew well what Meher Baba had said about drugs, and that they were not only unhelpful on the spiritual path, but actually harmful. He called it, "A delusion within the illusion." Baba was ultra-clear on this point for his followers, and in his role as Spiritual Master, he allowed us no compromise. The magazine offered a full spectrum of viewpoints. On the one side was the argument that Buddha had said to his disciples not to use "intoxicants," so that would naturally extend to all modern drugs. On the other side of the spectrum, one article asked, "How can you call yourself a Buddhist and not use drugs to help you attain enlightenment?" I was rather horrified reading all this, and then I saw in the back of the magazine a directory of Buddhist centers around America with contact information for each one.

I made up my mind to create a little Baba project. I decided I would buy a lot of copies of Baba's message concerning drugs, which was in a short pamphlet titled *God in a Pill?* I would then send that pamphlet out to the centers listed in the back of Tricycle with a cover letter saying, "Haven't you heard what Meher Baba said about drugs?" I felt I needed to admonish the Buddhist community while there was still time and shake them up a bit around drugs on the spiritual path.

I went to the Sheriar Bookstore in Myrtle Beach, and at that time Ann Conlon was running the bookstore. She was an old friend from the City. I asked her how many copies she had of *God in a Pill?* Before answering my question, she asked me, "Why do you need so many copies?" I told her my tale of *Tricycle* magazine and their various perspectives on using psychedelics. She responded that she didn't feel comfortable selling me so many copies of that pamphlet for my project.

I argued with her that I wasn't asking for her opinion; I just wanted to buy them. Then she clarified that it wasn't about the project; it was actually that the old drug pamphlet was extremely outdated. It had been written in the 1960s and needed to be rewritten for a modern audience. She turned to me and said, "Laurent, would you rewrite it?" I immediately reacted with, "No." However, I felt my heart say yes. She didn't let it go, and offered a final, "Would you at least try?"

I bought one copy of the pamphlet. For the next several years, I did research and slowly started writing. I kept the original quotes from Baba about drugs and performed a great deal of research in terms of finding more quotes from Baba on drug use. I decided to volunteer at drug rehab programs to help counsel drug abusers and even worked at a drug testing laboratory during that period. Still, I felt unworthy of the project. In the 1960s, when drug use in the US skyrocketed, Baba had chosen three of his disciples (Rick Chapman, Allan Cohen, and Robert Dreyfuss) to speak out against drug use in America. I was a nobody. I reached out to the three of them, and each of them gave me tremendous support for this project. Allan flew to Arizona where I was living, and met with me over two days about the work. We had a blast together. All of them wrote forewords for the new book. Rick was particularly supportive throughout the writing and editing phases. All in all, it was one of the best experiences of my life working on that project with such fine gentlemen, and we have remained friends since then. This became my first published book which was titled, *A Mirage Will Never Quench Your Thirst: A Source of Wisdom about Drugs.*

Meher Baba was firm in his drug message, and it was not the popular thing to say during the '60s. Any drug used without medical supervision for "what one can get out of it" is harmful physically, mentally, and spiritually. Furthermore, he was ultra-clear that drugs are not in any way a shortcut to the Truth, or any help on the spiritual path. Most likely they will become a detour (or worse) on the path back to who you really are; one with the Divine, and the essence of Divine Light. Baba said that the only shortcut spiritually is to hold onto the feet of the Spiritual Master. We have discussed this thoroughly in the book *Surrender with Meher Baba.*

Notes on LSD

LSD can be used for rare medical conditions,
but abuse of it can lead to madness or even death.
As Baba explained,

> Medically, there are legitimate uses of LSD. It can
> be used beneficially for chronic alcoholism, severe
> and serious cases of depression and for relief in
> mental illnesses. Use of LSD other than for specific
> medical purposes is harmful physically, mentally
> and spiritually. LSD and other psychedelic drugs
> should never be used except when prescribed by
> a professional medical practitioner in the case of
> serious mental disorder under direct supervision.
> Use of LSD produces hallucinations, and prolonged
> use of this drug will lead to mental derangement,
> which even the medical use of LSD would fail to
> cure. Proper use of LSD under direct supervision of
> a medical practitioner could help to cure insanity.
> It could lead to insanity if used for purposes other
> than strictly medical. In short, LSD can be used
> beneficially for specific medical purposes, but
> for spiritual progress it is not only useless but
> positively harmful.[64]

Ayahuasca

Shortly after I wrote *A Mirage Will Never Quench Your
Thirst*, I was introduced to Ayahuasca. I had never
even heard of it, but I recognized the pattern to which
it belongs: a medicinal mixture of natural plants that
provides hallucinogenic experience. It's the new LSD.
The ceremonial use of drugs is an ancient practice,

and by no means do I disrespect this or put it down. When it is used with a genuine master or Shaman in a ceremonial way, with the right setting and the right intention, I can understand the *how* and the *why* of Ayahuasca.

However, almost all of what I have seen of Ayahuasca is a far cry from its original sacred usage. There are many fake shamans popping up to make money from rich, white people looking for a native trip, or an eco-friendly, psychedelic sightseeing tour. Don't fall for this. They even sell Ayahuasca's active ingredient, Dimethyltryptamine (DMT), online so you can sit at home and smoke it. Please God, no!

While there are few recorded deaths related to using Ayahuasca, there is no doubt that it can be harmful to users. As with other drugs, Ayahuasca doesn't provide any lasting experience of spirituality or enlightenment. Once the drug produced by mixing the herbs fades, so does the experience, and the user is left once again with nothing. The best scientific article I have read regarding Ayahuasca and its main active ingredient (DMT), is "Neural correlates of the DMT experience assessed with multivariate EEG," by Timmermann, Roseman, Schartner, et al.[65]

My Relationship With Substances

I have never purchased marijuana. I certainly smoked it when my friends offered it to me, at a party or socially. Of course, I inhaled it (this is referencing former US President Bill Clinton when he said he smoked but never inhaled marijuana—for those of you born after 1990). Before I "came to Baba," it was my "drug of choice." However, it was really not that important to me. When I heard that Baba said, "No drugs," I stopped and never smoked weed again. That was in 1986.

In the '90s, I quit drinking alcohol for a number of years because I wanted to be more spiritual. At that time, I also embraced a vegetarian diet, thinking that it would help me move closer to God. In 2003, I moved to England to work with Don Stevens, a disciple of Meher Baba. The first time he invited me over to his London flat for dinner, he served pork chops and red wine. I decided to eat the meat and drink the wine with him, and I haven't been vegetarian or quit drinking since.

Do I feel a *pull* from alcohol? Is it a comfort to me? Do I feel like I could become an alcoholic? I think that it is a sort of nerve comfort when I feel stressed out from life, or work, or the state of the world. I don't feel like I could, or would, become an alcoholic. The main feeling is that I don't want to avoid drinking out of fear. When fear is a motivator, I become suspicious.

Rationalizations

One can rationalize the use of any substance, especially one's favorite drug, as not really a drug. They can believe that it's not a problem and that there is no addiction. The story sounds like this: "I can stop anytime." This is an old ego tactic and it's easy to see through as a type of denial. All substances must eventually be given up on this journey back home in order to realize our own unalloyed Divine Nature, to taste the nectar of the soul, and to consciously become that essence of spirit.

Lessons

- Children eat things that taste good and play games to have fun. Drugs may make you feel good for a short time (like mental or emotional candy), but when the fun of the drug wears off, you are in much worse shape than before. Ultimately, what is at stake is your mental, physical, and spiritual health, as well as your relationships. Be prepared to lose one or all of the above when you embrace drugs as a playmate.

- It is the tendency of avoidance that leads to drug use. One may want to escape pain, reality, oneself, others, truth, intimacy (which may be intimidating), or whatever is perceived as causing suffering. When one understands this and embraces the path of no escape, then this tendency will naturally fall away. In its place will appear a healthy longing for Divine Love, God, Truth, and Oneness.

- No drug is a shortcut to the Truth.

- No genuine spiritual experience comes from drugs, as real experiences are all latent within you, and come from your Divine Nature; your soul's innate oneness with the Divine.

- Those who have no spiritual bearings and nothing real to which they can compare their experiences may believe that a drug experience is spiritual. It is more like the belief that the mirage is life-giving water. A mirage is just an illusion. Those who drink the mirage are left licking hot, dry sand.

Journaling Prompt

In what ways has my relationship with drugs been a part of my spiritual journey?

...I Have Done Drugs

An Addendum by Laxmi Dady

I'll be radically honest here: I have done 'em. Psychedelics mostly. I am trusting that my transparency is in service of something much greater than my fragile ego. It has been like pulling teeth to get myself to sit still long enough to write this addendum. It pulled on me in my sleep, wrestled with me in my waking hours, and demanded attention in all possible ways. If I could live with being a hypocrite, I'd probably keep this part of my storied past to myself. That said, I cannot publish a book with a chapter emphasizing "Don't Do Drugs" when I have busted out the fungi to help heal my ancestral wounds. What would be the point of creating this book? I would have subverted my own vision for the perception of safety. I set out to do it differently; to do self-development and transformation in a radically honest, down-to-earth, easily approachable way, told through lived experience and shared through story.

My good ol' friend Fear and his cronies, Self-Preservation, Ego, and Image-Consciousness loudly remind me of society's condemnation of people who do drugs. I can hear this motley crew crying out in despair, "Oh Laxmi! Don't do this. What if this addendum impacts your potential run for Congress that you've been striving for since third grade? What if Papa or Uncle Johnny reads this? What if a future employer or investor holds it against you?"

Well, if I can't be my whole self and be honest in a position of power, it was never the position for me. Decisions based in fear aren't decisions worth making, so I'm sharing how drugs have been a part of my spiritual awakening.

My intention behind sharing this is to lift the veil of mystery that surrounds drug use for spiritual awakening and to show both sides of the psychedelic coin.

Everyone's Got Something

The most basic definition of a drug is a substance that changes your body and brain chemistry. But so does sunlight, the darkness, and being in and out of water. Any food you ingest changes your chemistry, too. People often think of drugs as substances that are highly addictive and harmful to your body; something that does real damage, like methamphetamines. However, white sugar and high fructose corn syrup are also extremely harmful in very different ways. Google "the damaging effects of white sugar and high fructose corn syrup on the body" and you will be horrified that these substances are even allowed in food.

Then, we have the substances traditionally thought of as drugs. Those include weed, psychedelics of all kinds, party drugs (coke, MDMA, and alcohol), and then the more intense ones (meth, steroids, speed, opioids, and prescription meds). Let's not forget about the addictions that are not thought of as drugs, like social media, over-exercise, herbal medicine, gambling, reading, plastic surgery, tanning, cell phones, porn, caffeine, shopping, chocolate, cigarettes—and the list goes on. Google "What can I be addicted to?" and you will be surprised at what comes up. The list is endless.

Another colloquial definition of a drug is something that you become addicted to and can't get off of, and then it ruins your life. Hmmmmmm, like being a Tinderoni? Serial dating or hooking up as if the apps were actually paying you per match? Anything can be a drug. Anything that runs you, anything that you are compulsive about, anything that you cannot stop yourself from engaging with, and anything that has power over you. It's all about the individual person and what their drug of choice is. To me, a drug is something that I'm using to escape my reality in a way that negates my responsibilities, or harms myself and/or the people around me. Simultaneously, I know many incredible people who do powerful work helping people through deep trauma and PTSD with the controlled and supervised use of drugs such as ketamine, MDMA, psychedelics, and plant medicines.

Drugs = Enlightenment?

Can you find God at an EDM concert, high as a kite on ecstasy? Yes and no. You may have a profound, heart-opening experience or sense of universal oneness in the moment. However, I don't think that fist-pumping in a football stadium with 80,000 people can truly hold you through life's ups and downs. That said,

I have had life-changing experiences while communing with plant medicines that have assisted me in deep trauma healing, massive personal growth, and spiritual breakthroughs. All of these experiences have stayed with me and continue to support my unfolding. Despite having had positive, life-changing experiences through plant medicine, A.K.A. drug experimentation, there is no magic pill, button, or plant to make our suffering go away. Coming up against our anxiety, depression, and fear is a daily practice of facing ourselves and choosing love (which also means choosing God—because my God is synonymous with love).

A Tab of Oneness

Picture this: I'm twenty years old, sailing around the world with 600 college students. We're deep in the Amazon Rainforest outside of Manaus, Brazil. A friend I'd just met on the boat offered me LSD. Being the wild woman I am, I accepted. It was the second time I'd ever tried L. I was six hours from civilization, floating on piranha-filled waters in a wooden canoe, surrounded by lush rainforest and water buffalo, with a new friend, and in a foreign country where we didn't speak the language. It felt like a good time to try it again. During that trip, I experienced an overwhelming feeling of deep interconnectedness with all living things, the entire planet, and even the multiverse. The vivid colors and veins in the plants surrounding our hand-carved, aboriginal canoe will forever be emblazoned in my memory. There was a peacefulness as I felt the beat of my heart in sync with the lush rainforest around me and all of God's creatures. It made everything make sense, if only for those precious few hours. Tripping balls in the Amazon was such a profound experience of God flowing through me and connecting me to all living things of the past, present, and future. It has never left me. Acid has the effect of releasing the illusion of separateness. Ken Kesey and the Grateful Dead were definitely on to something. Even after "coming down," I continued to tap into that sense of oneness in a multitude of ways. It still happens when I'm feeling the warmth of the sun on my skin, when I'm observing the leaves growing on the trees in my backyard, when I'm watching the buds of roses gradually open, and when I'm witnessing a hummingbird feed. That experience with LSD cracked my heart wide open. The awareness of Mother Earth's beautiful, interconnected, and bountiful creation has remained with me since I used it over ten years ago.

Fire on the Mountain

Another LSD-induced, life-changing experience was when my brother GP and I split a tab of L. We were at a Dead and Co. show in Connecticut. At this point in my mid-twenties, I'd tripped about a dozen times and each time was a positive, heart-opening experience. I was expecting a joint experience of universal oneness with him. However, instead of the rainbows and unicorns journey I'd envisioned, I watched my baby bro get trapped in a twisted horror film inside his mind. GP was on an ADHD medication called Vyvanse. The meds, combined with the LSD, created a chain reaction in his brain that resulted in psychosis. His bulging eyes are forever emblazoned in my mind.

My partner and I stayed up with him until sunrise,
waiting for him to "come down," but he never did.
It was the day before Thanksgiving, and he was a shell
of himself for the rest of our family vacation.

A few days after returning to his university to finish
the fall term of his freshman year, he told our mother
that he was "off," and she picked him up from
the dorms. Mama called me and asked what had
happened over Thanksgiving break. I had to confess
to my very anti-drug, nurse mom, who'd never even
smoked pot, that I had given him LSD. Owning that
I had given my sweet, kind, funny, wonderful baby
brother drugs was a major hit to both of our hearts.
It burst the "Queen" status I had given myself in my
family structure. None of my siblings had ever done
psychedelics. Although I was the wild child of the
family, I was also the first to graduate from college, a
former Miss America title holder, and a Rose Festival
Princess. I had thought those meant I was "good."
In actuality, those were just accolades I used to feel
imagined superiority as the youngest daughter. They
had no real impact on my social standing in the sibling
pecking order. Regardless of how I thought I was seen
and how this would change that, it was painful to own
up to consensually "dosing" my brother.

Mama took him to his university's counseling center
and the healthcare professionals there sent him to
the Portland, Oregon ER. As soon as I learned that he
had been admitted to the hospital, I got on the next
flight from where I was living in Minneapolis.
I naïvely thought that my coaching background

and training through the MAPS Zendo Project (which aims to support people who go through challenging psychedelic experiences) would be of service to him. I flew with the hope of keeping him out of the fluorescent lights of a hospital. What I found upon entering my mother's home was a petrified young man, unable to decipher his intrusive, repetitive thoughts and newly surfaced traumatic memories. Foolishly, I hoped I could bring him out of his extended bad trip by taking him to the beach for a getaway. It was nothing that a few days by the sea, totally unplugged, eating a vegan diet, doing art therapy, exercise, and meditation couldn't fix, right? Wrong. Very, very wrong!

We stayed at the Sylvia Beach Hotel, an iconic Oregon coast getaway where each room is themed after a different author. They completely deck it out in furnishings that match the era and energy of their best-known book. Ironically, the room they put us in was Oregonian native Ken Kesey's One Flew Over the Cuckoo's Nest. This novel is about a charming rogue who serves a short sentence in an airy mental institution, rather than in a prison. Spoiler alert: the story ends with him being forced to receive a frontal lobotomy. After GP experienced a harrowing nightmare that included feeling a ghost standing over his bed while in sleep paralysis, I asked if we could be switched out of the room that was decorated like a 1960s mental hospital. We felt much more at home in the classically decorated 1920s-themed, Agatha Christie room. It was complete with a live cat and a wood fireplace.

Despite my best "hippie healer" efforts in the technology-free, boutique hotel, we reentered society and GP's mind began slipping back into mumbo jumbo. In hindsight, I would never take someone in psychosis anywhere but the ER. Not only was I attempting to handle a medical crisis without the expertise or understanding required, but untreated psychosis is biologically toxic to the brain! The longer an illness goes untreated, the more grave the impact and long-term side effects.

In the end, eating half a tab of acid resulted in GP needing to be hospitalized in a psych ward for six weeks. As a result, he dropped out of his freshman year of college and moved across the country to live with my sister and father, where he could rebuild his life post-psychotic break. This experience deeply impacted all the members of my immediate family's lives. After seeing how intensely one bad trip impacted the course of my brother's life, my relationship with drugs will never be the same. The shame I felt about having provided him with the acid resulted in me wanting to hide and distance myself from my family for years thereafter.

GP takes ownership of the experience as part of his own journey. It taught me the seriousness of engaging with psychedelics. I learned how they can uncover long-repressed trauma and awaken mental illness if it's already present, even if dormant, in someone's chemistry. Lastly, it demonstrated to me just how dangerous it can be to combine drugs, medications, and supplements. Drug interactions are common and get real, real fast. Please, always be aware of the cocktail of substances you put in your body at any given time—including vitamins, minerals, Ayurvedic and Chinese herbs, pharmaceuticals, and the food you eat with them.

One Year: No Booze, No Blunts, No Boys

After all the experimentation and wildly synchronistic, powerful, trippy nights at music festivals with my best friends, I still consider sobriety the purest path to enlightenment. During the process of writing this book, I did a year of sober-curious living. With the exception of a few (literal) f*ckups that year, I abstained from alcohol and weed. Being without these social and emotional binkies I'd been using to assuage my anxiety since high school boosted my confidence in my self-control and ability to see things through. I pretended that I was pregnant with potential and birthing my adult self. Resuming having an occasional drink or hit of the joint after my sober year reminded me how fun these things can be when they're used with the goal of pure enjoyment, rather than self-medication. Living a fully present life where there is time to listen to that soft, still voice makes space for a consistent relationship with God.

Go Your Own Way

Listen to your own intuition and embark on the journey that is right for you. You are your own chooser and creator of your life. There is no one-size-fits-all answer or path up the mountain of self-discovery. What works for you is unique to you. From my experience in co-authoring this book, I now know that sobriety is an amazing way to live. It can take me everywhere I wish to go in my life. Doing drugs is really fun, but when living sober, it is easier to hear your deep knowing. Even though you may have incredible highs and epiphanies when doing drugs, it can cloud your sense of reality and potentially open you up to addiction. Plant medicines and psychedelics can at times be the way to go for people who battle with blocks and barriers, such as PTSD, physical violence in early childhood, or psychological and emotional manipulation. These substances also tend to attract the curious, wild ones among us; the ones who want to experience everything life has to offer. When exploring anything potentially dangerous, doing so in a safe, controlled environment with trusted people is key.

Ask An Expert

Should you feel called to participate in casual drug exploration at a public event, please have a human guide physically present with you to be your trip sherpa. When you get drugs, test them! The Bunk Police and Dance Safe have similar missions of promoting health and safety within music and nightlife communities. Both sell at-home and on-the-go testing kits and provide free safe-drug testing at many EDM shows and music festivals.

The "wise drugs"—ancient plant medicines and psychedelics—primarily circumvent the rational thinking, conscious mind to trigger non-ordinary states of consciousness. This can aid in healing our fractured selves. These drugs are often most effective when used with a medicine person or specialist trained in the use of psychedelic psychotherapy. Integration sessions are crucial to ensure that the discoveries made are honored and brought from the subconscious mind to the conscious mind.

MAPS, the Multidisciplinary Association for Psychedelic Studies, was founded in 1986 and does research and training on the healing powers of psychedelics. Their website has a plethora of resources to prepare and educate oneself on healing with the clinical use of MDMA, LSD, marijuana, ibogaine, and ayahuasca.

These substances have the power to severely damage your brain, destroy your memory, and in the same breath make you feel your inner-God consciousness. Psychedelics create deep, expansive feelings of connectedness and oneness that you may have never felt before. They can open your heart and your mind and temporarily bring you into your version of wholeness. Whatever you choose, choose it for your future self's best interests. I believe in You. I trust You.

Journaling Prompts

If you are curious to explore drugs for recreation, spirituality, or therapeutic purposes, ask yourself these questions:

Where does my curiosity to experience a particular drug stem from?

What was I told about drugs as a child?

How might those messages impact me now?

Think of your five closest relationships. What kind of relationship do each of these people have with substances?

Fill in the blanks: if I could wave a magic wand, my desired outcome from experimenting with _______ will produce the result of _______.

What are some other things I can do to create a similar result?

Practice

Create a safety plan. The first thing on your list should be to test the substance you are considering taking. Once that is done, write down your answers to the following questions:

Who is my safety point of contact if I become unwell? Be sure to tell this person in advance and share your location with them. Ensure that the people around you have this person's info and/or your phone's passcode.

How will I integrate this experience into my conscious state? Is there anyone I'd like to ask to help me do this?

How much time am I allotting myself to recover or integrate from whatever might come up from this experience?

Have I been conscious of the food and beverage choices I've been making in the time leading up to my exploration?

What will I do for my aftercare in the days following my experience?

Lesson 12
Surrender
Divine Alignment

"Unfold the wings of your essence."—Rumi

Carl G. Jung of Switzerland was one of the preeminent psychiatrists of the twentieth century. He, along with Sigmund Freud, helped the world to better understand psychology and the nature of the ego. Jung was also a spiritual seeker. When asked in 1959, "Do you now believe in God?" he responded simply, "I know. I don't need to believe. I know."[66]

Meher Baba clearly explained to us that every step on the path back to Self-realization is a surrender, until the final surrender of the separate ego self and the merging into Oneness.[67]

I recently wrote a book called *Surrender with Meher Baba.* Many lessons around surrender on this spiritual path are fresh. I can smell the scent of the flowers of this graceful offering back to God, Truth, and Oneness. What does surrender mean in the context of spirituality? It is not like a Hollywood surrender, laying down your weapon of choice and putting your hands in the air. That would be much too easy. This spiritual surrender is internal. Naturally, there will be external circumstances, but spiritual surrender is an internal process.

It is more about self-will and the ego asserting itself than anything else. How can we offer over to God our self-will, our self-reliance, and our ego's many desires and wants? For me, this is extremely difficult. The ego doesn't like this spiritual path at all.

It is much easier to love than to surrender. Love, loving, and being loved is juicy, full of natural highs, great, lovely, and wondrous. Eyes sparkle, your partner smells great, your relationship with God is thriving and flourishing, and there is inspiration and insight; movement and flow. You're glowing and there is Grace.

Surrender is different. According to Baba's sister, Mani, Meher Baba said to his close disciples (Mandali), "You either want what you want, or you want what I want. You can't want both."

What does it mean to want what Baba wants?
He is not speaking as a man when He says this.
He is speaking as God in human form, as the Avatar.
He is saying that God's Will is what is important; not
your ego's wants and desires. Surrender must then be
related to giving over to God the self-will and trying,
step by step, to come into perfect alignment with
God's Will for each situation.

When a vehicle goes out of alignment, it starts to drift
off the road and can become dangerous. In the same
way, when we become out of alignment with God's
Will, we can veer off the spiritual path because of ego
desires that have nothing to do with spirituality.

Another way Baba explained this, especially to his
early disciples in Europe and America, was that
spirituality means NOT doing that which you have
been doing for ages. And what is that? He said that for
ages, we have been only chasing after our desires and
wants. We've been trying to fulfill them and still, we
are not happy. He said that so many lifetimes of sex,
seeking money, fame, and power, and violent struggle
for these have not given lasting fulfillment. Spirituality
is the not-doing of that. It is instead focusing on what
will make others happy, and what will help them. It is
trying to be selfless, in place of selfishness. Instead of
having lust, we aim to become more loving. Instead
of greed, we become more generous. Instead of
responding with anger, we become more tolerant and
accepting of others. Instead of trying to control others,
we allow God's Will to work through our
every thought, word, feeling and action.

Lesson

The spiritual path which ends in Self-realization of our own divine nature is made of a series of surrenders. It ends with the final surrender of the separate, limited, false ego self, the experience of divine Oneness, and unity with the Real Infinite Divine Self (God).

Journaling Prompt

In what ways do I need to surrender
more deeply to the Divine?

Lesson 13
Saints and Spiritual Masters
Receive The Help They Are Giving

"Every God-realised personality is Perfect.
However, those who come down and act as Masters—
the Sadgurus and Avatar—come down with their minds
universal,and use divine powers to work for others."

—Meher Baba

Once we realize that Spiritual Masters are always helping humanity, it becomes clear that coming into harmony with the help they are giving is vital to spiritual progress. Throughout the ages, we have incredible examples of those real human beings who beautifully exemplify spiritual reality by living it. It is easy to speak as if one is spiritual, but I have found it difficult to walk that talk. I still struggle with lust, anger, and greed. I have come to embrace my weaknesses. I strive to overcome them with more and more love, tolerance, acceptance, forgiveness, generosity, kindness, and surrender.

Meher Baba was extremely generous in sharing his knowledge of who in the past was spiritually advanced, and to what extent they helped humanity. The long and short of it is that there are different types of spiritually advanced souls. For an in-depth description, it is best to read his seminal book, God Speaks. I will summarize here and then delve into a few examples more deeply. Baba said that there are seven planes of spiritual consciousness, with the material world being zero. The first planes are the experience of the energy of the "subtle world," followed by the direct experience of the mind (not the brain) in the "mental world." According to Baba, the mind of the mental world has two parts. The first (meaning nearest to energy) is thought, and the second (meaning nearest to God) is feeling. According to Meher Baba, souls on the inner planes are either in the spiritual realm of energy (subtle world) or in the mental realm. In rare cases, Baba explained that there are souls who are God-realized (or Self-realized). They are on the seventh plane of reality, which is beyond all planes. The ones consciously in the subtle realm can perform miracles with this energy. The ones with consciousness of the mental realm have mastered the mind; either thoughts, or thoughts and feelings both. However, they are not spiritually perfect, as they still feel separated from God. The ones who merge into oneness with the Divine Beloved become spiritually perfect. If the Perfect Ones return to consciousness of this material world, and have a duty to perform to disciples, they become Perfect Masters. Baba gave examples of all of these types of souls throughout history. Here is a poem by Rumi, one of the greatest masters:

> Don't believe you're healing yourself.
> Prayer is an egg.
> Hatch out the helplessness.
> Your defects are the ways that
> glory gets manifested.
> —Rumi [68]

I wanted to take a little time to let this poem sink in, steep, and sleep on it for whatever it contains to settle into my mind and heart. I am sure I can only grasp a fraction of the meaning, but let's take it line by line.

"Don't believe you're healing yourself."

I really love this line. To me, it means a number of things. Healing of the body is deep and happens at a level that is cellular and organized by the body in amazing ways. You may already know this from biology class. That kind of intelligence is wired into the human form, and to me, this is because of the ensouled vitality that is present. This is nothing short of the presence of God within. When the soul (God) departs, all that physical healing stops. And that is just the body. What about the energy, the mind (thoughts, feelings, and emotions), and what about spiritual healing? To me, anything beyond physical healing gets into a spiritual conversation that becomes metaphysical.

Healing beyond the physical is all about one's relationship with the Divine; the divine within and the divine in others. It is about unlearning falsity. It is about letting that which is blocking the way fall away; letting it go consciously. This is not easy, and healing has not been an easy path for me in this lifetime. I am reminded about what Baba said about "healing:"

> Real healing is spiritual healing, whereby the soul, becoming free from desires, doubts, and hallucinations, enjoys the eternal bliss of God. Untimely physical healing might retard the spiritual healing. If borne willingly, physical and mental suffering can make one worthy of receiving spiritual healing. Consider mental and physical suffering as gifts from God, which, if accepted gracefully, lead to everlasting happiness.

At the end of the day, I feel that God and Baba are healing me. I choose to participate in that process. I do my part.

"Prayer is an egg.
Hatch out the helplessness."

This is also an incredible line, and rich with symbolism. Thinking of prayer as an egg is new to me. I never saw this before, even though I have had that Rumi book for years and keep rereading it. Eggs symbolize new life. Prayer is something I have struggled with. When I first started on my spiritual path, I was seventeen. I didn't like to pray, and didn't want to pray.

I wanted to meditate. As I have continued on this path, I find I want to pray more and more, and I don't want to meditate. Why? I believe what has happened is that meditation sounded more like the spirituality I wanted, but prayer was more of the spirituality I needed. In prayer, my heart activates, and I need an activated heart more than I need the stereotypes of spirituality. There is nothing wrong with meditation, but now I can see that for myself, prayer is helping my fledgling heart to grow feathers on stubby love wings. I am drawn to pray now. I drive to the beach to pray, and I go to waterfalls to pray. It has become a highlight of my day.

Hatching and Helplessness

Hatching means being born. Helplessness is a state that most don't want or like. Spiritually, Baba has indicated that helplessness is good because when we feel that spiritual helplessness, we become reliant upon God. It is the ego that feels it doesn't need God's help. This line is pregnant with meaning for me. I would sum it up as "pray and become spiritually mighty by embracing your newborn helplessness."

Finally, we arrive at the last line of the poem:

"Your defects are the ways that glory gets manifested."

Here is classic Rumi. Elsewhere he wrote,
"The wound is the place where the Light enters you."

This is similar, except it reminds me of a story of Jesus.
He was walking with disciples, and they saw a blind
man whom they all knew. They asked the Master,
"Was he born blind because of his own sin, or because
of the sins of his parents?" And Yeshua said, "Neither."
Walking towards the blind man, he said, "He was
born blind so that the glory of God could be made
manifest." Then he healed the man, and removed his
blindness, and he could see.[69]

This notion that defects are the way God's glory
manifests is counterintuitive. Yet, if it's true, it is
a marvelous and wondrous Truth that inspires me.
It helps me to be more vulnerable, which in turn
helps me to accept and love myself.

Lesson

Saints and Masters are here to help humanity, and the best thing we can do spiritually is to accept, embrace, and receive this help gracefully, living in this spiritual life more and more.

Journaling Prompt

In what ways have the saints and masters encouraged me in how I walk my spiritual path?

Avatar Meher Baba in India. Christine Cook shared what we know about this beautiful image of Baba: According to Padri this photo was taken in 1927 in old Mandali Hall, at Meherabad. It may have been taken by Naval Talati, who had a large camera, took many early photos from 1925–1938, glass negatives. Mani's writing on back of a print: "KAMLI (pron. as comely) Meherabad 1927. In the old Kamli coat and the sandals. Kamli is the inexpensive hand woven Indian blanket from which coat was made."

Lesson 14
The Avatar
God in Human Form

"God is a verb."—Vanessa Weichberger

The Avatar returns as the world teacher, age after age, to help us all. What does it mean for God to be a verb? It must mean many things. If you want to know what God has done, or is doing, or will do, research the life of the Avatar and see for yourself. In Meher Baba's time, he added, "I have come, not to teach but to awaken." So, awakening is part of God's doing; awakening humanity to their own Divine Nature within.

One day, I was sitting in my car in the parking lot of a supermarket, with my son Francis in the backseat. We were waiting for my wife Vanessa to come out with fresh groceries. While sitting, my Pandora station played one of my favorite songs; Connie Dover singing "Ubi Caritas." I had heard this song many times over the years and I loved it. While I recognized that she sang in Latin, I had never taken the time to research the song's meaning. Since I had some time, I did it right there in the car. When Vanessa returned to the car, the song had passed, so we played it again on YouTube. We read the lyrics out loud in Latin and found an English translation.

However, when I returned home, I decided to double-check the translation. I had seen poor translations in the past—mostly of Persian and other Eastern poets. I wanted to be sure that I was getting every drop of goodness from this song in Latin. Sure enough, while doing deeper research, I discovered the first translation I read was not as accurate as I would like. It was certainly not poetic. I yearned to translate this song myself, so that night and the following morning, Vanessa and I did. Here is what we came up with:

Ubi Caritas ("Where there is Charity")
by Paulinus of Aquileia

God is present where there is charity and love.
We come together as one in the love of Christ.
Rejoice, celebrate, and be merry,
Let us love and revere the living God,
As we love each other purely from the heart.

God is present where there is charity and love.
Simultaneously, we gather together as one.
Take care, don't let thoughts separate us.

Cease these toxic fights and struggles, stop arguing.
And may our anointed one, Christ our God,
be at the center.

God is present where there is charity and love.
Concurrently let us behold the blessed ones.
The splendor of Christ our God, Your glorious face!
Limitless joy which is honest and good.
Eternally the infinite, eternal truth.[70]

Let's take a moment to go over this wondrous song,
or poem, line by line, to appreciate the nectar of this
lovely bouquet of words.

It says, "God is present where there is charity and
love, we come together as one in the love of Christ."
This means that the formless infinite divine makes its
presence known when humans express love and give
charity. The dictionary defines charity as generosity
and helpfulness, especially toward the needy or
suffering. It also defines it as aid given to those in
need. This indicates that love in action, as charity, and
helping others is important. Some people think that
love is a feeling and they never move past the passive
state of feeling love towards one another. When love
is a verb, it is put into action as charity and more.
Vanessa said, "We are loving God by loving each
other." It is also showing the importance of oneness,
and how through our love of Christ, the Avatar, we
are able to come together.

On the topic of loving God by loving one another, Meher Baba said it perfectly when he shared, "The greatest virtue is called charity, not this ordinary charity. Real charity means tolerance due to big-heartedness. Tolerance and forgiveness are included in real charity. It is also charity to offer the other cheek when slapped. In fact, to lose to make others gain is charity. It is a vast thing."[71]

When the song says, "Rejoice, celebrate, and be merry, let us love and revere the living God, as we love each other purely from the heart," this is about the atmosphere created on the spiritual path. We don't need to be somber, glum, overly serious, or pious. In fact, Baba recommended that everyone remain cheerful while they love God.

In November of 1955, at his spiritual center in Meherabad, Meher Baba had a "sahavas" program, for the four major language groups of India. He posted this for everyone to grasp the concept of a sahavas:

Just remain here like one family; be in my proximity and derive benefit from my company [sahavas]. Be absolutely free and comfortable and think that you are in your own homes. Forget all your troubles and household atmosphere, and be mindful only of your presence here. If you go on thinking of your wife and children, then you will be in the sahavas of your family and not of Baba. If you fold your hands before me mechanically, but go on thinking of your ailing wife at home, you will be folding your hands to her and not to me. Eat, drink, sleep, remain happy and cheerful, and taste as much of my love as you can.

Here, we can sense the atmosphere Baba was creating with those attending his program. Each language group spent a week with Baba in intimate companionship. We can see Baba didn't indicate that he wanted pious (devoutly religious) people, or meditation, or any serious lectures about God and the Master. He wanted love, cheerfulness, and mindfulness. On another occasion, he explained to my spiritual mentor, Don Stevens, that while the Avatar has manifested and is present, the "Path of Love" is wide open to one and all. While the path of love with Avatar is so open, it is a relative waste of time to meditate. The best thing is to love God, and love the Avatar.

Don and I spoke about this concept, and he shared this story.

'Each time I arrived in India, Baba would ask, 'How are things coming along? How are you getting on?' I said, 'Well, Baba, frankly, I've got something that confuses me. It is bothering me, and I've got to straighten it out with you. How come you created so many meditation discourses, and yet you stopped us from practicing them when we became Sufism Reoriented? You've still never given me a meditation.'

Immediately, a little voice inside his head said, 'I'm treading on terribly dangerous ground here.'

'Instead, Baba said, 'Good question, Don.' Don let out a big sigh of relief. [This is a terribly important point; note the word 'Manifestation' here.]

'Baba says to you that during the period of his Manifestation, and for some time afterwards, the Path of Love, which is the highroad of all roads to Realization, is fully opened to all of humanity. But gradually, the Path of Love will slowly narrow, and finally will be inaccessible to all but a very small percentage of devotees. Then, the second major road, not as great as love, but the second major road to Realization will have to be used and that is meditation.'

'First, Baba is simply saying that, yes, love is terrific. He explained to me that love, of all human qualities, can marshal and focus better than any other human quality, the psychic energy to do the job. Love. But then, he went on to say, 'But the Path of Love will gradually narrow, and then meditation, the best of the secondary roads, will be used.'

'I must say, even the very few Mandali to whom I mentioned what Baba had said were shocked to pieces and they regurgitated it. Really, they could not accept it. They said, 'Don, Baba has emphasized to us so many times about love, the importance of love, and the utilization of love, and we just know that it is open eternally now.'

But how can that be true if Baba himself told me, 'No, the path of love will gradually narrow…'? Then, Baba went on, 'Don, I have to prepare for the next seven hundred years, so I have to plan for the time when meditation must be used before I come again.'

That means that the Path of Love is going to become relatively inaccessible. Not maybe before four or five hundred years from now, but pretty damn soon. We've got to be realistic.[72]

Back to the song "Ubi Caritas," the lyrics in the next stanza are, "Take care, don't let thoughts separate us. Cease these toxic fights and struggles and stop arguing. And may our anointed one, Christ our God, be at the center."[73] This reminds me of what is going on in America right now around the Black Lives Matter (BLM) protests, as well as the counter-protestors from various groups such as those who are pro-President Trump, Proud Boys, Patriot Prayer, white supremacists (White Lives Matter), and the Blue Lives Matter (pro-police) movements. In 2020, there was a clash in Portland, Oregon where a BLM protester shot and killed a Patriot Prayer member.

Then, on February 24, 2022 (one day before Meher Baba's birthday), the world was shocked when we saw Russia invade Ukraine. A number of people have asked me what Baba said about Russia, and so here is one of many things Baba has said:

> On Friday, March 13, 1953, Baba explained about the farce of illusion and the evolution of opposites: 'The nature of evolution is of opposites. Never before was the world divided into two blocks of opposites—America on one side with its allies, and Russia on the other with its satellites. This is what Masters have worked out. They know how to do it.'[74]

The quote continues, but that is the only part about Russia. This toxic fighting and struggle in this Russian-instigated war must stop. But how? I have a wife and five children. I often say that if I was not married and only had one son, he and I would probably have flown over to Ukraine to help! I naïvely thought that the world was past this point of such unprovoked warfare being inflicted by one nation upon another.

I am still learning about the ways of this dark world. My son wrote a song for Ukraine after hearing about this war, titled "Flower Pockets." This was inspired by a Ukrainian grandmother who yelled at a Russian soldier, "You should put sunflower seeds in your pockets, so at least flowers will come up from your body when we lay you in the ground!" Also inspiring was the response that Ukrainian president Volodymyr Zelenskyy gave to the USA when we offered to airlift him out of his country: "I need ammunition, not a ride."

There are many other things Meher Baba said about Russia, and you can find them by doing some research in Baba literature. To me, the most important thing is to remember what he reminded us: God alone is real, and all else is illusion. Focus on Him and the Oneness. He said, "Remember me and I am with you, and my love will guide you."

This level of violence and war goes way beyond the lyrics "don't let thoughts separate us," but what we know is that thoughts lead to words, and words lead to actions. This is a Latin hymn over one thousand years old about a spiritual master, who was the Avatar, Yeshua ben Yusuf (Jesus Christ). He lived two thousand years ago. How do we modernize this spiritual message for one and all?

As fate would have it, God does that for us. As you see, the Avatar returns to Earth on a regular basis, and His "advent" is profoundly awaited by humanity. Baba said that the Avatar has been manifesting on Earth for thousands of years and included (but was not limited to) the lives of:

Zarathustra, the Prophet of Persia

Lord Ram and Lord Krishna, the Avatars of India

Lord Buddha

Lord Jesus

The Prophet of Arabia, Muhammad

(Peace be upon Him and his family)

All faiths await the return of their Avatar, Christ, and Prophet. It is my firm belief and conviction that he has manifested once again as Avatar Meher Baba.

Recently, at a dinner gathering at our home in Wilmington, North Carolina, we had a guest named Madeleine. This young woman who self-identifies as a "recovering Christian," and as a seeker of peace, shared this when I asked her about spiritual lessons:

> My prerequisite for spiritual growth and healing is unlearning shame. Particularly as someone who grew up with Christianity and around Christians —I think all young people who grew up with Christianity struggle – I've had to unlearn the idea that shame is at all conducive to any sort of spiritual connection. Brené Brown says guilt is, 'I did something bad,' and shame is, 'I am bad.' Believing I am inherently bad or wrong has never made me feel closer to a god.

What can I say about The Avatar? Since I am not spiritually advanced, anything I say which is metaphysical is borrowed from what Meher Baba has explained about this subject, or what the saints and other spiritual masters have intimated. If I speak from my direct experience, I can share that I have heard Baba communicate to me strongly and clearly. I can also share about dreams I have had of Jesus Christ, Avatar Meher Baba, and other Avataric manifestations. If I speak intuitively, I can share what I have heard or felt in my heart with Meher Baba, as the Avatar in my esteem. When I speak from experience, I can say that the divine presence and love that flows from the Avatar to me, as well as all of humanity, the entire universe, and all of Creation, is so deep, vast, and immeasurably infinite that it is like a flea trying to explain how a horse gallops through sunny open fields.

I can say this much; the Avatar, in any advent, is to me the mountaintop of all experience. By that, I mean what the Avatar IS, what the Avatar shares, and my experience of that. It is the most incredible, real, soul-awakening experience to be in relationship with Him.

Intellectually, I can read that the Avatar is the externalization of the Higher Self in all, and yet, until I have that experience of Oneness with Him, I do love Him. I do strive to obey Him, and ultimately surrender my all to Him. And why?

He has brought me from darkness to light, from confusion to clarity, from relying upon my intellect to tuning into my heart's intuition, and from being aloof and detached to being intimate, more vulnerable, and surrendered. I have not reached any spiritual goal, yet I experience participating with Baba more and more in this journey to the destination. It is not so much waiting to finally meet him in some Heaven state. It is more of an active and dynamic relationship with God, in the present moment; moment by blessed moment.

Based on my research, conversations with Meher Baba's disciples, my dreams, and my intuitive knowing, The Avatar (while always purely God manifested in the world) is also always a different personality, which is the best personality to fit the culture, time, place, and people to whom He is sent. He integrates and manifests divinity for all. By this, I mean that my experience of Jesus' human personality is much different than that of, say, Buddha, Krishna, or Meher Baba.

It is like ice cream at an ice cream parlor. So many flavors are there, but it is all ice cream; just with different tastes based on various ingredients. God is pure being—the Soul of all Souls. Essentially we are all that, and yet the flavor that manifests has a different taste. That's why some are drawn to Buddha, while others prefer Krishna, Jesus, or Mohammed. At the end of the day, what matters is your movement towards the Truth of your own Divine Nature within.

As Jesus said, the Kingdom of God is within you and nowhere else. Baba said the same. All real masters redirect you to find and know yourself, as the divine essence you really are. As you probably guessed by now, my favorite Avataric flavor is Meher Baba. Why is that? Maybe it is because he lived so recently that I can deeply feel his resonance within my heart. I get him, and I feel like I know him. He visits me in my dreams and he guides me intuitively. He has never let me down, ever. Lately, I have come to feel that the more I surrender myself to Him, the clearer I hear my own intuition, as his voice within.

Another aspect of The Avatar that I feel is important
to describe is accessibility; who is given direct access
to their guidance. For example, we know historically
that John the Baptist was a great spiritual master,
about whom even Jesus said, "This is the one about
whom it is written: 'I will send my messenger ahead
of you, who will prepare your way before you.'[75] Jesus
also said, "I tell you, among those born of women,
there is no one greater than John; yet the one who is
least in the kingdom of God is greater than he."[76]

And yet, the world knows almost nothing about John
the Baptist, and almost no one follows him or is a
disciple of John. They are instead followers of Jesus.
If he was so great, then why is that? It is because
John was a Spiritual Master, but Jesus was The Avatar
(the Christ). Jesus has been accessible to people for
thousands of years, and many people have entered a
mystical relationship with Jesus long after his physical
death. In the same way, Ramakrishna of Calcutta
was a great Spiritual Master, had disciples, and there
are still monks in his order. However, it is Krishna
the Avatar who has millions of followers around the
world, many thousands of years after his passing.
Why? Because the Avatar is present and available
to his followers after his passing.

People read the sublime Sufi poetry of Hafiz and Rumi,
who were not only poets but great Spiritual Masters.
Rumi also had his own Sufi order, and yet it is the
Prophet Muhammad (peace be upon him and his
family) who has inspired them and millions of other

people around the world to follow him on his path of Islam. It is like this in every faith. There is the founder of the faith, followed by saints and masters in the faith. But the saints and masters pass away and while remembered, they are not accessible to the world after they pass away.

The Avatar remains present in a way that is sometimes known as the ever-living master. This is inspiring and real for me and I experience Meher Baba as alive and present in my life, guiding me internally, on a daily basis. As Vanessa has said, "Baba is seated in your heart, and he is always available."

To give you another taste of the flavor of Meher Baba, here is a message from Him, known as "How to Love God." Enjoy:

> To love God in the most practical way is to love our fellow beings. If we feel for others in the same way as we feel for our own dear ones, we love God.
>
> If, instead of seeing faults in others, we look within ourselves, we are loving God.
>
> If, instead of robbing others to help ourselves, we rob ourselves to help others, we are loving God.
>
> If we suffer in the sufferings of others and feel happy in the happiness of others, we are loving God.

If, instead of worrying over our own misfortunes, we think ourselves more fortunate than many, many others, we are loving God.

If we endure our lot with patience and contentment, accepting it as His Will, we are loving God.

If we understand and feel that the greatest act of devotion and worship to God is not to hurt or harm any of His beings, we are loving God.

To love God as He ought to be loved, we must live for God and die for God, knowing that the goal of life is to Love God, and find Him as our own self.[77]

Finally, while walking this morning around Beaver Lake here in Asheville, North Carolina, I was inspired to add to this chapter the prayer Meher Baba dictated. It is really a Oneness prayer titled "The Master's Prayer," (or sometimes the "Parvardigar Prayer"). I will add my commentary between the lines to help the reader with the meaning since it employs multiple languages and spiritual traditions. My notes are in italics, and the prayer from beloved Baba is in regular text.

LAURENT

"The Master's Prayer"

O Parvardigar, the Preserver and Protector of All,

You are without Beginning and without End,

Non-dual, beyond comparison, and none can
measure You.

*In the Persian Zoroastrian tradition, which is pre-Islamic,
there were three aspects of God: The Creator, the Preserver,
and the Destroyer. The Preserver (Protector) aspect is
named "Parvardigar." Meher Baba said that of the three
aspects of existence, this Parvardigar is the most important.
The Hindus name this aspect "Vishnu."*

*This existence is so infinite, total, and complete that all that
lives is a part of this being; so there is nothing else. That
is the meaning of non-duality. Anything which appears to
be "other" than God does not exist. This infinite, Divine
Nature cannot be measured and there is nothing that can be
compared to God.*

You are without color, without expression, without form,
and without attributes.

This infinite being is also infinitely impersonal.

You are unlimited and unfathomable, beyond
imagination and conception, eternal and imperishable.

*There is no limit to the infinite, Divine Nature and none
can reach the depths of the divine except through direct
experience of Self-realization. The mind alone can never
reach the infinite. The limited mind must be transcended.
That Divine Nature has no beginning or end, is never born,
and never dies.*

You are indivisible, and none can see You but
with eyes Divine.

*The Divine is so incredibly, infinitely One that it can never
be divided. The Divine is so infinite and all-pervading that
it is everywhere. So, paradoxically, it can't be seen unless
you have Self-realization. Then, it is all you see.*

You always were, You always are, and You always will be.

*God always was, always is, and always will be infinite
existence (being); the One within the many.*

You are everywhere; You are in everything;
and You are also beyond everywhere and beyond
everything.

*This means that God entered the Creation as the soul of each
living thing, and yet, God can never be dependent upon
anything. While in Creation as the living soul, God is also*

beyond the Creation. It is a paradox. It is like saying, "Yes, you dream at night, but you are more than your dream."

You are in the firmament and in the depths.

This firmament is the old English word, rarely used now, for "the Heavens" or "the vault or arch of the sky." The depths means deep below, like the bottom of the sea.

You are manifest and unmanifest on all planes
and beyond all planes;

You are in the three worlds and also
beyond the three worlds.

Manifest means that God is manifested in the three worlds: material (gross), energy (subtle), and mental (dual aspects of mind: thought and feeling), and yet also beyond these realms in the infinite, real realm where there is no Creation at all. In this sense, the Creation is the dream of God.

You are imperceptible and independent.

Most humans perceive with their bodily senses: seeing, feeling, tasting, touching, and hearing. These senses are not capable of perceiving the Divine Presence. For that, the heart's senses must be engaged and the experience is that of intuition, inspiration, illumination, and guiding insight. God's being depends on nothing. It is the cause, and nothing created the Creator.

You are the Creator, the Lord of Lords,
the Knower of all minds and hearts;

You are Omnipotent and Omnipresent.

The Divine Being created all that is, is the ruler of all those who believe they are in power, and knows the essence of all created beings. Omnipotent means universally powerful; God almighty; possessing unlimited powers. Omnipresent means the Divine Presence is everywhere at once. There is nowhere God is not.

You are Knowledge Infinite, Power Infinite,
and Bliss Infinite.

This is a reference to what the experience is of the soul who realizes the Divine Nature, and it is the experience of the triune attributes of knowledge, power, and bliss on an unlimited scale.

You are the Ocean of Knowledge, All-knowing,
Infinitely-knowing the Knower of the past, the present,
and the future; and You are Knowledge itself.

Here, Baba is driving the point home that there is nothing not known by the Divine, and that the knowledge and the knowing what is known are also all One.

LAURENT

You are all-merciful and eternally benevolent.

*Benevolent is from the Latin "bene," which is "well"
or "good." All that God does is for the well-being of all
concerned. Mercy is connected to compassion and blessing.*

You are the Soul of souls, the One with infinite attributes.

*Here, Baba is talking about Oneness again. All souls are
really One, and they are one with that Oversoul which is
the Divine Being. Even an ant's soul is really one with
God; it just doesn't realize this fact. The "One with infinite
attributes" is a contradiction of the earlier line that says
"without attributes." This shows the paradox of the Divine
Nature which is beyond all rules and promises. How God
can be both impersonal and have no attributes while being
more personal and having infinite attributes is part of the
divine mystery.*

You are the Trinity of Truth, Knowledge and Bliss;

You are the Source of Truth, the Ocean of Love.

*Here, Baba goes into a few of the infinite attributes of God:
love, truth, knowledge, and bliss. Also, that truth comes
from the Divine. God is an infinite ocean of Divine Love.*

You are the Ancient One, the Highest of the High;
You are Prabhu and Parameshwar;
You are the Beyond-God and the Beyond-Beyond-God
also;
You are Parabrahma, Allah, Elahi, Yezdan, Ahuramazda,
and God the Beloved.

Now, Baba turns up the heat and delves into the attributes further. "Ancient One" means that the being goes back eternally into the past and is above all else. Whatever is high, the Divine is higher. "Prabhu" is a Hindu word and it means "the Lord." "Parameshwar" is a compound word in Hindi. "Param-" is a prefix meaning supreme or ultimate. The suffix of "-eshwar" is a reference to Ishwar (Ishvara), which is another name for the Divine being.

The states of God named as "Beyond-God" and "Beyond-Beyond God" refer to the impersonal states of God, such as those listed after: Parabrahma for the Hindus, Allah for the Muslims, and Sufis.

The word "Elahi" that is used by Baba is a bit obscure. I discussed this with my close friend Yaakov Weintraub, who helped me break this down. In the Bible book of Genesis, from Moses, we see the Hebrew word, "Elohim." It means "Divine Beings" (it is plural). In Hebrew, the singular form would be "Eloh."

It is my sincere belief that Meher Baba was bowing to the Hebrew root and made this word "Elahi." Perhaps it is a Persian version of the Hebrew singular form. I say this because Baba, having the opportunity here in the prayer, may have corrected the plural to show his focus on the Oneness (singularity) of God, and away from the plurality.

"Yezdan" and "Ahuramazda" are for the Zoroastrians.

"Ahura" means Lord, and "mazda" means wisdom, in old Persian. This would best be translated as "The Wise Lord."[78]

"Yezdan" is derived from an ancient Persian word, "Yazata," which means "divine entities" or "the good powers under Ahura Mazda … greatest of the yazatas." What is important here is that Baba once again used the singular form, "Yezdan," going back towards Oneness. This can also be translated as "Creator."

"God the Beloved" is for both the Jews and Christians.

You are named Ezad: the only One worthy of worship.

Finally, Baba ends this special prayer on a Persian note once more, saying that the Divine being alone is worthy of being worshiped. The word "Ezad" is Farsi, and for Zoroastrians, it is used as a name of God. However, a deeper look shows that "Ezad" is related to the Avestan word, "Yazata," which means "worthy of worship or veneration." In this sense, Baba himself defined the meaning of Ezad on the same line of the prayer, meaning that God alone is worthy of this level of deep awe and respect.

Lesson

- Meher Baba explained that in order to realize the Truth, we must come into harmony with everything in Creation. Since the first Avatar, this includes the presence of the Avatar.

- Humanity is always being given help from the Avatar, age after age, and this pattern has been going on for thousands upon thousands of years.

- If we don't have a living spiritual master, we can always turn our hearts to the Avatar who is alive and responsive within the hearts of those who love him.

Journaling Prompt

On my spiritual journey,
how do I feel about the Avatar?

Lesson 15
Intuition
Gentle Guide & Bitch-Slappin' Bestie

"Insight is not a lightbulb that goes off inside our heads.
It is a flickering candle that can easily be snuffed out."
—Malcolm Gladwell

Intuition is something that is talked about constantly
in the world of New Age spirituality. Its definition
quite literally depends on who you are talking to.
To me, intuition is that still, quiet, centered place that
I find inside of my true self when I pause and listen.
When you read the word "intuition," what images
does that invoke for you? What does your inner voice
tell you right now? What do you feel in your body?
Take a moment to write down your experience.

Intuition is the ability to understand something without the need for conscious reasoning. Other definitions of this word are instinct, a sixth sense, divination, clairvoyance, second sight, ESP (extrasensory perception), and the opposite of intellect. What is your relationship with intuition? Do you hear your own inner voice guiding you? Do you trust it or do you ignore it? Do you have the desire to follow your own council, but get overrun by outside influences? Take another moment to write down the immediate thoughts and feelings that come when you think about your current relationship with your intuition. Below is a visualization for you that helped me develop a much deeper relationship with my own intuition.

Practice

The Taproot Channel

Imagine there is a strong, sturdy, vibrantly alive taproot growing up from the earth's fiery core. This taproot is moving through all the different layers of the earth's mantle. It goes up through the crust, springing free and up into your feet, anchoring you in steady, sturdy earth energy. Further up this taproot grows, into your red root chakra at the base of your spine. It travels higher into your creative center – your orange second chakra – and into your solar plexus. This is your inner sun; your yellow power center that connects and infuses your three lower foundational chakras with raw, nurturing energy. When connected and aligned, these three chakras (red, orange, and yellow) are what hold you. They make it so that you can walk your path in this embodied life, secure, centered, and self-trusting.

Let's keep traveling. The taproot channel grows further up still, into your heart. This is your green fourth chakra of love, empathy, kindness, and service. It is also called the bridge between the lower and upper energy systems, or the earthly and the spiritual realms. You reach your throat – your blue fifth chakra of self-expression – and continue beyond that to your third eye. This is located between your eyebrows. Here, your sixth chakra is vibrating purple. This is the wisdom seat of your intuition, and it gives you the ability to see beyond the bullsh*t. Finally, you travel up to your crown chakra, located at the top of your head. That soft spot of the skull that we can feel when babies are just born – this is the portal through which it is believed our souls enter and exit. This seventh chakra of divine wisdom and direct connection with the heavens is often visualized in indigo tones. That is what intuition is. It's this total alignment of the self, connected deeply in the earth *and* high in the heavens. It's this deep, clear, unf*ckable-with self-trust that guides us like an energetic pole, spanning galaxies through this funky, crazy, chaotic thing called Life.

Intuition is sometimes a whisper in your ear, a feeling in your gut, a flash of an image across your third eye, or a dream fragment that will not leave you. It can show up in the form of thoughts, dreams, absentminded journaling, and doodling, or a song lyric that keeps running through your mind. Intuition is so many different things and it manifests in so many different ways. Really! Intuition is exactly what you wrote down just a little while ago…and more.

Intuition is not asking for other people's opinions, approval, or feedback before acting on something that you already know is a great fit for you. It is not weighing and/or swaying because someone

else says they know what is "right for you." It is
not second-guessing or taking pictures to share for
validation. Intuition is not doing what society tells me
to do. Instead, intuition is a still, quiet, aligned, and
always present part of self. It is going deeply inward
to listen to the constant voice that guides me wisely,
in alignment with my true inner compass. It can be
heard in my heart's calling. It can be felt in my deepest
desire. It is my eternal knowing. It is a loving kick in
the butt when I choose to do what my intuition tells
me *not* to do, and then I end up in a blind alley. It is
then re-aligning my compass needle so it points to
my True North, and finding my way back to my true
path. Intuition is always there. It's just a matter of
tuning in and paying attention, just like tuning the
knob on a static old AM/FM radio so you can hear the
programming clearly.

Let's look at intuition in the 21st century. As I write this,
millennials and Gen-Zers, especially women, are being
diagnosed with depression and anxiety at rates much
higher than ever before seen in recorded history.[79] To
me, that's a sign of not listening to our intuition. It
tells me that women are diminishing their third-eye
knowing; the wisdom source that generations
of women before us have tuned into and relied upon.
It tells me that when we are not living in integrity
and alignment, and when we are not listening to our
intuition, life gets really uncomfortable, really fast.
That can take a lot of different forms. It can look like a
ton of anxiety and depression; it can look like diarrhea,
Crohn's disease, migraines, and insomnia; it can
manifest in addiction and self-sabotage in all manner

of ways, including hopelessness, cynicism, infidelity, aggression, and violence. What are some other ways you have seen it manifest? What dissociative patterns are present in your life right now? More than ever, we are steeped in diagnoses caused directly by not listening within. Our bodies and souls are screaming to get our attention but we're deafening our inner wisdom voices with pills, drugs, alcohol, or other quick fixes. We have dissociative behavioral patterns, like overwatching TV or hiding in the infinite weeds of social media.

How can we meet these 21st-century challenges? How can we reset these unhealthy lifestyle choices and unconscious, fractured ways of living that we've created for ourselves – ways of living that literally make us sick? Here in the Western world, we have more of everything than any other generation before us, but we are sicker, more dysfunctional, more diagnosed, and more disconnected than ever before. We are isolated from our communities, depending most often on ourselves. We have overworked, stressed out, often single parents who are raising children alone, instead of with grandparents, aunts, uncles, and cousins around. Neighbors don't know neighbors. Teens and young adults leave home in the hopes of finding a place of support somewhere, and attempt to be self-sufficient in a fractured, faltering, f*cked up world. Lost are the villages and extended families collaboratively raising children, and the neighborhoods centered around community. We are confused, often alone and isolated, and we live longer than ever; often without meaning and purpose.

We isolate young children from early morning to late evening in institutions, put old folks into warehousing facilities where they're largely alone, and let our mentally ill and frail populations wander the streets without shelter. We work hard to keep bodies alive while simultaneously killing the heart and the spirit.

Intuitively, we all know this is wrong. The guilt drives us. This is why exhausted parents overcompensate with material possessions and why we feel excruciatingly bad when we leave from our rare visits to our grandmas and grandpas; we walk away from them sitting in their small cells, waiting for a four o'clock dinner and bed-depositing by six o'clock. We feel bad when we leave them because they're lonely. We know this because we are too. And still, we do it, because that's what "we do." We're supposed to leave our babies to feed the capitalistic demon and we're supposed to put the old out of sight because we don't have the resources to care for them. It's this deafening of our ears to our intuition that's destroying our world, our country, our communities, our families, our friendships, and ultimately, our spirits. Technology has resulted in us becoming so f*cking individualistic that we are alone and increasingly incapable of connection. Given the growing rates of anxiety, depression, and death by suicide, our current system obviously isn't serving us. We know that the society we've created here in the Western world is not only destroying the planet, but it's destroying the fabric of what it means to be human beings. It is slowly killing us. We are the richest, sickest society to date, rivaled only by the old Roman empire as it fell into decline.

There is a powerful essay called "The Paradox of Our Age" that speaks to our declining society. I first read it during undergrad. It was printed upon a tapestry that hung inside of a home in Eugene, Oregon. This poem is often miscredited to the Dalai Lama, but upon digging deeper into the origin, I discovered that it is from a collection of prayers, homilies, and monologues called *Words Aptly Spoken*. It was written in 1995 by a former pastor of Seattle's Overlake Christian Church, Dr. Bob Moorehead.

The Paradox of Our Age

The paradox of our time in history is that
We have taller buildings, but shorter tempers

Wider freeways, but narrower viewpoints
We spend more, but we have less
We buy more, but enjoy it less

We have bigger houses, but smaller families
More conveniences, but less time
We have more degrees, but less sense
More knowledge, but less judgment

More experts, but more problems
More medicine, but less wellness

We drink too much, smoke too much,
spend too recklessly,

Laugh too little, drive too fast, get angry too quickly,
Stay up too late, get up too tired,
Read too seldom, watch TV too much,
And pray too seldom

We have multiplied our possessions,
but reduced our values

We talk too much, love too seldom,
and hate too often
We've learned how to make a living, but not a life
We've added years to life, not life to years

We've been all the way to the moon and back,
But have trouble crossing the street to meet the new
neighbor

We've conquered outer space, but not inner space
We've done larger things, but not better things

We've cleaned up the air, but polluted the soul
We've split the atom, but not our prejudice

We write more, but learn less
We plan more, but accomplish less
We've learned to rush, but not to wait

We have higher incomes, but lower morals
We have more food, but less appeasement

We build more computers to hold more information,
To produce more copies than ever,
But we communicate less and less

We've become long on quantity, but short on quality
These are the times of fast foods and slow digestion
Tall men, and short character
Steep profits, and shallow relationships

These are the times of world peace,
But domestic warfare

More leisure, but less fun
More kinds of food, but less nutrition

These are days of two incomes, but more divorce
Fancier houses, but broken homes

These are the days of quick trips,
Disposable diapers, cartridge living,
Throw-away morality, one-night stands,
overweight bodies,
And pills that do everything from cheer,
to prevent, quiet or kill

It is a time when there is much in the show window
And nothing in the stockroom

A time when technology has brought
this letter to you,
And a time when you can choose either
to make a difference,
Or to just hit delete

Remember, spend some time with your loved ones,
because they are not going to be around forever.

Remember, say a kind word to someone who
looks up
to you in awe, because that little person soon
will grow up and leave your side.

Remember, to give a warm hug to the one next to
you,
because that is the only treasure you can give with
your heart and it doesn't cost a cent.

Remember, to say "I love you" to your partner and
your loved ones, but most of all mean it.
A kiss and an embrace will mend hurt when it comes
from deep inside of you.

Give time to Love, give time to speak, give time
toshare the precious thoughts in your mind.[80]

Very apropos that such powerful words were written
by a spiritual man who probably let the very things he
is pointing out as unfulfilling lead to his demise. Sadly,
it seems that this is common; particularly among men
like Moorehead who build large parishes. He had over
6,000 members and a $3.9 million annual budget. At
62, Dr. Bob Moorehead was found guilty of molesting
men. "Many of the alleged incidents occurred before
baptism and wedding ceremonies, mostly in the
1970s." The allegations were "particularly devastating
to the congregation and the evangelical church
community, given Moorehead's public condemnation
of homosexuality and gay rights."[81] As a survivor
of child molestation myself, I seriously considered
whether or not to include an abuser's poetry in my
book. However, I ultimately decided to because it
speaks to how someone is never all one way. This man
was obviously an oppressor of others. He was also
oppressed in himself, deeply flawed, and a hypocrite.
Simultaneously, he created something beautiful that
many people have reattributed to a more palpable-for-
them Eastern author's name—so they don't have to
hang a Christian believer's words in their home. The
whole thing is asinine when I put it like that. It's all
one God. I am really not concerned whether someone
wants to believe that the Dalai Lama wrote it, or an
evangelical Megachurch pastor; the message
is resonant.

Rates of depression are also increasing because the
younger generations are destigmatizing mental health
and are more open to receiving help for it. Back in
the day, there weren't studies and accounts kept of

depression rates and deaths by suicide. Therefore, it is hard to be historically accurate and create an exact comparison of just how many more of us are ending our lives by suicide, compared to those in the Middle Ages, or the average hunter-gatherer. Still, I feel clear on the perspective that the more technology-oriented we are and the less connected we are to each other, the less happy we are as a species.

If you are struggling with understanding and getting in touch with your intuition, think about what intuition is not. Sometimes the easiest way to crack the code on something is to look at what we believe about its opposite. Ask yourself, "What do I believe about my intellect and its importance in my life?" Write it down. Ask yourself, "Do I believe that I have natural intuitive powers?" Read your responses out loud to yourself and see how it lands in your body. Write down what you are feeling in your body as you are reading your answers to yourself out loud. Take a deep breath and blow it out with all your might. Blow that breath out! Get on your feet and shake your body. Move yourself to a different space in your room. Now, close your eyes and become still. Listen deeply inside, down into your heart and into your soul, into that quiet, still place of no thought. Listen for that heart voice. Maybe it is so faint that you must strain to hear it. What is it saying to you? When you find it, introduce yourself and ask it, "What am I wanting, deep, deep down? What is it that exists in me that wants to be born, that wants to come to light? What is it that wants to come out and be known? How can I live that, be that, and create that?" Listen, and when you are ready, write down what you hear without editing, judging, or analyzing. Your brain will bark for your attention. Ignore it! It is so used to ruling the roost that it will be in disbelief that you are not snapping to attention. Now, the same thing again: read what you wrote out loud to yourself and feel how it lands in the body. Write down your experience. That's a practice in creating space for and listening to your deep knowing. That's intuition!

Intuition can be as small as a voice guiding you to "take a right turn here, and take a left turn there." It can be a voice that is guiding you away from your normal route, and what you don't know is that you just avoided a horrific accident. You'll never know what you just missed because you acted intuitively. You simply listened instead of analyzing and overriding it with the thinking mind. That's what we call the "butterfly effect" of intuition.

There's also the "fun" kind of intuition. When I "let go and let God," magical things always happen. Some are big, some are not. The other day, I suddenly realized I had to go to Costco at 2 p.m. Because I have come to trust my intuition, I got in my car and drove to Costco. I figured that if I had to go there, I could "community shop," so I had a short list from my dad. There I was, searching for the right kind of trail mix bars for my father, and lo and behold—I bumped into an old friend whom I hadn't seen in a long time. This friend had lost all their contacts due to some phone shenanigans and had gotten a new number.

They were trying to get a hold of me but couldn't find me. It turned out that it would have been hard to find me because they weren't on social media and I didn't have their address. I didn't even know where they hung out or worked. It was so good to see them again and catch up. We swapped numbers and I left Costco with a full cart and an even fuller heart.

The weirdest part (actually, not really weird at all if you believe in listening to your intuition) was that they had just been in my dreams a few days earlier. When I woke up, I had resolved to reach out to them. I was feeling curious about where the heck they were in life, but I promptly forgot about it as I got busy with my coaching clients and other projects. I remember sitting in my car after bumping into them thinking, "Of course, it makes sense that I had to come to Costco at this exact time. Thanks, intuition." I was both blown away (yes, it still blows my mind every time my intuition proves to me that it's worth listening to) and simultaneously thinking "Of course!"

Intuition makes itself known within us in infinite ways, all the time. It's the deep knowing that, for example, a relationship is not meant to be. Maybe you feel mostly happy in it, or it makes sense on paper. Maybe your family loves them, your lifestyles align, and you have shared values or religious beliefs. Blah, blah, blah. That's all the head stuff. The deep knowing of intuition does not come from the head; it lives in the heart. It lives in the "gut" and in the third eye. It's the divine God self within you. We always have it and it's always available to us. All we must do is slow down, get present, and listen. No money, favors, or drugs necessary. How cool is that?!

Today, before I sat down to frame this chapter that had been wrestling around inside of my being and vying for time to become a part of this book, I was hustling and bustling. I was having one of those days where I was getting sh*t done, being productive, and checking things off my list like nobody's business. I somehow felt unaccomplished and was beating myself up (in my head) because I believed I was not doing enough; I was actually falling behind. As I was getting out of the car to go into the gym – another action item on my to-do list – "something" inside of me (my intuition and guiding, self-loving compass), yelled "NO!" I stopped in my tracks. I heard, "For goodness' sake, woman! Slow the f*ck down. Meditate, find your sanity and balance, and then dictate that chapter on intuition that's been desperately calling for your attention. Then, get your workout done. It will be so much better for you if you are actually present in your body when you work out." That's my intuition for you. No longer a faint whisper. Now, it's a demanding boss bi!ch who knows how to keep me honest with myself. She wakes me back up when I fall into "unconsciousness" and old, bad patterns. So, thanks to my intuition, I got my chapter dictated instead of putting it off. And, who knows what I missed out on in the gym? Maybe someone with Coronavirus was going to sneeze on me or a weight was going to fall on my foot and break my toes. That Butterfly Effect has probably saved my a$$ more times than I can count.

Even though I won't know exactly why my intuition was so insistent on me waiting to enter the gym until after this intuition-download was done, I know and trust that everything is in divine order when coming from that calm, still place. So, I listen. I listen because I have learned over time that it's better to honor what it has to say to me when it's speaking. It's worth it to be a little bit uncomfortable in my cold car while I work on this chapter, instead of suffering the consequences of overriding my own truth. Any discomfort or pain that comes from listening to my intuition is usually nothing in comparison to the discomfort that arrives in my life from ignoring my inner knowing. I lived for years ignoring "her" until she b!tch-slapped me so hard, I thought my head was going to fall off. By choosing to read this book, maybe you don't have to make all the mistakes I've made to learn this lesson. Maybe you are more willing to listen than I was.

A Look Back Often Reveals the Ignored Answers

It's always interesting and worthwhile to look back at old journals during times of tumult in our lives. Hindsight really is 20/20! Every time I move, which has historically been every six to eleven months, I look back and say, "Oh my God. The writing was really on the wall with that one," or "I can't believe I was so desperate to get that job. It's so out of alignment with what I want for myself!" I have thought, "Wow, I was so unhappy, and still, I stayed in that relationship for another two years! What was I thinking!?" The roblem is that I was thinking! And thinking, and thinking, and thinking, and analyzing, and judging, and justifying, and overriding my own truth. It would be so easy to beat myself up and fall into the pit of regret. It can be crazy-making. Still, if I listen to my inner voice, whether it's presenting as a gentle guide or a b!tch-slappin' bestie, it's all lessons, gifts, and opportunities to practice living from our intuition. Let me tell you a little secret: we always *know*, even when we don't want to know, or pretend not to know, or wish we didn't know. Even if we're hearing ourselves say "I don't know," we definitely do—even if it's somewhere deep down. My coaching clients often tell me, "I don't know." I challenge them, saying "Oh, but you *do* know. Maybe you don't want to know that you know. Maybe your conscious, thinking mind doesn't want to know, but your subconscious mind does, and so does your body. We've just got to move whatever is blocking the connection into conscious awareness."

If you're numbing yourself with drugs, alcohol, lack of sleep, unhealthy foods, antidepressants, sleeping pills, anti-anxiety meds, and TV, then yes—it may feel almost impossible to know what's *actually* going on inside you. Even with the constant cocktail of distraction, once there's a crack in the "not knowing," you cannot stay there, no matter how much you think you want to. Then comes the process of decluttering and re-learning to listen. Even as you drink that soda or eat that Popeyes Spicy Chicken Sandwich, you know it's no good for you. You know it as sure as you know the sun is going to rise tomorrow. You cannot hide from it any longer, even if you don't want to admit it to yourself or don't fully believe it yet. Your knowing is growing! You'll begin to feel the difference in your body from making different choices. You'll have more energy, a little bit more pep in your step, and you feel a little more "alive-awake- alert-enthusiastic" (as one of my favorite camp songs goes).

Observe and be. Find stillness, listen, and allow yourself to slow down and be guided. This is especially important to keep front and center when you don't want to. When you find yourself in heightened states of stress, nervousness, frustration, exhaustion, anxiety, or thinking that you're too busy to stop, that is when it happens! In my past experience as someone who didn't listen to their intuition, I would be running around on the hamster wheel of life. I'd be thinking about how busy I was, how important my task list that day was, and that I couldn't possibly stop. Then, I would get in an accident. My immediate reaction was, "Oh my God. I don't have time for this!" Well, ya busy, tuned out, ego-driven self; that's exactly why you arrived at that moment of collision. If we don't slow down, the Universe will force us to.

Think about it this way: listening to your intuition is the best insurance policy you could ever have. It's free! No exorbitant premium or deductible. Your intuition creates space for the divine flow. Intuition is God speaking directly to you. When I'm "alive-awake-alert" and flowing with the divine wisdom in God's plan, I am divinely protected. I believe that everything is working out for me, even if it might not seem like it. It's only when I get caught up in this human thinking ego-world that revolves totally and completely around all those things we believe are so important, that I screw myself up. Most of the time, the belief that our to-do list must be attended to RIGHT NOW is all illusions and ego. No one is on their deathbed. Speaking of deathbeds, when you sit with the dying and listen to what they have to say, none of them say, "I wish I had worked more!" Instead, you will hear, "I wish I would have spent more time with my family;" "I wish I would have laughed more;" and "I wish I would have danced under the stars on the edge of a lake with my girlfriends, skinny dipping while howling to the sliver of the moon." You will hear them ask questions about why they were so afraid, why they spent so much time worrying about what others thought of them, or why they thought that more money would make them happier. They reflect on why they didn't listen to their inner voice and follow their dream of being a drummer, baker, horticulturist, monk, or flyfisher. Insert your own dream here and see what it feels like to say those words on your imagined deathbed. It makes for an interesting exercise!

We spend a lot of time being busy and making "other plans," but these things that the dying reflect upon are what will truly make us feel alive. Our intuition fights desperately to override our thinking brain, all the live-long day. We are fighting ourselves, trying to be heard by our own selves. It's kind of ironic and crazy when you think about it, as well as very informative. We are such powerful creatures. What we put our minds to and focus on becomes our reality.

In conclusion, we all have an intuition. It lives in
different parts of our bodies at different times.
It is there 24/7, even when you can't feel it. Maybe
especially when you can't feel it. Those are the times
when you are working extra hard to be numb to
it. You may be thinking, "Me, actively avoiding my
intuition?! Impossible! I'm walking barefoot on the
earth to connect to the vibration of the planet, maaan.
I'm vegan, buying all local and organic produce,
doing yoga, and meditating daily! I've studied with
a guru in India! I've climbed Machu Picchu and done
Ayahuasca in the Sacred Valley of Peru!" And still,
you can't f*cking feel or hear your intuition. Well, my
peeps, maybe it's the artificial sweeteners. Maybe
you're keeping your Wi-Fi on at night. Maybe it's your
ego trying too hard to be perfect, right, good, and
liked by all your sorority sisters. I don't know what
your barriers are, but your intuition is working its a$$
off to get your attention!

If there's anything I've learned in my short, chaotic,
wildly adventurous life with more than twenty-five
moves across the country in the last decade (yes, you
read right. I've literally packed up my belongings
and moved across the country so many times in the
nine years since college), it is that our intuition is
with us all the time. It is there, especially in the hectic
moments. You don't need to be on top of a mountain
with mala prayer beads in your hand to access the
internal, wise, or divine. The Divine is present on the
subway track in Brooklyn where a pack of rats attack
a sick pigeon. The Divine is in line at the DMV where
the toothless white man in his 60's is screaming at the

security guards about having to wear a mask to enter. The Divine is in the meat-stick at the gym, who you're pretty sure has steroids in that protein shaker cup of his. The Divine is in shopping for lettuce, picking up your old neighbor's mail, hugs, smiles, tears, laughter, raindrops, and broken bicycle chains. The Divine is everywhere, all the time. And so is our intuition. We don't need to sport the latest Lululemon matching set while sitting on a Moroccan pouf, breathing in a fine mist of essential oils in order to listen to ourselves. We don't need anything to tap into our intuition and live from it, except for breath and the willingness to begin. The old yogis and shamans who lived and practiced thousands of years ago knew this. So, beloved ADHD/ADD generation of mine, don't be fooled by the gizmos and gadgets, or the blinking lights that can reset your gamma waves. Don't fall for the $10,000 healing machine that links up to your meta-heartbeat, connecting it to the biodynamic energy field of the quartz crystal wand that you're holding. You don't need a machine to clear the vortex around you or to realign your vibration and chakras to the quantum field. Don't be fooled by that stuff. All that you need is already within you. All you need to do is turn the dial on *your* radio and clear the static so that the station can come in clear. That's it.

Intuition is magic! It can guide you to your dreams and your most beautiful goals. All you have to do is listen. Intuition is your North Star; your guiding light that will tell you what you need when you need it. Right now, I'm grateful that my intuition told me to

sit here in this strip mall parking lot to finish this
chapter while watching people run around. Many
don't look like they're following their intuition,
as they're pulling out in front of each other in their
stressed-out, non-present haste to get onto the next
thing. I am sourcing a lot of inspiration from my
parking lot pause in this Connecticut strip mall.
If that's not an example of how divine consciousness
is everywhere all the time, and how I can live
spiritually in the 21ˢᵗ century, I don't know what is.

Practice

Body Scan Practice

Ask a good friend if they'll practice utilizing their intuition with you. Lay down on yoga mats facing opposite directions, but with your heads in a line next to each other.

Take some deep breaths and do a body scan together. Go from your feet to your head. Pause and focus on particular parts of your body (for example, toes, ankles, calves, knees, thighs).

Then, do it again in reverse order (head to feet). This time, work to tune into the other person's body.

Do another scan. This time, scan your body from feet to head. When you get to each stopping point, be really present with what sensations you are experiencing in that place, as well as any that your friend may be feeling.

Take turns sharing what is coming up for both of you. Refrain from agreeing, dispelling, or reacting to your partner's share. The practice is around intuition, not identifying sore areas or tight places within your body.

At the end of the scan, take turns sharing how the other person's feedback resonated with you. Reflect on the sensations you both felt in your own bodies.

The more you do this, the stronger you are flexing the intuition muscle. It will get stronger.

Journaling Prompts

When was the last time I had
an intuitive premonition?

Did I listen? Why or why not?
What was the outcome?

How can I differentiate my fantasy or daydream
thoughts from actual intuitive knowing?

Lesson 16
Listen!
A Spiritual Practice

"Things that are real are given and received in silence."
—Meher Baba

The quote above means so much, coming from a man who gave up speaking at the age of thirty-one and was silent for more than forty years until his death.

Hearing and listening are not the same! Hearing is an automatic process that occurs without our active involvement. Sound waves travel from the source, through the air, and into our ears. They are translated into information that is identified by our brain and then "understood." We can hear music, the sound of the rainforest waking up, the sound of an oncoming train, the sound of voices around us, and so on.

Listening, on the other hand, is the active giving of attention to decoding sound frequencies and making meaning of them. It is the process of paying attention while comprehending the message.

Writing this lesson on listening came at a transformative time for me because I joined an app called "Clubhouse" when it was at the height of its craze. This social app allowed users to interact in themed chat rooms that could accommodate thousands of people. It launched in April of 2020 and quickly captivated all of us quarantined at home. For weeks, I listened to people and their wisdom anywhere from four to eight hours a day! As someone who had always sought out the spotlight, I would have preferred being the podcast host or workshop facilitator that people were listening to. However, in this space, I was a silent participant. Clubhouse helped me practice listening instead of impatiently waiting for a break in the conversation to say the next thing on my mind. This was a necessary evolution in my development. You couldn't even speak in the larger rooms within the app; you had to be invited onto the "stage" by the chat room facilitators. That quickly became an internet popularity contest that I was not Insta-famous enough to win.

The friendships I still have from that app and the chat rooms I curated (with the help of my friends) showed me that I gain so much more when I'm listening and creating space for others to share. I already know what I think. Being with the thoughts I've already thought isn't going to create new epiphanies for me.

Actually *listening* to others was something that I had been wanting to unlock for a long time. Once I uncaged my listening bird, I had a sense of fulfillment without needing to "do" anything. If all I did today was really listen to someone and for them to feel heard, is that not the foundation of relationship building? Isn't that the meaning of life? When I am listening more than I'm speaking, I feel a greater sense of everything being right, perfect, and exactly what it needs to be. I sense it unfolding according to its own Divine timeline.

Before this, I liked to see myself as a stellar communicator and an expert active listener. I have logged so many personal development hours in multiple seminar rooms and put myself through so much communication training. I can spout communication theory from morning 'til night. The truth is that I was just bullsh!tting myself. Now, I listen. Although I sometimes feel myself wanting to jump into talking, I do my best to focus and listen more. I recognize that I have wished that I could be on stage with the game changers who have the platform and resources to "make it happen," so that I can add my two cents. However, when I really listen, I notice that someone else is saying exactly what my two cents were going to be, and maybe they are expressing it in an even clearer, briefer, more poignant way. It's in these moments that I'm reminded that the most powerful thing I can practice is listening.

Mark Nepo, a highly gifted spiritual poet and writer of our time, wrote, *Seven Thousand Ways to Listen: Staying Close to What Is Sacred*. In this book, he states,

> Becoming a better listener takes practice, but if you succeed, you'll find yourself learning new and interesting things about the people you communicate with. You may also find you're better at picking up subtle messaging cues others may miss. A number of specific strategies can be applied to listening, but they all share one key element: being present and attentive during conversations and respectful of those involved. This ability can help you be a more effective partner, parent, student, and coworker.[82]

I practice being present, attentive, respectful, and more effective. I fail but strive to practice what Mahatma Gandhi said: "Speak[ing] only if it improves upon the silence." I want to leave so much space for listening that I leave space on this page. I want to leave this chapter short so that you can find time and space right now for your own deep listening; the deep listening to self that turns inward to your own innate wisdom.

I invite you to take a deep breath in through your nose. Blow it out through your mouth. Slowwwwly, inhale and exhale. Again, in through your nose, and out through your mouth. This time, make it an audible exhale for extra credit. While you breathe, LISTEN. Listen to your breath. Hear those ocean sounds that your breath makes as it enters and exits your body.

What else can you hear? Maybe you can hear your heartbeat. Listen to your thoughts. Hear that constant inner dialogue we keep with ourselves. Listen to your emotions—yes, it is possible to hear them too. What are they telling you right now? More importantly, what are you pretending and trying not to hear? Whatever it is, the more we listen, the more insight we gain. We can never lose anything from listening. We can only gain!

In general, as a modern society, we do not allow space for listening. Most of us are so set on being heard, understood, and perceived as right that we don't actually listen to anyone else around us. That is, unless they agree with us in all of our points of view. Oh, that lovely collusion! How we adore it. We don't have the ability and the discipline to just listen to our inner voices, and we are sorely lacking in the ability to resist the urge to add our own thoughts when someone else is talking. Stroll around a corner in any big US city and you will find someone screaming at you in a desperate attempt to save your soul. They're trying to convert people to their religion, political agenda, belief system, or capitalistic agenda. They believe that they have the answers and know what's best for others. The interesting and sad observation is that the path of self-interest leads most people to miss out on God's wisdom altogether. God's wisdom is given in silence. God lives in silence. God is silence. Many forms of spiritual awakening can come to us in the silence.

Thus, when we think about listening, we also have to think about hearing. What sounds and messages are being produced in our surrounding environments? What are we choosing to hear, and what are we creating space for as we listen? You see, as we have already talked about in earlier chapters, our subconscious mind hears all and stores all! Our subconscious mind houses our deep belief system and is the source of our thoughts and internal dialogue. It is the source of what we wish for, what we dream, and what we manifest and create in our lives. It is also the source of our self-image and how we feel about ourselves. We always hear, and only sometimes we listen. The spiritual practice then becomes hearing and active listening simultaneously, and then choosing mindfully.

Not only have I learned what active listening really requires, I have also learned to paraphrase back to the speaker, to let them know that I understand what's being said. I've learned that this whole process of quieting my voice, focusing on the message, processing it, and showing that I understand it takes place in the present moment. It happens when I am present in my body, and outside of my own head. Here are some pointers and skills to practice.

Practice

Active Listening

- Be present, outward-focused, and attentive.

  As a good listener, I am outward-focused, fully engaged, and present in the moment. I am in my body and not in my head. I shut out all distractions and focus on the person in front of me. I use attentive, engaged, positive responses (nodding, touch, small vocalizations), showing that I am actively listening and heart-connected with the speaker.

- Make and keep eye contact.

  I maintain eye contact with the person speaking, showing them that they have my undivided attention. I put my phone on silent and away. I turn off and put away all distractions (for example, my computer, TV, music system, gaming station, or book). Scanning the room or looking at my phone are actions that signal to the other that I am unfocused, uninterested, and disconnected. It interrupts my active listening process. Each time I go up into my head, I am no longer in the present and therefore no longer listening.

- Don't interject, interrupt, or otherwise bogart the conversation.

  When I am in a place of waiting to interject just the right thing, I am not actually listening. Instead, I am self-focused and thinking about how I can be clever, funny, give good advice, tell a better story, give my two cents on the matter, and so on. I am no longer connected with the person in front of me and I am not actually hearing what they are saying.

I am communicating that I don't really care about what's being said. Interrupting or interjecting myself into someone else's story and making it about me displaces the other, cutting the connection.

• Be curious. Paraphrase what they are saying to make sure you have understood the meaning of their message. Ask follow-up questions.

If I do not quite understand the message that is being communicated or if parts are unclear, I can paraphrase back for clarity and understanding (also known as confirming questions). I can also ask clarifying questions to gain more information. Confirming questions would sound something like "It sounds like you're saying ______. Is that correct?" This will send the message that I am engaged and actively listening, and it can help me gauge if I've accurately understood what's being said.

The spiritual practice of active listening is listening without attachment. It's the practice of really living in the *Four Agreements*. It's not taking things personally. It's being impeccable with my words. It's doing my best to be fully present and outward-focused. It's being non-judgmental and curious. It's being open in body, heart, and mind. I encourage you to explore these concepts and practices. I encourage you to find ways to listen. First, listen to nothing. Listen to the void, which silence can feel like when we are not used to it. It is here in the silence that God enters. It is here in the silence that you can hear yourself. Instead of hearing your constant, critical, self-loathing diatribes, you can hear your true, spiritual, self-loving, self-accepting, whole self. God is with us all the time regardless, but particularly so in the silence; in the stillness of the present moment. When I'm just sitting quietly, when I allow the world to calm long enough to be able to be present and listen, I can hear what is always there. Namely, that is God's love and wisdom. We just have to shut up and listen.

God will make me still, even bringing me to my literal knees at times. In November of 2019, I didn't listen to God's wisdom and chose to ski while exhausted. I had been celebrating successfully completing a crowdfunding campaign for my former business, Artemis Wild. It was the last run of the day. I heard the quiet, still voice in me saying, "You're not wearing your knee brace. You have been partying for three days in a row. It's too late in the day to start!" Regardless, I pushed through and ignored the many signs God had sent me to opt out of this adventure.

The result of not listening was the trifecta of knee injuries. I tore my ACL, MCL, PCL and fractured my tibia in one seriously hard fall from grace. It felt as if God was quoting Kendrick Lamar: "Sit down, b*tch, be humble."[83] For sixteen painful weeks, God forced me to listen. I was on crutches and in a wheelchair relearning how to walk. I had to ask strangers in the grocery store to reach things off of shelves so that I could put them in my automated scooter basket, or in the backpack I wore while crutching around. The month I reached full mobility, the world shut down and COVID-19 precautions took over. Having already felt like I was on lockdown for four months, I was already accustomed to the quarantined life that so

many struggled with. One of many silver linings in
the harrowing lesson of sitting in stillness was that it
prepared me for what was to come before I ever saw
it coming. It be like that! Every storm I weathered
in the past prepared me for my future. God doesn't
always create such strong circumstances in which I
have to practice listening. Yet, when I ignore my inner
wisdom and neglect the stillness, or choose not to pay
attention, God makes it unavoidable.

Practice

Write some of these affirmations to on sticky notes. Put them in places you see daily.

Affirmations for the Active Listener

This is a combination of Coach Laxmi's exercises, an article from Maryville University, and WINGS wisdom.

As an Active Listener, I help others feel
secure in expressing their opinions.

As an Active Listener, I am able to reduce tension
during arguments and communicate both curiosity
and respect to the speaker.

As an Active Listener, I pay attention to both verbal
and nonverbal cues, and ask for clarification when
needed.

As an Active Listener, I am engaged.
I make and maintain eye contact.

As an Active Listener, I am present in the conversation.

As an Active Listener, I seek to fully understand
the speaker's message.

As an Active Listener, I build stronger relationships.
I understand that communication is a two-way
street. I show interest, ask open-ended questions,
acknowledge what's being said, and help to reduce
misunderstandings by repeating what I heard.

The Four Types of Listening[84]

1. Deep Listening
   This occurs when you're committed to understanding the speaker's perspective. It involves paying attention to both verbal and nonverbal cues, such as the words being used, the speaker's body language, and their tone. This helps build trust and rapport, and helps others feel comfortable in expressing their thoughts and opinions.

2. Full Listening
   This involves paying close and careful attention to what the speaker is conveying. It often involves the use of active listening techniques, such as paraphrasing what's been said to the person you're speaking with, to ensure you understand their messaging. Full listening is useful in the classroom, like when someone is instructing you on how to complete a task. It's also helpful at work when you're discussing projects with superiors.

3. Critical Listening
   This involves using systematic reasoning and careful thought to analyze a speaker's message, separating fact from opinion. Critical listening is often useful in situations when speakers may have a certain agenda or goal, such as watching political debates, or when a salesperson is pitching a product or service.

4. Therapeutic Listening
   This means allowing a friend, colleague, or family member to discuss their problems. It involves emphasizing and applying supportive nonverbal cues, such as nodding and maintaining eye contact, in addition to empathizing with their experiences.

5. It is very powerful to ask people how they want to be heard. Sometimes, you just want to vent, whereas other times you want to be probed.

Ineffective Listening

1. Selective Listening:
    This is as if you're listening with a highlighter. Instead of considering the totality of the speaker's message, selective listeners only pay attention to the parts they think are most relevant to them.

2. Inattentive Listening
    Inattentive listeners don't give speakers their full attention. They're often distracted and focused on other things, which can mean they're missing most of what the speaker is saying.

3. Defensive Listening
    Defensive listeners hear innocent statements, such as "I don't like people who are indecisive," and perceive them as personal attacks. Defensive listening can cause strain in both personal and professional relationships.

Journaling Prompts

How can you create more stillness
in your daily life?

How can you listen to the silence? If it is too
overwhelming, just start by listening to your
breath. It's a process.

Write down one thing that someone told you
today about themselves or their day. This will
help you remember to listen. You may even be
surprised at how much we talk and how little
we actually communicate in todays "zing beep
bop" electrical world.

Lesson 17
Befriending My Shadow
Hello Darkness, My Old Friend

"Until you make the unconscious conscious, it will direct your life and you will call it fate."—Carl Jung

In analytical psychology, the "Shadow" (also called the repressed id, the shadow aspect of the self, and the shadow archetype) is defined as "the unconscious aspect of the personality that does not correspond with the ego ideal, leading the ego to resist and project the shadow."[85] In plain English, the shadow refers to parts of me that I cannot accept. The parts of me that I don't want to acknowledge, identify with, or embrace. Those embarrassing or shameful parts can be behaviors, emotions, personality traits, judgments, thoughts, or feelings.

Are we doomed to live with our shadow selves running the show for the rest of our lives? Everything that happens to us from the day we are born (and most likely even before we gulp in that first breath of oxygen) teaches us what is considered acceptable and unacceptable. Our family systems, our social systems, and our cultural systems all have specific guidelines. They come to us as lessons, and they're coming at us from all sides. Initially, they're from our parents, grandparents, siblings, uncles, aunts, and cousins. As we grow and our social circles expand, we receive messages from our friends and their family systems, as well as teachers at school, religious figures, television, social media, society at large, and more. Everyone and everything attempts to teach us how to behave and how to become the person they think we should be.

The shadow self represents everything we've learned about how to behave in every single context we encounter. Someone tells you in preschool that you shouldn't be aggressive with toys or other children, and a pattern of suppressing your anger is potentially created. You watch your mom and dad act like they are not angry, and the pattern of anger suppression is further strengthened. You are told the message at home of "Don't be loud," and thus, you begin to put away your exuberance, love of singing, and maybe your voice altogether. Your first romantic partner puts you down in front of friends at a party for your clinginess and jealousy, and in this state of undesirability and feeling unloved, you make an unconscious contract with yourself to never allow jealous thoughts and feelings to show themselves again. See what I mean? Messages like these shape and refine our identity over time. Everything teaches us and shapes our acceptable social selves. As we are molded by acculturation and socialization into "good people," we suppress anything that doesn't fit this image. Many parts of our natural selves disappear into the darkness and oblivion…or so we'd like to pretend.

The psychoanalyst Carl Jung is famous for being the first to develop the concept of shadow selves and shadow work. Jung used the term "shadow self" to describe the things about ourselves that we do not like to acknowledge, and therefore repress; the parts of our personalities which, through the course of our lives, we relegate to the darkness of the unconscious. While Jung is awarded the golden star for being the first to bring the concept of the shadow into public awareness, this aspect of our human nature has long been recognized as an ubiquitous feature of what it means to be human. In 1886, before Jung made his mark, Robert Louis Stevenson wrote his famous story called *The Strange Case of Dr. Jekyll and Mr. Hyde.* Dr. Jekyll represents the respectable part of the main character's personality, and Mr. Hyde stands for the transformed shadow personality that gains dominance over him and wreaks havoc on his life.

What Carl Jung tells us about the shadow is that it is the unknown, dark side of our personality. It is instinctive and irrational, and therefore prone to psychological projection. This means that when

we consider something to be wrong and inferior
in ourselves, we will often recognize it as moral
deficiency in others. He also makes it clear that
although the shadow is an innate part of what it is
to be human, the vast majority of us are stubbornly
and willfully blind to its existence. We hide what
we deem to be our negative qualities *so* deeply in
our subconscious that we are not even aware of it
ourselves. To keep up this charade, we often criticize
and condemn others so that the spotlight does not
illuminate our own faults and destructive tendencies.
Without exploration of our dark selves, we go through
our entire lives with false airs of moral superiority,
along with a deep belief that others act immorally and
destructively while we ourselves are always in the
right and on the side of virtue.

In a nutshell, shadow work is a process of excavating
the gems hidden in the dark. We own them as key
and integral parts of ourselves and step into a deep,
self-integrated wholeness. Our shadows are the
parts of ourselves that, due to past trauma and social
conditioning, have been dislodged, disowned, and
deeply hidden away.

Below are a few examples of some shadow selves that
you might recognize within yourself—or maybe in
others around you. It's always a good clue that this
lives in the darkness deep within you as well; you
know that ol' saying, "You spot it, you got it!"

- Let's start with **The Perfectionist.** This is someone who can never, ever, ever relax because they're afraid of making the slightest mistake. They live in constant monitoring and vigilance, and so their nervous systems are always alert, taut, and overtaxed.

- Then there's **The Workaholic.** Ah, the college buddy who's constantly focused on their achievements, goals, and deadlines. This shadow self is all work and no play.

- Bring around **The People Pleaser**. We all know at least one of these. The one who is constantly bending over backward, contorting themselves into the most horrible shapes to help others. They aim to please, but they cannot say "no" and give too much of their energy away. These are the good girls, the humble servants, and the doormats; the boundaryless who apologize for the slightest thing, even when it's totally out of their control. The ones who silently scream, "I'll do anything for you if you just love me, validate me, and see my worthiness."

- Next, we have **The Control Freak.** These are the ones who must dictate, micromanage, and guard against every aspect of existence; the ones who can't stand to let anyone else make a decision. They always know the best way to do things.

There are many, many more shadow selves.
Jung himself talked about twelve shadow archetypes:

1. The Sage
2. The Innocent
3. The Explorer
4. The Ruler
5. The Creator
6. The Caregiver
7. The Magician
8. The Hero
9. The Rebel
10. The Lover
11. The Jester
12. The Orphan

He says, "Each of these archetypes has many aspects within it, including a shadow side of itself."[86]

Ohh, yippee! More uncomfortable emotional work to do! That's what I thought when I sat in my first five-day personal development/shadow workshop. There's a shadow within the shadow? The f*cking work truly never ends! I had come there understanding that I had a shadow and that things weren't working in my life the way I wanted them. No matter how many self-development books I read, mantras I chanted, or positive affirmation post-it notes I stuck around my house, I eventually learned that I needed to embark on a journey of inner alchemy in which I brought the unwanted parts of myself to the surface. I had to bring them into my consciousness to heal and integrate into my true self. I had to step into a whole, authentic, real Me. I understood that everyone has a shadow and that my shadow wasn't something I should be ashamed of, vilify, or hate. Great! Good to know! [Insert dramatic, high school cheerleader eye roll here.] Well, what now? How did I go about spotting it, this elusive part of myself that I had worked so hard to suppress or forget, and how did I start this work of seeing what I didn't even know was there? It turns out that there are some very easy ways to spot our shadow parts. There are clues all around us when we begin to tune in and start to pay attention. Quite simply, we can catch glimpses of our shadow selves by paying attention to our behavior and how we interact with those around us.

A surefire way to spot my shadow is to become aware of it, and observe when and where I harshly judge others. Judgment often reflects the shadow self at work. You see, the way we judge others is based completely on our need to hide from our own perceived weaknesses. For every finger you point at someone, there are three fingers pointing back at you. Our judgments reveal more about ourselves and our insecurities than about the person we judge.

Meet Judgment's other half; "Projections." When we project our flaws, problems, behaviors, and issues onto others, we are in shadow territory.

Projection, in psychology, describes a self-defense mechanism by which we humans ascribe our perceived weaknesses, wrong thoughts, and unwanted emotions onto others. What we see in others lives within us. I'll add a quick note here: it is important to remember that we repress just as many "good" parts of ourselves as "bad," because family and society equally devalue and misunderstand both.

If you are constantly accusing your partner of being disloyal, maybe it would be valuable to take a look at how you behave when your partner is not around. Go through the weeds of your DMs. Or, if you spot arrogance and rudeness everywhere, maybe you can try to focus the spotlight inward and check yo'self. There's a great old-world saying that goes, "Thief thinks every man steals." This basically explains projection. Our interpretations and experiences of the world around us, and how we act and interact with it, inform both what we pay attention to, and what lives within us.

Put plain and simple, once we start looking for our shadow selves, we cannot go back. Once we see, we cannot unsee. Once we begin to know and understand, we cannot unknow and return to amnesia; at least not for more than short periods. Making peace with what we uncover begins, just like the healing process, with radical self-acceptance.

This is our shadow work. It is that courageous deep-dive into the darker, unknown parts of ourselves, and the bringing forth of what we find there. Bringing out those hidden aspects of ourselves that we have long denied and fought so hard to keep suppressed, unnamed, and forgotten. It is the brave, tender, and curious self-loving path of acceptance and re-integration of these parts without shame, blame, and judgment. Once you have self-love with the shadow self working for you, rather than against you, your life will be lighter, easier, and sooooo much more fun.

If you feel like something is a bit off in your life, if you are working hard towards something and you fail to get the results you want, if you are stuck in cyclical patterns, or if you feel that you are not contributing anything of value to the world – it might be time to explore shadow work. Other telltale signs that your shadow is running the show and ruling your life are the inability to forgive easily, strong and very critical inner self-dialogue, experiencing difficult emotions and/or strange flashes of anger or lust at unpredictable or inappropriate times, a denial of your reality ("This is not what my life is supposed to be like!"), noticing that you have changed who you are to suit another person, and the denial of your own needs and wants.

Learning how to honor all the different parts of myself, especially those tucked away in my shadowy corners, has made me feel more integrated. Once I started down this path, I quickly understood that if

I kept working hard to repress and ignore what was so obviously there, it would just keep coming up bigger and louder. I knew I would just keep making myself sicker and more unhappy. Alternatively, I could face it, acknowledge it, and then see if I lived to tell the tale. Spoiler alert: although it might feel like walking the plank, you will not die from acknowledging your hidden parts. It is actually an incredibly freeing and empowering experience.

When I was in middle school, I used to have these crazy anxiety and panic attacks. About once a quarter, I would lock myself in my closet, scream at the top of my lungs, and pull my hair out. These intense attacks would overtake me. I'd be full-on body shaking, screaming, and ugly crying until there was so much snot and tears between my eyes and nose that my face felt like sad mush. I'd rage out until I had no strength left to even lift my head. I had a loft bed in this nine-foot walk-in closet with no windows, and would sit in the dark, with the darkness inside of me. It was the place I went to hide my young, wounded, and fractured-feeling, hormonal teenager self.

Since childhood, the only emotions I allowed myself to express were "positive:" joy, excitement, curiosity, happiness, openness, laughter, giddiness, and playfulness. My inner guardians had learned early on that these displays were acceptable, and therefore safe. On the other hand, overt displays of "negative emotions" (anger, jealousy, blame, resentment, fear, and so on) were considered inappropriate, wrong, and bad. So, my inner guardians disallowed me from expressing these emotions, and I became a master of short-cutting them. I routinely ignored, disowned, and repressed them.

Looking back as an integrated adult upon these closeted anger episodes and the denial of expressing my negative emotions, it all seems completely bizarre. Now, I hold my younger self with such tenderness. She was completely alone with this huge flood of uncontrollable emotions that ruptured the fabric of her existence. My young self was constantly guarding against all those "undesirable" emotions. Because I wasn't allowing them to come out, they had to go somewhere. Where they went was into the darkest corners of my unconscious mind; into my shadow. From here, they would erupt with regularity, like a volcano when the pressure has reached maximum capacity. They leaked out in all kinds of sideways, misunderstood ways.

As I grew older, I learned through therapy, personal development work, and my spiritual practices to navigate my emotions in a much more egalitarian way. I befriended all my emotions. The most healing part of the shadow integration process has been learning how to express both my anger and my sadness. It is so freeing to allow oneself to express the whole gamut of human emotions in healthy and productive ways, right when I'm feeling them. I broke through my early-learned "The Show Must Go On" suppression pattern. Gone is the consistently sweet, pretty, coy front that I believed everyone else wanted to see. Now, I see the beauty and the gifts in all emotions. I am so grateful for each and every one of them.

Most of the work I do now as a spiritual life coach is helping people integrate all parts of who they are. I encourage people to think about and look at how they can better integrate their whole selves into their daily lives. How can you best honor and be with all of who you are? I really encourage you to begin your shadow work by tapping into the fledgling awareness of your shadow self; holding yourself in tenderness and grace as you start your journey towards your wholeness.

There are so many ways to work with our lost parts, to help them find their way back from being disenfranchised. There are several reintegration exercises at the end of this lesson. One exercise I particularly enjoy is writing separate letters to my lost parts. I acknowledge them and all the work they have each done to keep me safe. Then, I share kindness and compassion with them, show them my deep gratitude, and welcome them back. In this way, I make conscious what was previously unconscious. Old patterns come into the light and get re-made. New behaviors and thought pathways are thus created. I still do this as often as I need to. I write to myself from the different parts of my psyche, so that I can hear their voices clearer. I write to the different parts of my shadow self that I am still struggling with healing and integrating. I write, and then I read it out loud to myself. Sometimes I write under the new moon (dark moon), or perhaps under the full moon (bright moon), or maybe under the canopy of stars. In this way, I speak my full palette of emotions into existence.

Often, I burn the letters when I am done reading them aloud to the universe and myself. This releases and transforms their energetic hold on me. I believe there is so much power in writing, speaking, bearing witness to, and even burning our letters as a form of releasing pent-up emotions. Sometimes, it takes talking to people outside of our community who don't think in the same familial ways in which we were raised, to discover our lost selves. Consider working with a shadow practitioner, energy healer, life coach, or therapist on uncovering, understanding, accepting, and integrating the lost parts of yourself; especially the parts of you that are hard for you to reach. They may be locked away due to trauma.

Trust me, it's a process. It's a journey. And often not a pretty, logical, linear, forward-moving journey. It spirals and loops back on itself again and again; you fall into the same potholes and think "F***, I'm here again! Dang, I thought I was done with this!" New shadows and versions of old, seemingly known-to-you shadows come up all the time. That's the human condition. It's the journey without a final destination (other than death, that is...and even then, maybe not. Who really knows?) Someone will piss you off and you will get triggered. The old, limiting shadow beliefs and patterns will start to rear up. And then, the new, curious, "working-to-be-non-reactive" shadow explorer you have become will take a moment, pause, breathe, and reflect: "Am I really upset at this person, or are they displaying a characteristic or an aspect that I myself wish I could or didn't embody? Is this person simply standing in for someone or something else from my past? What old survival pattern am I wanting to run right now?" Be present with all that comes up. Face it, lean into it, own it, and honor it. Then, give yourself a break. Be gentle with yourself. From this less reactive vantage point, you can choose your internal state differently. From there, you can choose how you want to show up. Remember that everything that is meant to be will be, and that the most important thing you can do in this life is to show up as yourself; your whole, honest, authentic, integrous self. And that means honoring all of you, including the deepest, most hidden shadow parts.

When interactions with others leave you bothered, irritated, agitated or judging, there's a big chance that you are in shadow territory. You are most likely in contact with suppressed and disowned shadow parts of yourself. Keeping a journal of negative interactions that you have with others can be a great way to begin exploring and recognizing these lost parts of yourselves.

Practice

Reflecting On Our Reactions

Take a few minutes at the end of each day to get quiet and review the interactions and conversations you have had with others.

- How did they go?

- What happened? Be as detailed as possible.

- How did you react?

- What feelings did you experience in the moment?

- What feelings are you experiencing now?

- What are your judgments about the other person(s) involved?

- What character traits do they possess that turn you off?

Once you unpack the elements, judgments, and feelings involved in these interactions, you can begin to examine how you express these same qualities. The more grace you have for the "uglier" parts of yourself, the more grace you'll be able to give to others. Remember, the gift of these interactions is simply pointing to where you have some work to do, and where you need to give yourself more love. This kind of reflection can assist you in making decisions about how to proceed further.

Maybe you want to:

- Express your inner shadow artistically (dance, paint, draw, sew, compose...)

- Start an inner dialogue with these parts of yourself

- Begin a meditation practice to observe your triggers

- Decide that you want to seek some form of therapy or shadow work workshop

- Take yourself and your ego out to lunch and practice spotting your inner shadow as it is reflected back to you

- Think back to your childhood and write your life story as if you are looking down at it from the top of a mountain, instead of from inside it

- Find some books and take a deeper dive

The 3-2-1 Shadow Process

If you are looking for a detailed guide on how to work on your shadow, I recommend finding a copy of *Integral Life Practice* by Ken Wilber, and checking out the 3-2-1 Shadow Process he has created.

Here is an introduction to the steps:

- Step One:
  First, choose a subject (a family member, friend, or partner) to think about. Pick someone you struggle to get along with or have an emotionally charged relationship with. This is the easiest place to start for this activity.

- Step Two:
  The next step involves imagining this person. Think about the qualities that upset you the most or that attract you the most, using third-person language (they, she, he or ze). Write what you are feeling in a journal.

  "He annoys me. He talks too much and never gets to the point."

  "They make friends so easily. Everyone loves them right away, and they make it look so effortless."

- Step Three:
  Now, create a dialogue or conversation with the person using your imagination. Speak to the person using second-person language ("you"). Speak directly to the person and imagine they are there. Tell the person what irritates or bothers you regarding how they behave. This can be done out loud or on paper.

- You can ask these questions:

- Why do you do these things to me?

- What do you want from me?

- Are you trying to show or tell me something?

- Why do we keep having the same argument?

- Do you have something to teach me?

Think about how they will respond to each question. Speak these imaginary responses out loud. You can also record these conversations in a journal.

- Step Four:
Now, become the person taking on any qualities that fascinate or annoy you. Embody all the traits that you described in the second step. Use first-person language (such as mine, me, and I). This might feel awkward and strange, which is perfectly normal. The traits that you take on happen to be the traits that you deny in yourself.

- You can use statements like:

- I am jealous

- I am angry

- I feel insecure.

- Step Five:
  Look at all the traits you've uncovered and start identifying how these aspects exist in you. These are your shadow traits. Sometimes, these are shadow traits you need to work on. Other times, they are things we need to lovingly accept about ourselves.

For me, journaling is one of the primary tools of shadow work. You'd be amazed by how much you can discover about yourself when you pour yourself onto the page. Inevitably, you will find yourself faced with some deep, soul-exposing questions when you engage in shadow work. Truly, it is like putting a magnifying glass up to the most vulnerable parts of yourself. It's not the kind of thing we most like to engage in! These prompts provide you with insightful questions that are designed to help you get at some core issues. While the process itself might not be the most fun, the rewards are transformative.

How To Use Shadow Work Prompts

I wouldn't recommend doing more than one prompt per day, to give yourself enough reflection time. Let yourself go deep and give your unconscious mind a chance to respond. Many times, responses come when we are distracted and busy doing other things; "looking the other way with our conscious minds," so to speak. Often, they will begin to show up in your dreams. You can even scale it back to a couple of prompts per week. Check in with yourself honestly and then start wherever you are. Shadow work is a complicated process that takes time. You don't need to go in any particular order. Let the journey guide you.

What Can You Do With a Shadow Work Journal?

A shadow work journal can help you explore your thoughts and feelings in a safe, private space and can act as a record of your progress over time. It is a really good way to help you spot patterns. It's meant to be a tool in your self-discovery process. Some people use their shadow work journal to jumpstart spiritual or personal exploration. Others might use it as an activity in conjunction with traditional talk therapy. And still, others may use it as a way to track their progress and record insights as they work through challenging issues and emotions present in their lives. No matter what your goals are, having a shadow work journal can be invaluable for helping you get in touch with the deeper parts of yourself and starting your healing process.

The best way to use shadow work prompts is radical honesty and complete vulnerability. Choose the prompts that get to the core of your growing edges, and then be willing to dedicate time to dive deeply into them. If a particular memory comes to mind and you don't know why, just follow it and see what part of you is asking to be interacted with. It's an intense process that reveals your true, inner, beautiful, unique self, and a journey that also serves as a glorious catharsis into healing traits you want to change.

Journaling Prompts

Thank you to the founder of Soberish, Alicia, for permission to distribute these.

1. Do you feel misunderstood?
   What misconceptions do people have about you?

2. What triggers you? Why?
   Where does it come from?

3. What are the primary aspects of yourself you'd like to approve of? Explain your choice. Has anyone told you to work on these things before?

4. Do you find it easy to forgive yourself?
   Why or why not?

5. Do you forgive other people easily?
   Why or why not?

6. What are your core values? Why have you chosen them? How do you live your values daily?

7. What are/were your caregivers' core values? Do yours align or differ? Why do you think that is?

8. What version of yourself do you try to project to the world? Are you being authentic?

9. Where do you derive your sense of self worth from? Is this a healthy or unhealthy source?

10. What are some ways you could be more patient with yourself?

11. What lies have you or do you tell yourself? Why?

12. Do you have recurring dreams or nightmares? What happens in them? What do you think your subconscious mind is trying to communicate to you?

13. What's something you're afraid of doing? What's scary about it? How can you overcome that fear?

14. Which negative emotions do you try to avoid? Why is that? Have you always been this way?

15. Do you ask for help? Why or why not?

16. What keeps you up at night? Where does this worry come from? How long have these issues been troubling you?

17. How do you act when you're angry? Is this similar or different to how the people in your childhood acted when angry?

18. Describe a time you self-sabotaged. What happened? Why do you think you did it?

19. Do you accept compliments well? Why or why not? Are there any compliments you receive that you struggle to believe about yourself?

20. Write an apology letter to yourself.

21. Do you hold grudges? What's hard for you to let go? Why?

22. Describe a time you felt self-conscious or unsafe. What triggered these feelings for you?

23. What areas of your life do you feel are ignored or disregarded?

24. If you could change one thing about yourself, what would it be and why?

25. What triggers envy in you? Where does that come from?

26. Are you overly sensitive to constructive criticism, or do you respond well? Why is that?

27. Are you easily influenced by other people's opinions? Do you find it easy or difficult to assert your voice? Why?

Examining Your Past

1. Think about a relationship you had to leave. Why did you leave or stay longer than you should have? Why was it the right choice for you?

2. Describe a time you felt wronged as a child. What happened? How did you react? What did you learn from this experience? Has it affected your life as an adult?

3. Write a letter to your shadow self, thanking it for keeping your ego safe.

4. What's an early childhood memory that has stuck with you into adulthood? Why do you think that is?

5. What were you like as a child? How have you changed?

6. What is your worst childhood memory? How did your parents or guardians respond? Were you cared for? Were your needs met?

7. Write about a time you experienced something that seemed negative but turned out to be a positive thing in the long run.

8. What do you wish you could change about your childhood? Why?

9. Which memories bring you the most shame? What other feelings do they provoke? What do you do when you start feeling these things?

10. How has your past trauma affected you? How do you carry it in your everyday life?

Finding Your True Gifts

1. Imagine meeting yourself for the first time. What would be your first impression?

2. How would your loved ones describe you? Are they accurate? Why or why not?

3. What are your toxic traits? How do these traits affect others? How do they impact your daily life?

4. Make a list of your positive traits and negative traits. What are some things you can do to strengthen your positive traits? How can you start healing your negative traits?

5. Create an avatar for your shadow self. What are
    their traits and qualities? What do you want to
    say to your shadow self?

6. Think of one or two traits that you dislike about
    yourself. Where do these traits come from? Were
    they learned? Are they defense mechanisms?
    Explore as many ideas as you can.

7. What makes you jealous? Why? What does it tell
    you about your own needs? Are these things
    you can work towards, or something you should
    let go of?

8. What is a trait you see in other people that you
    wish you had? What are some ways you can
    cultivate this trait in yourself?

9. Which personality traits in other people drive you
    nuts? Why? Do you see yourself in any of these
    behaviors?

10. How do you handle stress?

11. What is your relationship to drama? Do you like it
    or involve yourself in it? Do you cause it or avoid
    it? Explore this.

12. Are there any negative emotions or traits that feel
    normal to you that you express every day? What
    are they? When did you adopt them?

Examining Your Relationships

1. What kind of relationships do you have with your parents/caregivers, siblings, or other close family members? Is it better, worse, or the same as when you were growing up? Why?

2. Have you ever developed an obsessive or unhealthy relationship? Why do you think this happened?

3. Do you struggle with commitment? What challenges have you faced in your dating life that you want to work on?

4. Is there a person you can't seem to forgive in your life? Write them a letter. What do you want to say to them?

5. Was there a time you opened yourself up to someone and felt rejected? What happened? How has that affected you?

6. Do you allow yourself to be vulnerable in relationships? Why or why not?

7. In what ways are you similar to your parents or guardians? How are you different?

8. Is there anyone in your life who belittles you or downplays your emotions? How does that affect you?

9. Who has the most influence over you? Do they know? Is it healthy?

10. Have you ever been in a codependent relationship? What about your family members? Talk about your experience with codependency, as well as thoughts or feelings that come up about it.

11. Write a letter to someone who has really hurt you. Let it all out. Feel free to destroy the letter when you're done.

12. Which relationships in your life no longer serve you? List them out. How would it feel to be free of these relationships? Why aren't you?

13. Think about a conflict you had with someone. How did it play out? Is there anything you wish you had done differently? What was your role in the conflict? Did you take responsibility?

14. Who have you let down in the past? Why did you do it? Where do you stand with this person currently?

15. What is your love language? How did you learn it?[87]

Lesson 18
Forgiveness
A Story of Learning to Love Myself

"Forgiveness has deeper rewards than excusing someone for how they have hurt us. The deeper healing comes in the exchange of our resentment for inner freedom. At last, the wound, even if not acknowledged by the other person, can heal, and our life can continue. It is useful to realize that the word "forgive" originally meant both to give and receive—to "give for." In keeping with the original meaning, we can see that the inner reward for forgiveness is the exchange of life, the give and take between our soul and the Universe."—Mark Nepo

What is forgiveness? An ongoing process that can take years upon years? Or a single decision made in the blink of an eye? What is the impact of its opposite; holding on to perceived transgression and choosing to live with hurt and searing resentment? Choosing to retell those victim stories over and over again until they become so codified that they look like the actual truth? Those juicy, delicious moments of collusion when someone else exclaims, "God what an a$$hole! I can't believe he did that to you." Score! Validation and vindication. Ohhhhh, the pleasure of feeling like sh*t while wanting to keep stewing in it.

In Galen Pearl's book, *10 Steps to Finding Your Happy Place (and Staying There),* she asks some deep questions about our idea of traditional forgiveness as taught by many faiths and secular wisdom. She suggests that forgiveness reimagined can actually be a radical spiritual practice and a path to happiness. She invites us to think about what traditional forgiveness looks like; it could be the continued dredging up of images of the person who has wronged us, hurt our feelings, broken promises, betrayed confidence, and/or lied. We forgive them, meaning that we release them from our judgment and release the hold that their wrongdoing has on our hearts. She asks us, "What is the power these wrongs have over us? Why is it that we believe so strongly that forgiveness is a good idea, and yet still nurse wounds long past?"[88] She then suggests that maybe it is all rooted in our collective definition of "forgiveness."

Her revelations about forgiveness made me curious, and like Galen, I went searching for definitions of "forgive" and "forgiveness." What I found, just like she suggests in her book, is that all the definitions out there are based on ceasing to blame or resent, and then granting pardon to those who have wronged us. So, the assumption of a trespass that has been committed against oneself underlies our common story of what it is to forgive, which means "I must be a victim!" This is where Galen gets radical with her forgiveness practice by suggesting that we question these definitions of "victim model wrongdoing." She asks, "What if we questioned that assumption? What if no wrong has been committed? *A Course in Miracles* teaches us that all perception of attack is based on a mistaken belief that we are separate from each other. Our whole view of the world is a creation of our egos, based on a past that isn't real. Forgiveness is the miracle that corrects that mistake."[88]

What if we could do it differently? What if we could take a page out of Galen's book and become Radical Forgiveness Practitioners right now? What if we could shift our worldview from "separateness" to "oneness" and erase all perceived transgressions as if they never happened? Transform our hurts and heal our wounds, not by traditional forgiveness that uses a "wronged victim" model, but by radical forgiveness that is based on a "victimless" model? Where would that get us? Galen suggests that it would take us to gratitude and happiness. Believe it or not, that is exactly what I discovered for myself along my wild journey.

Here is my own lesson in forgiveness: my first time living in Mexico, I had the experience of being asked to change a lot of my behaviors in order to appease someone else and be in a relationship with them. As it turns out, all of the requested changes required by this person were things I was already in the process of updating and upgrading within myself. So, in the end, it wasn't actually necessary for me to change myself for someone else at their request. Yet, it still irked me. I knew that a lot of what they were pointing out in me was already what I wanted to transform in myself. It was just the way they were going about expressing it and the ways in which they wanted me to "uplevel" for them. It irked me to be asked so blatantly and bluntly to be something other than who I was at that moment. And then, believe it or not, after all these demands were made, this person turned out to be withholding some very pertinent information about themselves. It was information that definitely shifted not only how I saw them, but also how willing I was to change my behavior for someone that wasn't honest to begin with.

The truth came out, as it always does. Trust me, it might not be today or tomorrow, but the truth always comes out. I've learned that lesson in spades. I put the brakes on, said that I needed time, and stepped into my processing space. I had to figure out what the heck was going on here and figure out what I actually wanted. We met up again for our scheduled date night. It wasn't the tantric massage date night we'd envisioned. Instead, it was a breakup talk on the water. They became contrite. No daggers and no swords. They were kind of deflated. They just sat there and said, "I take ownership of the fact that I lied to you. What I did was wrong! I was thinking with my 'head below my waistband' and not my head above my shoulders. I apologize. I know that it's completely out of integrity for me to ask for honesty and not give it fully in return. It's wrong to justify my own withholding for my own selfish desire to gain sexual pleasure." I really appreciated this honesty. It was so real and actually bonded us, sitting there on the water.

We ended our talk and decided to grab some dinner. It felt nice to be together; like the air had been cleared. It progressed into a walk home. They said, "Thank you for forgiving me." I heard myself quickly snap back, "I never said that!" Immediately, at that moment, a chorus of voices exploded inside of me. All the stuff I had ever heard or read about forgiveness poured into my consciousness, in a tangled mess of snippets and soundbites. I thought, "I could forgive him right now. I would feel clean." My ego responded with, "Don't give them the f_cking satisfaction of being forgiven so easily. Make them stew for a while." (Insert evil witch-queen laugh here.) Then, I noticed myself baiting forgiveness as if it were something that could be dangled like a carrot in front of a horse. What happens once they get the carrot? Forgiveness? Does that mean that somehow the horse has won, and we've lost? The horse is my ex in this analogy; maybe it's your ex too.

And here we get to the Buddha again. He was a pretty wise dude, as it turns out. Buddha said quite bluntly that "resentment is like drinking poison and expecting the other person to die." We end up poisoning ourselves in order to keep the other person on the hook for as long as possible. It might feel delicious and self-righteous for a few moments, but in the long run, we end up carrying this cancerous thing inside of us that takes a whole lot of precious life energy to carry. It has to be nurtured and fed, and so it gets more and more toxic. Forgiveness is actually a courageous act of self-liberation and self-care. Of course, it benefits the receiver of the forgiveness (the one we'd love to think of as the transgressor, the A-hole, or the dirty bag); but more than anything, it benefits the person doing the forgiving. I ended up getting so excited about understanding forgiveness within the self-care/self-love framework that I took a deep dive into much that was written about it. Now, in my bag of radical practices, which includes radical self-acceptance, radical self-trust, and radical honesty, I also practice radical forgiveness. It's totally liberating and puts a fabulous spin on the stuff that happens to us along the way. We grow and become more and more unshakable. I'd recommend a deeper look-see if you are curious.

In the middle of this karmic lesson, provided so generously by this person who had been withholding information about their health that could potentially impact my health, I had this massive, internal discussion with myself about forgiveness. As they say, things come to us in mysterious ways when we are ready to receive and understand. Apparently, I was ready to receive and understand!

Back to the story. All of this resulted in us separating, and in the face of that, I decided to be honest instead of playing games. I told them that in the past, I chose to have multiple lovers simultaneously so that I didn't get attached. I avoided having any kind of emotional connection so that I would not be hurt when it didn't work out, or turn into anything beyond sex. I knew I couldn't get attached because I wasn't giving myself the opportunity to. I did not show up in relationships vulnerably so that I would have nothing to lose. If someone demanded monogamy of me, I would rise to it grudgingly; but honestly, it's what I wanted too. I was just not quite sure how to fully trust one person wholeheartedly. It felt very foreign and super scary to me. The reason I dated so many people simultaneously, beyond the fact that I was enjoying it, found it fun, and it felt like an adventure (I am an Enneagram Seven and am therefore in love with "new and shiny" all the time), was because I have a deep, entrenched narrative that men are trash and will do whatever they can to get into my pants.

I can hear my mom's voice in my head. In her infamous "Don't have sex" talk for middle schoolers and teenagers, she would say, "All boys want is sex." She also made sure to impart this nugget: "As soon as they get what they want, they'll just dump you and move on to the next girl." Do you see what I'm saying? All this negative messaging I received regarding sexual motives definitely impacts how I show up in my dating life, and my choice to keep myself always safe (or unavailable) from love. It's not easy owning up to the darkest parts of ourselves and

being vulnerable. In the end, it is exactly the medicine
that will set us free and help us find the way to our
core; to our centered selves.

Turns out, this guy was a pretty good dude after all;
just like Buddha. He listened and let me talk. And in
that moment, I decided that I was not going to let this
experience with this man feed my negative judgments
of all men even further. I was not going to give any
more of my power away to outside forces, and I was
not going to be poisoned by this story any longer.
It's pretty powerful stuff, this radical forgiveness.
I was not only going to let this man off the hook for
his lying and putting my health at risk, but I was also
going to let all men off the hook. I was going to take
all the life lessons I had learned on my own to create
a new story that was mine; not one downloaded by
well-meaning adults imprinting me during my early
"sponge" years. I was taught to fear men; a story
I spent so much life energy combating by living the
life of the fearsome, unattainable, heartless dominatrix.
Nope! I was done with that old story. It clearly no
longer served me.

The truth shall set you free! Based on my experience,
that is absolutely true! Even the ugly truths we'd
rather leave buried deep in our shadows. Usually,
they end up being our biggest teachers and liberators.
Everything begins with baby steps.

Standing there with my lying man, being super vulnerable and in the midst of a karmic moment of super accelerated learning, I used this as an opportunity to practice remaining open. I could have gone with my old methods of armoring up, closing down, and giving 'em hell. I didn't know it yet right then and there, but looking back from this vantage point now, I understand that a big part of forgiveness is the choice to *remain open*. We can contract like flowers that close up in the night to protect themselves from the cold, or we can choose to remain open. Although there is risk in doing that, the rewards are usually a thousand-fold and totally unexpected. I feel grateful that I was able to forgive this man in that moment, instead of carrying yet another shred of proof that men are trash. It would have continued to poison me and shut me off from my deepest want: my desire to honestly and vulnerably relate to my monogamous partner. Like Mark Nepo so wisely says in his *Book of Awakening*, "What it really comes down to is the clearness of heart to stop defining who I am by those who have hurt me, and to take up the risk to love myself, to validate my own existence, pain and all, from the center out."[89]

Now, I have so much empathy and understanding for myself and for my mother, with all her concerns for my well-being, and for the men I have known on my path. They have all been most excellent teachers without whom I would not have been able to learn the lesson of forgiveness and come to understand the story I was carrying. You see, as paradoxical as it is, without something to forgive, we cannot learn forgiveness. So it is with all things in the universe. We have to have the inverse experience to push up against in order to be able to learn to come from love, not fear. It teaches us to remain open and curious. History is littered with examples of this.

Now, I see myself in everyone I meet. This is because I see God in them. For me, God is everything and God is love. I can also see myself reflected back through others. Of course, I want to show up compassionately and lovingly with myself. Therefore, that is how I choose to show up for others.

When this guy told me, "Thank you for forgiving me," and I stopped and said, "You know I haven't said that," I simultaneously realized that, actually, I *had* completely forgiven him. It felt like there was nothing to actually forgive. I became aware that, more than anything, more than anger and hurt, I felt sad that he wasn't comfortable enough with himself to speak his truth and truly share who he was. I could feel the pain and fear of inadequacy he must be carrying around inside of him. That requires no forgiveness. That simply asks me to show up with empathy, compassion, and the ability to see the other as God; and therefore, as perfect.

I understood! I understood that this did not mean that I needed to date him or give him a second chance. It just meant that by forgiving him, we were both off the hook and free to continue on our separate paths. It turns out that we were both better for knowing each other and going through what we went through. It meant that I was running clean in my life, and that he got to run clean in his life. We could both move forward from this heartbreaking experience wiser, more open, more connected, with a greater understanding of self and each other, and with the deepest sense of respect and admiration.

So, oddly enough (but not really, for the universe really does work in mysterious ways), the betrayal and the act of forgiveness led to a much closer bond for our shared human experience. On the other side of trauma, that is often what people will report as the outcome. That is what's known in psychology as the "trauma bond." For example, after the January 6th, 2021 terrorist attack on our Capitol building, the senators bonded. They hadn't been able to get along before that. This unthinkable event in our nation's history led to some previously unimaginable outcomes. The trauma of American citizens breaking into and taking the Capitol building by storm, federal guards drawing arms on US citizens, government chambers being barricaded with furniture to save senators' and congress members' lives, and people trying to keep our sacred temple of democracy safe was a huge wakeup call for our legislators and nation. When the Senate was able to reconvene, magic happened. What had, up until that moment, been unthinkable happened. Republican Senator Lindsey Graham and Libertarian Senator Rand Paul agreed to accept the ballot count in favor of a democratic president (the disagreement about the vote count results is what incited the January 6th, 2021 riots).

These two people, who hadn't agreed on just about anything in over thirty years, were able to see eye to eye. They could shake hands, and stand side by side. That speaks to the power of how a traumatic experience can bond rivals and unite people.

At the end of the day, we're all human and we all want the same basic things: to live our lives to the best of our abilities, to love, and to be loved. We want to feel safe. We want to be seen and heard. We want to be respected, and we want to matter to others. When traumatic things happen, big or small, we can choose to become like "bullets;" the term florists use for roses that are so tight in their buds that they will never open and bloom. Or, we can take a risk and remain open. We can risk being hurt again and again, and in turn, grow stronger, more resilient, and more beautiful. We can know that we are unshakably centered and choose how we respond in each moment. That is the power of forgiveness.

As I started this chapter by saying, many choose to live unconscious and unaware. For these folks, forgiveness can take years or even decades. For some, it never comes. They cling to the hurt and trespasses like a self-righteous life raft, steadily building lifelong resentment. It becomes a continuous drink of poison that darkens their spirits and drains the life, love, joy, and happiness out of them. There is this great quote about how people who resent other people basically let them live rent-free in their minds. Forgiveness can be a simple choice; a courageous act in a single moment. The choice of choosing love over fear. Forgiveness is choosing an open, loving heart, instead of walking through life constantly closed off. It empowers you to risk doing it differently. It is a choice for yourself, instead of against yourself. It's a choice to free yourself from bonds and attachments to other people and their belief systems (personal and cultural) that just don't feel good, don't uplift you, and don't nourish you.

When I look at forgiveness through this new lens of openness, love, and shared human experience, I see that the self-righteous holding onto anger, resentment, and blame only fills my life with enemies. It creates a constant battlefield that I have to spend my life slugging through. Exhausting, right!? No wonder so many of us are self-medicating cynics.

Through the lens of Radical Forgiveness, I also understand that the deeper I dive into exploring spirituality in all its forms, the deeper I understand that there is no "other." In reality, there is only "us." We are all embodied spirits on a journey through three-dimensional life, on this insanely beautiful and chaotic planet. We literally are all One. By that, I mean to say that we are all God's creation. Since God is love and light, we're all just love and light. We're human meat suits, walking around and wounding each other all the time because we forget that we're actually perfect, divine, spiritual beings.

We forget that we are magnificent beings because
so many of us are raised with contradictory belief
systems that trap us into a mediocre existence. I was
raised in a cacophony of religious and spiritual beliefs:
the culture of West Coast USA, East Indian messages
about what it means to be a woman, Catholicism,
Hinduism, yogic philosophy, and so many other
things. I was taught to say a daily prayer: "Lord, grant
us our blessings and forgive us our trespasses as we
forgive those who trespass against us. Lead us not into
temptation, but deliver us from evil. For thine is the
kingdom, the power, and the glory, now and forever.
Amen." I was taught this prayer when I was very
young, and I have said it over and over again without
ever considering what I was actually saying. So many
of us are raised with these unexamined messages
and beliefs about forgiveness that really don't make
much sense. So much is written in the Bible about
forgiveness, and ironically, many people who claim
to follow the Bible often misconstrue these words
and concepts of forgiveness. They can end up being
some of the most unforgiving, hurt people in our
communities.

Jesus forgave his trespassers; the ones that wanted
to hurt him and put an end to his talk about love and
peace. Right there is the perfect example of opening
instead of closing. It's an example of practicing
forgiveness for self-empowerment—not just to let
someone else off the hook. If we pause for a moment,
it's pretty interesting to think about the kind of
man that Jesus was, and how he is described by his
disciples. He, like Buddha, Muhammad, and other

teachers of peace and enlightenment, embodied the idea of just holding a little more space for others. He showed what it means to be just a little more tuned in and open-hearted, carrying just a bit more grace for our fellow human beings. He knew that at some point, every single person would need love, compassion, and forgiveness. He knew that we would all need to drop our resentment in favor of grace. This means forgiving your lazy, "no good for nothing" baby son whose liberal arts degree you paid for, and who now works at a gas station pursuing his music dreams.
It means forgiving your hyper-religious parents who forced you to go to church with them and sit through Sunday after Sunday of hateful rhetoric that viciously condemned your queer identity; rhetoric that left you feeling confused, worthless, scared, and "othered." Just a bit more grace, just a little more tuned in and open-hearted for all those beliefs and behaviors that are rooted deeply in fear. Through that tuning in and holding space, we come to understand that forgiveness is the path to setting ourselves free.

The power of forgiveness has been written about and researched a lot. There is so much out there if you want to take a deeper dive. I would totally recommend finding a book about the power of forgiveness. It has helped me a lot on my journey.

As I am sure you know, forgiveness and atonement are a part of every twelve-step program. If you are not familiar with such programs, one of the steps on the addiction healing path is to go to anyone that you've hurt and wronged—particularly as a result of your addiction and being an addict—as well as those you've hurt outside of your addictive behaviors. You are tasked with reaching out and taking ownership of what you have done or are doing that is out of alignment with your values, and has negatively impacted another person or people. You apologize and make amends. I have a friend who has been going through that process recently. She is keeping me up to date on her progress and her experience, and we have talked a lot about how forgiveness, in the end, is not about the other person at all. When someone is asking you for forgiveness, they are trying to feel forgiven. They want to have peace and understanding and connection. Forgiveness will make everyone feel better. It clears the air and the heart space, and it connects us back to each other.

Maybe you are struggling with this right now; especially if it's the first time anyone has ever asked you to think outside of the box about forgiveness. Maybe you are thinking, "But, but, but! Wait a minute. Someone did something heinous to me and it's impossible to forgive them." Still, I will say, "If you can elevate yourself to a higher perspective (in coaching language we call it 'chunking up') as if you're climbing to the top of your favorite mountain and looking at things from up there, then maybe it's easier to see that we are all the same. We are all spirits in human form that just want to be loved. We all get afraid and do stupid things in our smallness, out of self-preservation." I totally get your objections and your perspective. I was there right alongside you a few years ago. It is hard to comprehend how this works, but as Mark Nepo says in his *Book of Awakening*, "Yet the mystery of true forgiveness waits in letting go of our ledgers of injustice and retribution in order to regain the feeling in our heart. We can only hope to begin this exchange today, now, by forgiving what is broken in each other and imagining through love how these holy pieces go together."[89]

Take, for instance, our former President, Donald J. Trump. He's a great example of someone who really just wants to be loved and accepted. He doesn't know how, so in his pursuit to be liked and loved, he often disenfranchises others. This desire to be seen, loved, and be powerful is not God stuff; that's just human stuff. Although I may struggle to forgive the impact his choices have had on our country and the world, I can also absolutely forgive someone for feeling unloved. I can forgive them for wanting so desperately to be validated. I've done that, and in some form or another, so have you. Granted, I've never been at the helm of one of the wealthiest, most powerful countries in the world, nor have I been the chief of the world's largest military. For that reason, I haven't had the same power or jurisdiction to create as much damage or impact as he has. And still, through trespasses big and small, the concept and practice of Radical Forgiveness are the same. I know that it's too soon to say what the repercussions of his actions will be. It usually takes about eight to ten years for the full impact of a president's choices on the nation, macro-economically and geopolitically, to show itself. Without a shadow of a doubt, I can say that I have acted shamefully and in

ways that are out of alignment with my value system,
in search of validation and connection. I know that I
have impacted others and created damage the way
Donald Trump did. I, like Trump, want to belong.
I want to feel that I am wanted, needed, seen, heard,
and understood. I want to know that I matter and,
most of all, that I am loved.

Owning this is so liberating. I feel freer now than
I have ever felt. Reframing my ideas of what
forgiveness is has been a great, big step on my path
to becoming my unshakably centered, empowered
self. Now, when I feel my defenses activate and my
heart constrict, and when I am judging and defending
and feeling all my "victim feels," I put myself in the
shoes of the person I am judging. I then know that
we both need forgiveness. On the other side of that
forgiveness, neither one of us is being poisoned by
stories that do not belong to us, or doing damage to
each other. We are the same, standing together. We are
spiritual beings in a human incarnation, seeking to
love and be loved. Forgiving makes it so much easier
to live and love in this messed up, sometimes hateful
world. Trust me, the view from the land of forgiveness
is spectacular. You should try it.

Practice

A Short Forgiveness Breath Meditation

Sit quietly and comfortably in your favorite spot
(if possible. If not, this can be done anywhere! No
mountaintop or cushion is needed when it comes
to forgiveness or meditation in general).

Let your breath slow down and deepen. This will happen
naturally as you begin to focus on your breathing.

Let yourself feel the pain of a wound that you carry. It can
be old or new. It doesn't matter. Whatever comes to you,
let it surface.

Let yourself feel the pain of keeping this wound wide
open and well-tended, so that you can continue to
prove to the world that you have been wronged and are
suffering. As you inhale, feel the softness and freshness
of the new breath, carrying with it the promise of new
beginnings. As you exhale, let yourself release the
resentment, indignity, injustice, woundedness, and
victimhood.

As you continue to breathe, forgive the wound. Allow
the simple exchange of the part of you that is defined by
the woundedness for the part of you that, without your
consent, keeps healing.

Keep breathing, slow and steady. Inhale new, fresh
softness and exhale old, stale harshness. Allow this
simple exchange to continue until you begin to feel
more spacious, self-loving, and grateful for the ability
to validate your own existence.

A Radical Forgiveness Exploration

These are steps to working with Radical Forgiveness, as proposed by Galen Pearl in her book, 10 Steps to Finding Your Happy Place (and Staying There).

1. Acknowledge what has happened. Tell your story and feel your feelings about it. Galen's example is a childhood memory of when her best friend sided with the popular kids at a party. They made fun of Galen and excluded her from the group. As she says, "It still hurts."

2. Cradle your feelings and befriend them, rather than pushing them away and denying them. Galen shares the hurt manifested as anger and judgment that created barriers to forgiveness, and increased her suffering. She tried to control that which she could not. "I wanted my friend to be sorry. I wanted her to stand up for me and tell off all those prissy little you-know-whats."

3. Once our pain is honored and soothed, we can begin to look below the feelings at the underlying facts. Galen shares, "Instead of judging my friend's actions as selfish and mean, could I consider that she wanted the same things I did; to be popular, to belong, to be liked, to be accepted, to be valued? Might some of my anger towards her mask envy because she was included, and I wasn't?" When we create space to consider other interpretations, most often, our hearts soften and we begin to feel compassion instead of condemnation.

   a. Here's where the radical part begins. Challenge your assumptions, get curious, and take risks. Ask yourself, "Is it possible that what happened to me actually benefited me in becoming the person I am today?" Consider which ways your life has become better because of what happened. For us to reflect on this question, we have to loosen our grip on our victim identity and let go of the model of "wronged victim" that traditional forgiveness rests on. Galen says, "What comes to mind for me is how this event shaped my views about inclusion. I won't claim to be always compassionate, but whenever I see anyone being left out, being teased, or bullied, I don't hesitate to stand up for that person. If I am in a group, I am more sensitive to issues of inclusion, making sure that everyone has a place at the table. As a parent, I was more attuned to these issues in my children, helping them cope if they were the targets and imposing quick justice and education if they targeted others." Explore these questions for as long as it takes to begin to shift your worldview and see the original event with new eyes. Write, draw, compose, or dance. Use whatever creative practices support your exploration.

b. Give yourself the ultimate gift: Bring to mind the original event, now free of the victim story, and see it through the light of gratitude. This is the lens that transforms. Galen concludes: "Thinking of this long-ago event in this light transforms my friend's actions from an attack to a gift. The pain is transformed into compassion. I am transformed from a victim to a more sensitive friend, a wiser parent, and a more aware person."

Radical Forgiveness transforms into gratitude. Gratitude leads us to joy and happiness; to our own liberation and freedom to be ourselves. Galen concludes, "It is a miracle after all, and all miracles
are radical."[90]

Journaling Prompts

Is there someone that you haven't forgiven yet?
If so, set a timer for five minutes and "angry journal"
about all the BS that you're still holding onto. Don't
let your pen leave the page. Use your stream of
consciousness to verbally vomit all that anger,
sadness, or whatever comes up, OUT.

When you're done, destroy the paper. Tear it up into
a million pieces and scream into the wind as you watch
it confetti away, set it on fire, or bury it in the ground.
Do it however you want to do it. I find that the more
dramatic it is, the more cathartic it is—but that's just
my Sagitarius moon talking.

If that doesn't interest or apply to you, dig deeper.
Just kidding. Write about the last time you
apologized to someone.

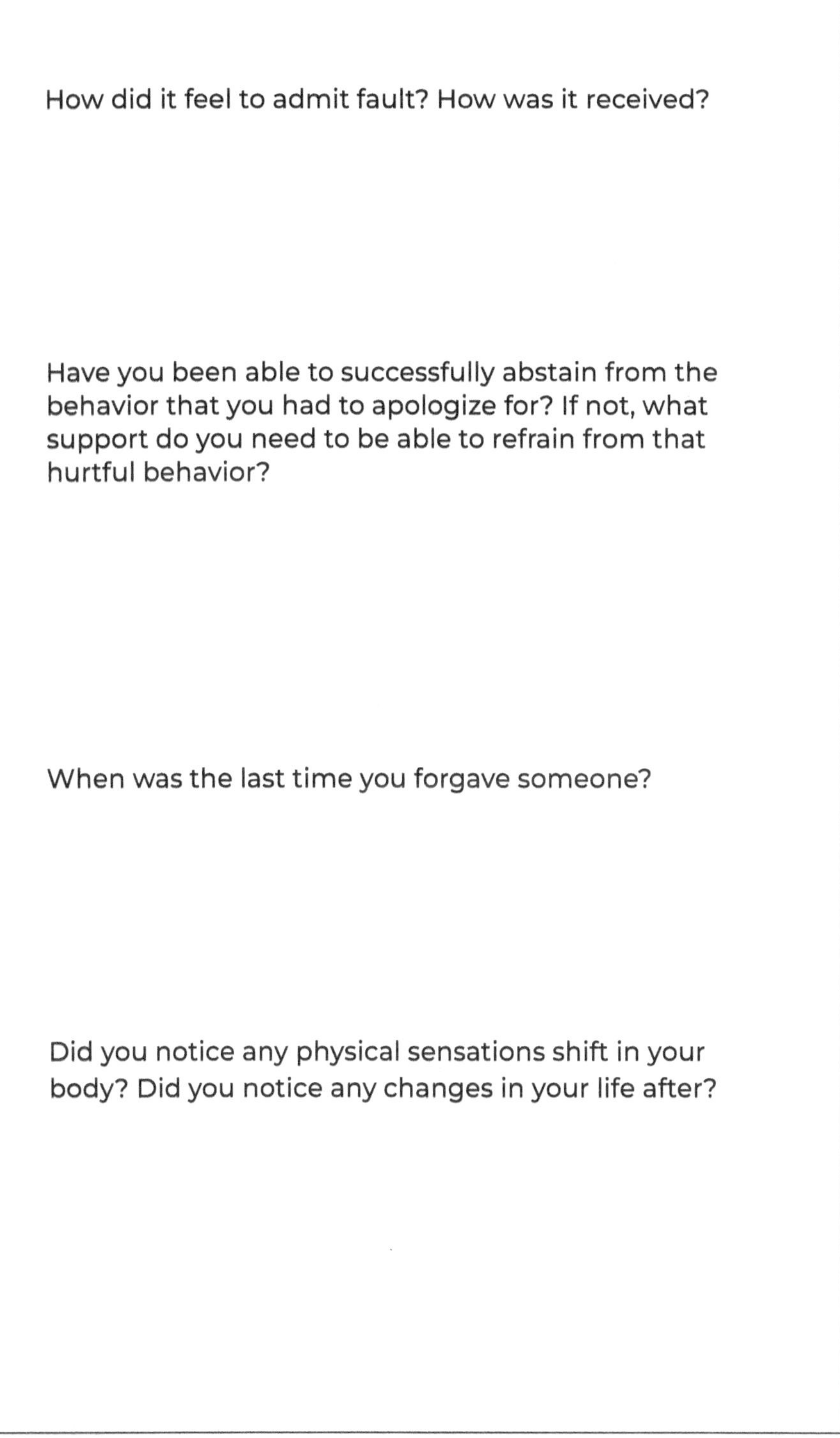

How did it feel to admit fault? How was it received?

Have you been able to successfully abstain from the behavior that you had to apologize for? If not, what support do you need to be able to refrain from that hurtful behavior?

When was the last time you forgave someone?

Did you notice any physical sensations shift in your body? Did you notice any changes in your life after?

Lesson 19
God Is Dog...Dog Is God
A Mutant Animal
Bred By Man From Wolves

"I look up and I see God, I look down and see my dog.
Simple spelling GOD, same word backwards, DOG.
They would stay with me all day.
I'm the one who walks away.
But both of them just wait for me,
and dance at my return with glee.
Both love me no matter what—
divine God and canine mutt.
I take it hard each time I fail, but God forgives,
Dog wags his tail.
God thought up and made the dog,
Dog reflects a part of God.
I've seen love from both sides now,
it's everywhere, amen, bow wow.
I look up and I see God, I look down and see my dog."

—Wendy J. Francisco

Before I became a dog mom, the above poem wouldn't have hit. Now that I've seen the light of what it is to experience the unconditional love, companionship, and comfort they both bring, I can't imagine my life without them.

God and dogs both embody everything that religion attempts to teach: loyalty, love, faithfulness, and being present. Some say we were made to make God smile, and dogs were made to make humans smile. Fun fact: dogs are "95% genetically identical to humans, which researchers are using to their benefit to deepen cancer research."[91] I got curious about why "God" is "dog" spelled backwards. Everything comes from somewhere. It turns out that there is a whole lot of mythology out there on this subject, throughout different religions and cultures.

Meet Bau, the ancient, Babylonian Dog-Goddess of Healing. She was often described as a divine midwife. She was initially thought of as a life-giving deity, and in some cases was linked with the creation of humankind. Over the course of the third and second millennia BCE, she also acquired the role of a healing goddess. Bau is depicted as a patron deity with a dog head. This ancient Dog-Goddess was worshiped by ancient peoples who gave dogs a very high position of importance in their culture. Because dogs were considered divine entities, their importance was signified by their use in ceremonies and oath-taking. An excavation in an area around the Ninishina temple in Isin, Mesopotamia produced dozens of ancient drawings of dogs, many dog deity sculptures, and more than two dozen mummified dogs laid sacredly to rest. The temple name literally translates to "Dog House."

Then there's Anubis, Egyptian Dog-God of the Underworld, and his companion Dog-God, Wepwawet, Way & Pathfinder. Anubis is said to have protected and guided all the sacred, dead spirits. Anubis is depicted as a man with a black jackal-like head, or as a black jackal. "Wepwawet" translates directly to "opener of the roads" or "opening a path." In Egyptian mythology, Wepwawet was responsible for leading the dead safely into the underworld and watching over them on their travels into the unknown. Much like our modern-day dog companions who watch over us, and who are often trained to help those of us who cannot easily find our way by ourselves. Ancient Egyptians had a deep, spiritual reverence for their dogs.

I found Dog-Gods who rule the elements. Among them are Filipino Kimat, Dog-God of Thunder and Lightning; Egyptian Set, Dog-God of the Storms; and Aztec Xoltl, Dog-God of Lightning and Fire.

Kimat comes from Philippine mythology. He was known as the Dog companion of Tadaklan, the Thunder God by the Tinguian people of central Luzon. The Tinguian people believed that Tadaklan and Kimat lived in the sky and that they were responsible for thunder and lightning.

Set, Dog-God of Storm, comes from Egyptian mythology. Set was responsible for all strange and scary natural phenomena that could not be explained. This includes solar and lunar eclipses, thunderstorms, and geological disturbances such as earthquakes and desert storms. For the Egyptians, Set was mighty powerful and these destructive and scary events were greatly feared. Set, like Anubis, is often shown as a man with the head of a dog.

The ancient Aztecs worshiped Xoltl, Dog-God of both lightning and fire. Xoltl was also understood to be the protector of the physically disabled and the sick, and was also the one who led the dead into the underworld and the afterlife. Xoltl is depicted as a man with a dog head; a monstrous animal with its feet often reversed. To this day, we still have the much-revered Mexican hairless dog breed known as the Xoloitzcuintil.

In Roman, Greek, Irish, and Norse mythologies, Dog-Gods contained power and strength. They were often worshiped as protectors and destroyers. In Norse mythology, we think of Thor's hounds and Fenrir, the monstrous wolf-hound and son of the god Loki. We have Cerberus, from ancient Greek mythology, who was a huge, three-headed hound. He guarded the entrance to Hades, where he prevented ghosts from sneaking out and rejoining the world of the living. In ancient Rome, Cerberus was known as the Watchdog Hound of Hades. Again, the dog comes up in history as a guard of the gates of the Underworld, preventing the dead from leaving. The Morrígan, from Irish mythology, is the goddess of war and conflict. She was seen as a shapeshifter who sometimes took the form of a gray-red wolfhound.

In Hindu mythology (my culture), they believe that being kind to dogs helps pave the way to Heaven. Dogs are depicted as the ones who guard the gates of Heaven and Hell. Dogs are believed to be messengers of the god of death, Lord Yamaraj. Therefore, according to the Hindu people, the dog is believed to be of a divine nature. They are celebrated and worshiped. They are part of the well-known Tihar festival (located in Northeast India and Nepal) which dedicates an entire day to dog worship. During Tihar, dogs wear marigold flower garlands, are given treats, and are marked with tilak (the colorful powder many Hindu people wear on their foreheads).

In Christianity, faithfulness is a positive attribute assigned to dogs. I also learned that the people of China, Japan, and Korea revere dogs as protectors. Shisha statues, a cross between a dog and a lion, guard Buddhist monasteries, decorate many buildings, and even keep bad luck at bay in convenience stores in Japan. The research just kept unfolding, on and on. Our canine companions have been worshiped as deities since the dawn of civilization. For thousands of years, our species has prayed to their species, relied on their spiritual protection and guidance, and/or lived in mortal fear of their Divine Canine Wrath. For centuries, human's best friend has often been our most-worshiped furry four-legged divine being. As the fun article "The Gods Must Be Canine: 9 Ancient Dog Deities" asks, "When you look at it that way, who's *really* wearing the collar and leash?"[92]

This divinity in animals, dogs specifically, reinforces that it does not matter if you're at an ashram at the top of some distant mountain, or in a Baptist church in the south of Florida, or somewhere in between; the essence of the message is the same. Love echoes from all directions throughout time. Love is what is downloaded to us in different languages and versions of our universal belief systems that have existed on our planet for millenia. Everyone is saying that God is Love, and that anything that is not love is not God. They're all saying that what is separate from God is an illusion and therefore doesn't matter; that the more we can focus on being within and with God, the happier, more fulfilled, and connected we will be to everything around us – and especially, to ourselves. Maybe that's why dogs are so cutely packaged in so many shapes, colors, and sizes. They make the message of love resonate with as many people as possible, in whatever way they are able to receive it.

Rumi astutely speaks on this in his poem,
"A Great Wagon:"

> Out beyond ideas of wrongdoing and right doing,
> there is a field. I'll meet you there.
> When the soul lies down in that grass,
> the world is too full to talk about.
> Ideas, language, even the phrase "each other"
> doesn't make any sense.
> The breeze at dawn has secrets to tell you.
> Don't go back to sleep.
> You must ask for what you really want.
> Don't go back to sleep.
> People are going back and forth across the doorsill
> where the two worlds touch.
> The door is round and open.
> Don't go back to sleep.[93]

Remove all the religious dogma, the stereotypes and judgments, and the "Us/Them" paradigm that says "WE have the right answers and YOU are screwed." Wake up and you will find the shared pot of gold at the end of the rainbow. This brings us full circle, back to Wayne Dyer's epic quote, "We are not human beings having a spiritual experience. We are spiritual beings having a human experience."[94] Spirituality is not a trend, nor is it to be underestimated. Spirituality always has been and always will be. Spirituality is connectedness, presence, and love. It is designed for your ultimate and greatest success.

I'm reading *A Course in Miracles* as I am writing this book. It talks about how everything is meaningless.

At first, I thought that was very nihilistic. From my
vantage point of spirituality, I wanted to reject that
premise, and the rest of the book too. That is, until
I sat with it and simply listened without judgment.
Then, I could hear what was actually being said. I
heard, "It is in the meaninglessness of life that we find
the true meaning of life." A-ha! Noodle on that one
for a few minutes and you might find that you land
exactly in the same field as Rumi did, all those many
centuries ago. He arrived smack in the middle of the
understanding and knowingness that "good" and
"bad" are man-made. We tend to judge everything that
happens to us throughout our lives, deeming them
black or white, true or false, and ugly or beautiful. We
forget the neutral, spiritual perspective. The "bad" is
what we do not like. The "good" is what we see in
ourselves as positive. Therefore, we cling to it. "Our
dualistic mind sections off emotions, thoughts, and
events—and we automatically follow it. This mental
division is often the main reason behind our inner and
outer conflicts," writes Elyane Youssef in her article,
"The Rumi Poem We Should All Read."[95]

I have arrived at a place, in a field, where I can feel
God with me in each breath. I can feel him in each step,
in each moment, and in everything I see, hear, and
touch. I struggle with duality, but somehow, grasping
this concept feels a bit easier now that I have made
room for spirituality in my life again. Now that I
have stopped judging others' ways of climbing their
mountain toward their understanding of the divine.
Even when I fall into those holes of old, judgy patterns
and limiting belief systems about "us vs. them," those

prejudiced and judgmental places of separation; it is easier to find my way up and out, back into the light of our spiritual human oneness experience.

I find organized religion to be deeply flawed. Let me pause here for a moment and reiterate, to clarify and avoid doubt in anyone's mind. I am referring to the human construct known as "organized religion," and not to spirituality itself. I am pointing only to that human creation designed for only one purpose; namely, to quell the masses into submission by denying them direct access to the Divine, and by promising a glorious afterlife if all rules are followed dutifully in the earthly life. So, although this socially entrenched ruler construct called "organized religion" is deeply flawed, filled with hypocrisy, and comes with a very bloody collective past (yes, this applies to all universally), I still seek it out.

I do this because I can feel God's presence in places of worship. I feel it in those places where we come together as human tribes to celebrate our divinity, as our ancestors have done for thousands and thousands of years, in reverence to their various gods and goddesses. There is POWER in numbers and a definite collective consciousness. I do not buy into the patriarchal structure of the Catholic faith, and still, I love to go to weekly mass with my father. It is structured time spent with spirit, as well as time to be heart-connected with one of my most favorite humans. In a group worship practice such as this, there is pause, there is quiet, and there is common experience. It does not matter where we are from or what degrees we hold.

I also find it interesting that a number of studies
show that when people are healing in community
(particularly in spiritually-based communities),
they heal much faster. I also love going to temple
with my Jewish friends and sitting with my
meditation group in the early morning as the sun
comes up. I love walking my dog and being totally
present with him as we experience the new, daily
wonders of our neighborhood park. Divinity and
spirit is everywhere if we can open ourselves to it and
get curious. In spirituality, one size does not fit all.
That is actually awesome. Imagine the boring, gray
world it would be if we all spoke the same language,
ate the same food, wore the same clothes, sang the
same songs and…you get the point.

So, as Rumi so eloquently expresses in his poem,
humans don't just *live* in the spiritual realm.
We *are* the spiritual realm! We have the opportunity
to see beyond our meat-suits and realize that our
true essence has been our purpose since the
beginning of time.

I'm going to end this chapter with a sweet, little
teaching story by Portia Nelson. I had it hanging on
my wall next to my front door for years so that
I would see it as I left my house. I find it to be a good
reminder to keep a mindful eye out for those pesky,
persuasive potholes.

Autobiography in Five Short Chapters

Chapter I
I walk down the street.
There is a deep hole in the sidewalk
I fall in.
I am lost... I am helpless.
It isn't my fault.
It takes me forever to find a way out.

Chapter II
I walk down the same street.
There is a deep hole in the sidewalk.
I pretend I don't see it.
I fall in again.
I can't believe I am in the same place
but, it isn't my fault.
It still takes a long time to get out.

Chapter III
I walk down the same street.
There is a deep hole in the sidewalk.
I see it is there.
I still fall in... it's a habit.
my eyes are open
I know where I am.
It is my fault.
I get out immediately.

Chapter IV
I walk down the same street.
There is a deep hole in the sidewalk.
I walk around it.

Chapter V
I walk down another street.[96]

Practice

Spirit Animal Practice

Dedicate time to discovering your spirit animal guides. There are lots of meditations on YouTube to support this, along with goofy quizzes.

One of the best ways is to spend time in nature around animals and see what feels familiar. Notice what seems to hold a message for you. Side note: on a recent Catholic pilgrimage to Lourdes Cathedral that I did with my father and sister, two bats flew into our hotel room. We woke up to them circling our beds. We woke Papa up to tell him, but he just said, "Those are your grandmothers coming to say hello." He went right back to bed. Take note of that sort of thing, and when it happens, look up the traits of that animal. It may have messages for you.

Journaling Prompts

Write about a spiritual experience that you have shared with an animal.

If you haven't had one, stare at a reptile's eyes and write down how that made you feel.

Make a list comparing all the ways you are like a dog, and ways that you are like a cat.
If you're more like a cat, consider changing.
JK, I love cats too.

Lesson 20
Sex Is God

Intimacy: Into Me I See

The more we trust, the farther we are able to venture.
—Esther Perel

If you want to know where your true power lies, go to the places you've been told to fear the most. Your orgasm. Your period. Labor and birth. Menopause. All processes that involve your p*ssy.   —Regena Thomashauer

We live in a sex-crazed world. Let's just call it like it is! We live in a sex-obsessed world. Sex has become so entangled with everything we do, say, think, and buy, that we have become almost oblivious to it. And still, sex sells everything; water, cars, dream vacations, and states of mind. There's no denying that it attracts attention. One of the earliest ads to use nudity as

a marketing technique came from a company
called Pearl Tobacco. In 1871, the brand included a
woman's naked torso on its packaging. The saucy
imagery created a buzz, and other companies started
embracing sexual imagery as a sales tactic. Bada
bing, bada boom: women became objectified and
sexualized in ways they had never been before. These
days, western society feels freer than ever to explore
and express sexuality and sexual preferences. Though
most people carry a lot of trauma and shame around
sex, we still have come farther than generations that
come before us, in the exploration of it. We talk about
it, create TV content about it, make restaurants and
bakeries about it, write about it, fight about it, have
parades about it, and wave banners about it.

I believe that this hypersexualization of everything
and everyone has resulted in a catastrophic, spiritual,
and social crisis through which we have become even
more lost to ourselves. We have lost sight of the true
meaning of sex. We've dragged it from its natural
place into a sky-high, teeter-tottering "dance around
the golden calf" that takes center position in our
minds, twisting and blinding us all.

The natural place of sex in all things has also been
grossly subverted by our patriarchal doctrine and
dominant religions. In both cases, sex represents the
power of control. Not power to sell products, but
power to dominate and grow richer. For example,
the Catholic Church's decision to deny its popes and
priests the ability to marry was a financial decision.

It would ensure that the church would inherit all the wealth that every priest accumulated throughout his life. Instead of wealth passing on to the priests' descendants, priests and popes were married in spirit only to God, and then all wealth would go directly back to the church. In case you didn't know this, the church used to allow all its clergy to marry and live in regular family units. "No marriage, no sex, just God" ensured a union that served the religious power structures economically. Denying men that were called to serve in the church their natural, earthly, body pleasures, and forcing them to form only a spiritual union with God resulted, as we now know, in one of the largest global pedophile rings.

Again, I return to my belief that everything is God, and God is everything. Everyone is God, and God is everyone. We are all created in the image and light of God. We are all spiritual beings on an embodied, earthly journey. So, the way I see it, sex is God and God is sex. Sex embodies creation; the lived experience of our human ability to connect in a space beyond ourselves. This alchemical unity is far from the twisted versions of sex we are inundated with today.

I also recognize that because everything is sex, and everything is sexualized, it can weaken the potency of the magic. When we really cut through the BS and connect in an open-hearted, vulnerable, personally empowered sexual union with another human, we create moments of magic. It starts with our inner world and then ripples out into how we show up in the outer world. Think about the pep in your step after

a good dicking down, or the amazing feeling you have
after a wild and free night with your lover where you
feel held, loved, seen, and supported in every way.

The reason so many of us are sex-crazed is that true
intimacy gets us out of our daily humdrum—out
of our victim stories, out of our wounded selves,
and out of our reality – and into a magical realm of
pleasure and possibility. For a few moments (or hours,
depending on how you like to play), the act of f*cking
forces us to be fully present with ourselves and others.
Sex cuts through all the noise and brings us directly
into the present moment (when we're doing it right).
The present moment is where we all hunger to live
because that is where we are truly free. That is where
we discover we can navigate whatever comes at us,
and even find pleasure in the surprises
or momentary discomfort that life also brings. Without
trying, we release the past and the future and become
fully swallowed up by the sensations of the present
moment. That is magic. That is God being present, and
the present is all we have. Most of the world is focused
on the past or worried about the future, and so they're
completely missing the present. We've all heard *that*
quote in some form or another.

Sex catapults us into a magical world where
everything is alive in us and around us. It transports
us into a world where people aren't disconnected
and escaping. They're not on their phones, watching
TV, gaming, overworking, overexercising, overeating,
over-shopping, and attempting desperately to fill the

love void. Instead, we are brought into the present, focused on this moment only. We're feeling everything and simply being. We are flowing with one another, tapping into the shared energy field that is around us all, and tapping into our own intuition.

We're sensing what the other person needs and wants. It's this subtle and powerful taking of time and of deep, shared breaths that transports us into the realm of the creative. We are brought into the spiritual space; into the orgasmic, cosmic space where we create divine magic. And that magic is God. That magic exists in all of us, all the time, and it is a direct line to that alchemical romance. When in divine sacred union with God (or another person – they can be viewed as one because God created us), we are completely naked, literally and metaphorically. We're fully exposed, vulnerable, and showing all of ourselves; even the parts that religion or culture told us is wrong, bad, disgusting, and needs to be denied.

Sex is God's grace. God created pleasurable feelings and reproductive organs because orgasm is part of the spiritual experience. God wants us to be happy. God wants us to feel joy. God wants us to be fully revealed and owning all of ourselves. Every wrinkle, every scar, every crevice. God wants all of that for us. To have really profound, powerful sex, we have to allow ourselves to be seen. In order to be fully seen for all of who we are, we must be present and allow ourselves to commune with spirit. That's what sex is all about. The Bible mentions the issue of marriage without sex in 1 Corinthians 7:5. "Do not deprive each other except perhaps by mutual consent and for a time, so that you may devote yourselves to prayer. Then come together again so that Satan will not tempt you because of your lack of self-control."[97]

It is a gateway, just like meditation, yoga, praying, or creating a mandala. There are many forms of mindfulness that allow people access to the divine and access to being in the present. Sex, when done intentionally, is simply another means of doing exactly that.

However, with anything that is abused or misused, the power and the potency of the magic diminishes. Sometimes, it vanishes altogether because it's no longer connected with God. Anything that is not God will never be fulfilling. I will say it again, for it bears saying over and over: anything that is not God will never be fulfilling! Another way to say this is, "You cannot get enough of what you don't need." That's why we hear stories like, "I was an über-rich Wall Street banker and I was totally miserable. I went to Costa Rica for a retreat and I decided to quit my job. I moved to the jungle and dedicated my life to saving salamanders." You hear versions of this, I am sure. Stories like that are everywhere. Stories of people waking up from the illusions they have been sold, and then being able to access the magic. Stories that show us again and again that anything that is not of God is just the sickening, life-squashing dance around the false idol. Dedicating ourselves to that almighty dollar, or whatever your currency of choice is, will only put us in constant, life-draining, and meaningless pursuit to fill a void that can only truly be filled by presence. We can believe that we can fill that hollow space inside that's crying for our spiritual connection to the present, on our own. However, that void exists in the past, and filling it is something we're trying to do in the future. We are doomed to fail, for in this equation, the present is completely missing. That is not God.

The same goes for sex. When you shag from the place of "*I'm* going to have an orgasm and *I'm* going to feel really, really good, because my life sucks and I need to escape from it," then you're missing the magic of being present with another. You're missing the opportunity to create meaningful moments together. The presence with yourself and another in sacred union is what feels good. And yes, when you're having a screamingly delicious orgasm, it can be very hard to do other things. Your brain is so flooded with dopamine and serotonin that you're on a kind of overdrive. You get catapulted into the present, even if it's just for a few moments.

I've not done DMT. I am told by friends who have that it's a ten-to-fifteen-minute experience that is comparable to that moment of ultimate orgasm. An orgasm with the big "O," if you know what I mean. I'm not talking about the small body tremors from a quick shag. I'm talking about the ultimate, mind-exploding orgasm we experience when we take a deep, sexual dive into sacred union with another human; the one where we come together and melt, with bodies, minds, hearts, and souls becoming one. The one where we are touching God.

As I understand it, DMT releases the same chemicals in our brains that are released only in the moments of birth and death. Our first and our last breaths; the bookends of that thing we call being alive. Talk about ultimate presence, right!? Whatever one's political or religious beliefs may be, we are talking science here. We know that bodies weigh less immediately after death. It has been measured many times. Scientists call this "the weight of the spirit." It's a teeny, tiny amount; about three ounces. It's right when our spirits enter the body, and when they exit.

And so, people use sex and drugs in desperate attempts to access this precious presence. They also try to make choices that are seen as healthy, like eating vegan foods and superfoods, taking handfuls of vitamins and herbs, and running Ironman distances. It is often an attempt to get back to that intoxicating feeling of aliveness that comes with being in the present. The question to ask then is, how can we live fully present in every moment? How can we live in sex in God? How can we live the experience of having sacred, union-inducing sex all the time? It may feel silly and awkward to think about calling in God during sex because we are conditioned to think in exactly the opposite way. Religious conditioning, in particular, wants us to believe that sex is wrong and bad. We're supposed to believe that it's evil, inappropriate outside of marriage, and even something that we should not enjoy. Depending on your flavor of religion, the messages around sex might be more brutal and condemning than others. Still, most religion carries some form of constricting narrative around sexuality and the body. In reality, sex is exactly the perfect time to commune with God and spirit. When you bring your full, open, curious, nonjudgmental attitude and attention to something, your relationship with it will only blossom and flourish.

Bring your whole self – body, mind, heart, and spirit – fully to sex. Whether it's with yourself or with others, seek to be fully present. Be present with your breath, with the feeling of touch on your skin, with deep eye-gazing, with exploration, with the giving and the receiving, all in sweet, delicious union. Sacred sex is so much more than the heteronormative and outdated definition involving penetration and humping. For many people, sex doesn't even include those actions. Embrace that this silly, funny, human, physical thing is a gateway into presence. With that precious presence comes true, sacred, big "O" orgasms. With that precious presence comes pleasure beyond measure, heart-opening delight, aliveness, and joy. With joy comes ease, and with ease comes freedom, and, and, and. On and on, it cascades through our systems, generating the ability to breathe freely; to really, truly be in our beautiful bodies; to feel and deeply understand what it means to honor ourselves; to live the miracle and magic that is our lives every day, remembering that we are not promised a tomorrow.

I like to walk through life as if I'm having sex all the time. I can still remember when my Tantra instructor told me, "Sex begins." The raw, sexual energy that we all contain is released into the space of creation the minute sex begins. When we find ourselves in a state of constant creation, we are fully alive and in the present. The moment that sex begins is the sacred moment when creativity begins. So why not always be in a state of sex?

Even as I write this, I'm feeling the sun on my skin. I'm noticing that my legs are getting slightly red. I'm feeling a few flies landing on me, joining me as I bask in the sunlight. I am smelling the spices in my teacup that is resting on my outdoor, makeshift writing desk. I am hearing the distant sounds of the ocean under the more demanding din of my neighbor's lawn mower. I am here in my body, fully present with what's going on around me and in me. As I have come to understand from my own inner work and my own sometimes gnarly journey, only from this place of tuned-in, turned-on presence can I find the energy, the insight, and the desire to channel-write this book. I am aware, sitting here and observing my hands write these words. I am in the present. Channeling these sentences from my inner wisdom is also God, right!? If I believe that I am made in the image and light of God, and that the sacred is found in the present, then anything that flows through me is also going to be of God.

Shifting focus then, let's understand that this is only now, and now, and now. Try it. Can you reach the moment that just passed and bring it back? No, for the moment that was "now" has vanished into the past. How about the moment just beyond this one; can you grab that and force it to come before its time? Also, no. No matter how much you strategize, it will not come until it is ready. So, what was "now" vanishes and what did not yet exist becomes "this now." It's a bit of a mindf*ck if you dive deep into it, and it's also the ultimate truth. So, I return to this moment of sitting here and writing these words. As I tap them out on my laptop, they are leaving my thinking mind. They are flowing down through my arms, through my hands and fingers, and onto the screen. They are no longer in the present, and I am in a new "now." In a mind-boggling, yet liberating way, this experience of life and being fully present with the "now" sets us free. It elevates us to a heightened perspective where we can see that everything is so fleeting, and therefore, so precious.

It is your choice to focus on the future (hope, fear, and worry) or the past (regret and self-condemnation). It is your choice to live in the precious present, fully awake, or to sleepwalk through life, caught in the illusion that if you hope, fear, worry, regret, and self-condemn enough, you will eventually develop the superpower to change the past and control the future. We are always at choice. The trick is to understand our choices and to know that each comes with a cost and consequence. For every choice we make, there is a choice that falls away. And so it is, with the choice to live or not live in the "now."

Herein lies the sacred magic of sex. Quite simply, it brings you directly into the presence of now. It transports you directly into your sensing body, into the experience of oneness with all, and into the experience of God. Whatever embodied tools you'd like to use to access the present, whether it's sex, meditation, yoga, dance, running, swimming, or something else, will bring you into direct communion with your body, and thus into the present moment. Our bodies cannot be anywhere but in the present moment! I invite you to leap, to fly, to climb down from that "Rapunzel tower upon high" which we call the thinking mind, and find your way into your sensing body. I invite you to stop thinking so hard about what the present is, what it would be like to be in the present, and how to get there. Instead, trust that your body already knows. I invite you to be in the state of experiencing each moment as it unfolds. Be in that state of pleasure, pain, sorrow, joy, delight, grief, ecstasy, and whatever else this moment brings. Feel yourself feeling the physical sensations around you. The body is the path directly to the present. The body is the vessel and the temple of our spirit. Being in the body helps our whirling minds quiet, and creates space for our soul experience. Then, we can be free to be in the sacred, precious present.

Practice

Intimacy Means "Into Me I See"

Set a timer for three minutes and stare
into your own eyes in a mirror.

I like to play angelic 432Hz music while I do this
and to use dimmed light or multiple candles.

Bonus if you can do it with your partner for five minutes.
Notice that each time you want to laugh, you're actually
dissipating the energy building between you two. You're
distracting yourself from the divinity staring back at you
and attempting to hide yourself. To be really and truly
seen is the most vulnerable and greatest gift of all.

Journaling Prompts

List at least three for each question.

In what ways do you see or want
to see yourself as a divine being?

What are some things you can do to
curate a sacred sexual ambiance?

Practice

- Create a "conscious" bump and grind
  playlist. Choose music that emulates love
  and positive energy.
  Example: anything Londrelle, India Arie,
  Lauryn Hill, Beautiful Chorus, etc.

Lesson 21
Gotta Have Faith
Faith: The Invisible String Holding Us Together

"Faith is an oasis in the heart which will never be reached by the caravan of thinking" —Khalil Gibran

"We lack faith in what exists within us because we lack faith in Who exists within us."—Marianne Williamson

"For we walk by faith, not by sight."—2 Corinthians 5:7

Faith is the bridge between current experience and the goal of self-realization. I walk the bridge because I'm not yet where I want to be, and because I'm also not only my current experience. I'm in motion. We are all in motion; a constant work of art. I'll close this interfaith book on spirituality with a final story that Laurent told me about the Dalai Lama:

> I used to go to this wonderful monastery for private retreats. The monks there were so much more open and real, and simultaneously, more spiritual and mystical than most of the 'religious' clergy figures I'd ever come across. I experienced these humble monks as infinitely more curious and graceful, much more than the pastors and preachers who, as you might remember from earlier chapters, suggested pointedly that I not return to their parishes after I began to voice my interpretations of the written word. At this monastery, I had the incredible, eye-opening experience of being on retreat with monks who truly embodied the word of God beyond anything that I'd known or understood before; more than I had witnessed within any church or organized religious gathering I had previously attended.

> On my third retreat there, I got really curious about their collective way of being, and their approach to the Sacred. I asked one of the head monks about this. He responded with a short story. He said, 'One day, His Holiness the Dalai Lama came here to our monastery.' I answered that I did not know that. 'Yes, he did,' he replied. 'Let me tell

you what happened. His Holiness was traveling in North America. When he got off the plane in Atlanta, he asked those who received him if there were any monks nearby in the area. They found our Conyers monastery, which is close to Atlanta. At the time,I was attending Conyers on a regular basis. An inquiry was made to the monastery, to Father Anthony, who agreed to meet with His Holiness.

His Holiness and his whole entourage drove to Conyers monastery because His Holiness wanted to meet us monks. We are Trappist Cistercian Catholic monks, and he didn't know anything about us. The Abbot came out to meet His Holiness and said, 'Welcome to our monastery. We had no idea you were coming, so we have not prepared for your visit.' His Holiness responded, 'No need for preparation. I just wanted to meet you.' The Abbot invited everyone inside. We sat down and had tea. As it was served and everyone was settled, the Abbot asked His Holiness, 'What can we do for you?' His Holiness the Dalai Lama, after a few moments of quiet contemplation, answered, 'Well, I simply want my monks to share with your monks.' After a few more moments of quiet, he continued. 'Not about theology. I wanted them to share with each other their experience of being monks.'

So, the Catholic Cistercian monks shared with the Tibetan Buddhist monks. They didn't talk about religion or doctrine at all. They spoke only about their sacred human experiences. Upon parting later that day, His Holiness and Father Anthony agreed that it was an incredible experience. I was there and it was an incredible experience. We all realized that we were having the exact same experience.

It built this giant, sturdy bridge between the East and the West because we avoided doctrine, dogma, and religion. Instead, we focused on our shared spirituality.' And that was the story the Head Monk told me in answer to my question. It made complete sense to me why they all were so much more open, real, and deeply spiritual; so much more humble, curious, and graceful. Their worldview of their sacred experience had been expanded into the realm of shared human experience. They were walking the 'One Path,' which, according to Baba and other great masters, is the same experience for us all. It is going back to 'the One,' 'the Oneness,' and the internal journey. There is no scripture for that. There is no building for that. It's all within. And that's my story.

Reduced to one kernel of wisdom, this is the essence of *21 Spiritual Lessons for the 21*st *Century*. It doesn't matter if you're a Catholic monk or a Buddhist monk. It doesn't matter if you're living in a newer monastery outside of Atlanta or in an ancient temple on top of the Himalayas. We are all spiritual beings. Meat-suits, yes, and nonetheless, we are having a spiritual experience. We're spiritual beings having an embodied, three-dimensional, spiritual experience. It's the same experience for us all when we take away all the trimmings. We are all just beings journeying through the unknowns of life. We all want the same

things, and we all need the same things to survive:
Love, Belonging, Purpose, and of course, air, water,
food, and shelter. We're all literally One. And not in
a racial or spiritual bypassing way. I am fully aware
of our meat-suit differences. Saying that we are all
one can be really triggering, especially in light of
movements like Black Lives Matter, #MeToo, Fairness
for All Faiths, LGBTQIA+ rights movements, and
many others. Some say things like, "I don't see color,
sex, gender, or religion." We must acknowledge that
in our human meat-suits, we do have very different
experiences. It is imperative to acknowledge and keep
talking about these differences so that we can build
those giant, sturdy bridges like the monks of the East
and the West. We can remember, as we talk about our
meat-suit differences, that underneath them, we are
all spirit energy beings. We are literally all from God.
Whether we like it or not, and whether we want it
to be true or not, we are all equal made in the
image of divinity.

Life is much richer when I live in faith that
everything is always working out for me. I took my
dog for a walk with the intention of figuring out how
to end this book. Along the way, I met an old man.
I expected him to reprimand me for walking on his
private road (right on the Connecticut River in East
Haddam, where I live). Instead, he took me into his
backyard to show me the bald eagle that nests in his
tree. We were both in awe of its regal and powerful
presence. This white dude was wearing a shirt with
an American flag on it. He lived on a gravel road with
signs like, "We shoot and then ask who you are… then

we shoot you again for trespassing," and "This street is protected by guns, God and ammo." We were totally present and connecting over God's green earth. To ignore that I'm a white-passing woman of color with a cute little dog would be ignoring my privilege, as well as an obvious factor as to why I was welcomed instead of shot. #Merica. Watching the eagle perch with its chest puffed reminded me that there is magic EVERYWHERE, all the time. If I look up, I see God. I look down and I see God. We can choose to see his grace and live in his trust at any point. When I choose to live and be in a state of presence and gratitude (which is God), I open myself up to goodness. I find that his goodness is better than my wildest imagination. God is good, all the time.

Oprah said it beautifully (as she does everything) in her book, The Path Made Clear: "I believe every one of us is born with a purpose. No matter who you are, what you do, or how far you think you have to go, you have been tapped by a force greater than yourself to step into your God-given calling."[98] The process of writing this book brought me one step closer to the person God meant me to be. I hope it aids you in your journey. As you continue on your unique path, the 19th-century Hindu monk, Swami Vivekananda, reminds us, "You have to grow from the inside out. None can teach you, none can make you spiritual. There is no other teacher but your own soul."[99]

I wish you all the joys this world has to offer.

If I were God...

What would I want for myself?

How would I speak to my most
challenging adversary?

Where would I spend more
or less time, respectively?

What are some ways I can live my
spiritual values in my daily life?

"The work of the eyes is done.
Go now and do the heart-work on
the images imprisoned within."
—Rilke[100]

Notes

Intro: Page 1

1. "Ep. 8 - Forgiveness, Spiritual Surrender, the Avatar, with Laurent Weichberger." Conscious. Hotline. March 24, 2021. Video, https://www.youtube.com/watch?v=uGyV7Mxq7xM.

2. Psalm 139:13-14. New International Version, Harper Collins, 1973

3. Charlotte McDonald. "How Many Earths Do We Need?" BBC News. June 6, 2015. https://www.bbc.com/news/magazine-33133712.

4. Schwartz, Barry. 2004. The Paradox of Choice. Ecco.

5. Schwartz, Barry. "The Paradox of Choice I Barry Schwartz." TED. January 16, 2007. Video, https://www.youtube.com/watch?v=VO6XEQIsCoM.

6. Daniel Burke and Laura Smith-Spark, "Pope Francis asks forgiveness for priests who sexually abused children." CNN, Updated Friday, April 11, 2014, https://edition.cnn.com/2014/04/11/world/europe/vatican-pope-sex-abuse/index.html.

7. Associated Press. "Pope Francis Calls for End to Anti-Gay Laws and LGBTQ+ Welcome." The Guardian. January 25, 2023. https://www.theguardian.com/world/2023/jan/25/pope-francis-calls-for-end-to-anti-gay-laws-and-lgbtq-welcome.

8. Inés San Martín. "For First Time, Pope Francis Installs Women in Two Church Ministries." Crux. January 23, 2022, https://cruxnow.com/vatican/2022/01/for-first-time-pope-francis-installs-women-in-two-church-ministries.

9. Orlowski-Yang, Jeff, director. The Social Dilemma. Netflix, 2020. 1 hr., 34 min. https://www.imdb.com/title/tt11464826/.

10. Jeffrey M. Jones. "Church Membership Down Sharply in the Past Two Decades." Gallup. April 18, 2019. https://news.gallup.com/poll/248837/church-membership-down-sharply-past-two-decades.aspx;

11. Wikipedia. 2023. "Evangelicalism in the United States." Wikimedia Foundation. Last modified August 14, 2023. https://en.wikipedia.org/wiki/Evangelicalism_in_the_United_States#cite_note-10.

12. "US Population." Worldometers. Worldometers Info, Accessed September 13, 2023. https://www.worldometers.info/world-population/us-population/.

13. Matthew 18:20. New International Version, Harper Collins, 1973

14. "Religion Among the Millennials." Pew Research Center. February 17, 2010. https://www.pewresearch.org/religion/2010/02/17/religion-among-the-millennials/.

15. "Prayer for Protection." Unity. https://www.ntunity.org/prayer-protection.

Lesson 1: Page 29

16. Mountain Dreamer, Oriah. 1999. The Invitation. San Francisco: HarperONE.

17. Dady, Lakshmi. "Finding My Grandmother in India." Cement Sailor, 21 Mar. 2011, https://cementsailor. blogspot.com/2011/03/finding-my-grandmother-in-india.html.

18. "Student Video: Finding Family." Semesteratsea. March 21, 2011. Video, https://www.dailymotion.com/video/xhzbcv.

19. Plato. 1922. Apology. 3rd ed. Oxford.

20. Mountain Dreamer, Oriah. 1999. The Invitation. San Francisco: HarperONE.

21. "It's Always Sunny In Philadelphia | Season 4 Ep. 10: Pepe Silvia Highlight | FXX." FX Networks. August 7, 2020. Video, https://www.youtube.com/watch?v=1NBfZcNU4O0.

22. Trista. 2019. "32 Inspirational Moments Eleanor Roosevelt Gave the World." History Collection. February 26, 2019. https://historycollection.com/32-inspirational-moments-eleanor-roosevelt-gave-the-world/.

Lesson 2: Page 63

23. Jessawala, Eruch. 1995. That's How It Was: Stories of Life with Meher Baba. Sheriar Foundation.

24. Stiller, Ben, Director. Zoolander. Paramount Pictures, 2001. 1 hr., 30 min. https://www.imdb.com/title/tt0196229/.

25. McGuinty, Patrick. "Positional Power Vs. Personal Power." Linked In. March 9, 2016. https://www.linkedin.com/pulse/positional-power-vs-personal-patrick-mcguinty/.

26. Alighieri, Dante. The Divine Comedy. Ware, England: Wordsworth Editions, 2009.

27. Smith, Dr. Evan M. "How Are Natural Diamonds Formed?" Only Natural Diamonds. August 15, 2022. https://www.naturaldiamonds.com/diamond-guide/how-are-natural-diamonds-formed/.

28. Williamson, Marianne . 1996. A Return to Love: Reflections on the Principles of "A Course in Miracles". HarperONE. https://bookshop.org/p/books/a-return-to-love-reflections-on-the-principles-of-a-course-in-miracles-marianne-williamson/8868251?ean=9780060927486.

29. "THE MATRIX: THERE IS NO SPOON." Pablo Parprado. March 1, 2011. Video, https://www.youtube.com/watch?v=uAXtO5dMqEI.

30. Frankl, Viktor E. 2014. Man's Search for Meaning. Boston: Beacon Press.

31. Van der Kolk, Bessel . 2014. The Body Keeps the Score: Brain, Mind, and Body in the Healing of Trauma. Viking.

32. Chumbawamba. "Tubthumping." Track 1. Tubthumper. Lossless, 1997, CD.

Lesson 4: Page 99

33. Hicks, Abraham. "Abraham Hicks - Everything Is Always Working Out For Me." Life: The Real World. January 7, 2023. Video, https://www.youtube.com/watch?v=cKa-XYN8V6k.

34. Mathers, Marshall . 2000. The Way I Am. Eminem.

35. Mulan. Walt Disney Pictures, 1998. https://www.imdb.com/title/tt0120762/.

36. Pocahontas. Walt Disney Pictures, 1995. https://www.imdb.com/title/tt0114148/.

37. Ludwig Jacobowski. 2018. Leuchtende Tage. Wentworth Press.

Lesson 5: Page 149

38. Thomas Merton. 2002 No Man Is an Island. Mariner Books.

39. Baba, Meher. 1987. Discourses. Sheriar Foundation.

40. Baba, Meher. 1973. God Speaks. Dodd, Mead & Co.

41. Luke 17:21. New International Version, Harper Collins, 1973

42. John 10:30. New International Version, Harper Collins, 1973

43. Kalchuri, Bhau. Lord Meher. Sheriar Books. https://www.sheriarbooks.org/product/lord-meher-volumes-13-14/.

Lesson 6: Page 175

44. Ruiz, Don Miguel. 1997. The Four Agreements: A Practical Guide to Inner Freedom. San Rafael, California: Amber-Allen Publishing.

Lesson 7: Page 183

45. Baba, Meher. 1973. Discourses, Vol. III. Sufism Reoriented Inc. https://www.amazon.com/Discourses-Vol-III-Meher-Baba/dp/B00377CC4K.

Lesson 8: Page 109

46. Meher Baba Discourses, Volume I, p. 161, "Love."

47. "SADE - Skin (Album Soldier of Love) + Lyrics." 00eschris00. February 22, 2010. Video, https://www.youtube.com/watch?v=NrqgLa2f6Yo.

48. Baba, Meher. 1967. Listen, Humanity. New York: Dodd, Mead. https://archive.org/details/listenhumanity00mehe.

49. Baba, Meher. "WHAT BABA MEANS BY REAL WORK." Avatar Meher Baba. Universal Spiritual League in America, https://www.avatarmeherbaba.org/erics/realwork.html.

Lesson 9: Page 199

50. Baba, Meher. 1995. The Everything and the Nothing. Myrtle Beach: Sheriar Press.

51. Baba, Meher. "Baba Pearls." The Awakener, January 1, 1976. https://www.theawakenermagazine.org/avol17/av17n01/av17n01p36.htm#Baba%20Pearls.

52. Baba, Meher. "WHAT BABA MEANS BY REAL WORK."
Avatar Meher Baba. Universal Spiritual League in
America, https://www.avatarmeherbaba.org/erics/
realwork.html.

Lesson 10: Page 207

53. Baba, Meher. 1973. Discourses, Volume III.
Sufism Reoriented.

54. Webster, Noah. "Humility." Webster's New
International Dictionary of the English Language.

55. "Humility." Online Etymology Dictionary. Douglas
Harper, https://www.etymonline.com/word/
humility#etymonline_v_16050.

56. Ott, Lyn. 1980. In Quest of the Face of God. Myrtle
Beach: Meher Prasad.

57. Webster, Noah. "Self-Effacement." Webster's New
International Dictionary of the English Language.

58. Webster, Noah. "Modesty." Webster's New
International Dictionary of the English Language.

59. Webster, Noah. "Pride." Webster's New International
Dictionary of the English Language.

60. Webster, Noah. "Self-Esteem." Webster's New
International Dictionary of the English Language.

61. Baba, Meher. 1973. Discourses, Volume III.
Sufism Reoriented.

62. Baba, Meher. 1967. Discourses. Sufism Reoriented.

Lesson 11: Page 223

63. "Buddhism and Psychedelics." Tricycle, September 21, 1996. https://tricycle.org/magazine-issue/fall-1996/.

64. Weichberger, Laurent. 2020. Surrender with Meher Baba. OmPoint Press. https://www.amazon.com/Surrender-Meher-Baba-Laurent-Weichberger/dp/057873804.

65. Timmermann, Christopher. "Neural Correlates of the DMT Experience Assessed with Multivariate EEG." Scientific Reports, (2019). https://www.nature.com/articles/s41598-019-51974-4.

Lesson 12: 253

66. "Carl Gustav Jung - "Face to Face" (BBC 1959/Better Quality!)." Peacefulness. July 25, 2017. Video, https://www.youtube.com/watch?v=oBYEFX2dqpM.

67. Baba, Meher. 1987. Discourses. Sherier Foundation.

Lesson 13: Page 259

68. Barks, Coleman. 2002. The Soul of Rumi: A New Collection of Ecstatic Poems. San Francisco: HarperOne.

69. John 9:3 New International Version, Harper Collins, 1973.

70. Wikipedia. 2023. "Ubi Caritas." Wikimedia Foundation. Last modified September 2, 2023. https://en.wikipedia.org/w/index.php?title=Ubi_caritas&action=history.

71. Baba, Meher, and Bhau Kalchuri. 1990. Lord Meher. MANifestation.

72. Stevens, Don E., Norah Moore, and Laurent Weichberger. 2003. Meher Baba's Word & His Three Bridges. Myrtle Beach: Companion Books.

73. Wikipedia. 2023. "Ubi Caritas." Wikimedia Foundation. Last modified September 2, 2023. https://en.wikipedia.org/w/index.php?title=Ubi_caritas&action=history.

74. Baba, Meher, and Bhau Kalchuri. 1990. Lord Meher. MANifestation.

75. Malachi 3:1. New International Version, Harper Collins, 1973.

76. Luke 7:28. New International Version, Harper Collins, 1973.

77. Purdom, Charles. 2021. Three Incredible Weeks with Meher Baba. 4th ed. Myrtle Beach: Companion Books.

78. Purdom, C.B. 1971. The God-Man. Myrtle Beach: Sherier Books.

Lesson 15: Page 291

79. "Nearly One in Ten Americans Reports Having Depression." Columbia Mailman School of Public Health. Columbia University Irving Medical Center, September 19, 2022. https://www.publichealth. columbia.edu/news/nearly-one-ten-americans-reports- having-depression.

80. "The Paradox of Our Time" or a Timeless Paradox?" Psychology Today, January 25, 2019. https://www. psychologytoday.com/us/blog/the-resilient- brain/201901/the-paradox-our-time-or-timeless- paradox#:~:text=Said%20to%20have%20been%20 penned,of%20Seattle%27s%20Overlake%20 Christian%20Church.

81. "Elders Now Say Moorehead Is 'Guilty' Of Misconduct." The Seattle Times, May 21, 1999. https://archive. seattletimes.com/archive/?date=19990521&slug=over21.

Lesson 16: Page 317

82. Nepo, Mark. 2013. Seven Thousand Ways To Listen: Staying Close To What Is Sacred. Atria Books.

83. "Kendrick Lamar - HUMBLE." Kendrick Lamar. March 30, 2017. Video, https://www.youtube.com/ watch?v=tvTRZJ-4EyI.

84. "How to Be a Better Listener: Exploring 4 Types of Listening." Maryville University. Maryville University, https://online.maryville.edu/blog/types-of-listening/.

Lesson 17: Page 333

85. Wikipedia. 2023. "Shadow (Psychology)." Wikimedia Foundation. Last modified June 16, 2023. https://en.wikipedia.org/wiki/Shadow_(psychology).

86. Cherry, Kendra. "What Are The Four Jungian Archetypes?" Very Well Mind, March 11, 2023. https://www.verywellmind.com/what-are-jungs-4-major-archetypes-2795439.

87. Gilbert, Alicia. "77 Shadow Work Journal Prompts For Beginners + Tips For Starting." Soberish. September 17, 2023. https://www.soberish.co/shadow-work-prompts/.

Lesson 18: Page 361

88. Pearl, Galen. 2012. Ten Steps To Finding Your Happy Place (And Staying There). Still Creek Press.

89. Nepo, Mark. 2000. The Book of Awakening. Red Wheel/Weiser.

90. Pearl, Galen. 2012. Ten Steps To Finding Your Happy Place (And Staying There). Still Creek Press.

Lesson 19: Page 385

91. Dunn, Lauren. "Genetic Similarities Between Dogs And People Are Helping Cancer Research." NBC News, February 10, 2018

92. Kauffman, Melissa. "Nine Ancient Dog Deities." Dogster, June 1, 2012.

93. Barks, Coleman. 2002. The Soul of Rumi: A New Collection of Ecstatic Poems. San Francisco: HarperOne.

94. Dyer, Wayne W. 1990. You'll See It When You Believe It.

95. Youssef, Elyane. "The Rumi Poem We Should All Read." Elephant Journal, December 21, 2016. https://www.elephantjournal.com/2016/12/the-rumi-poem-we-should-all-read/.

96. Nelson, Portia. 1993. There's A Hole In My Sidewalk. Hillsboro, Oregon: Beyond Words Publishing.

Lesson 20: Page 399

97. 1 Corinthians 7:5. New International Version, Harper Collins, 1973.

Lesson 21: Page 415

98. Winfrey, Oprah. 2019. The Path Made Clear: Discovering Your Life's Direction and Purpose. FlatIron Books. https://www.amazon.com/Path-Made-Clear-Discovering-Directiondp/1250307503?asin=1250307503&revisionId=&format=4&depth=1.

99. Vivekananda, Swami. 1947. Complete Works of Swami Vivekananda. Vedanta Press and Bookshop.

100. Rainer Maria Rilke. 1993. Letters to a Young Poet. W. W Norton & Company.

www.ingramcontent.com/pod-product-compliance
Lightning Source LLC
Chambersburg PA
CBHW020116180726
47992CB00018B/8